W9-BLG-418

796.334 BEN
Bennett, Roger, 1970- author.
Encyclopedia Blazertannica : a suboptimal guide to soccer, America's "sport of the future" since 1972

ALSO BY ROGER BENNETT AND MICHAEL DAVIES

How the United States Can Win the 2006 World Cup

Bavarian for the Modern Business Traveler

Puffin Breeding Today

Self-Loathing and How to Live with That Curse

John Terry: Symbol of Our Times or Misunderstood?

Tony Hibbert: Modern Day Jesus

Men in Blazers Present

Encyclopedia Blazertannica

Men in Blazers

Present

MEN IN BLAZERS

Viri Recte Vestiti

Encyclopedia Blazertannica

A Suboptimal Guide to Soccer,
America's "Sport of the Future" Since 1972

Roger Bennett and Michael Davies

Ghostwritten by Zlatan*

Fountaindale Public Library
Bolingbrook, IL
(630) 759-2102

Alfred A. Knopf · New York · 2018

* *Not really (we had to add this asterisk for legal reasons)*

THIS IS A BORZOI BOOK
PUBLISHED BY ALFRED A. KNOPF

Copyright © 2018 by Roger Bennett and Michael Davies

All rights reserved. Published in the United States by Alfred A. Knopf, a division of Penguin Random House LLC, New York, and in Canada by Random House of Canada, a division of Penguin Random House Canada Limited, Toronto.

www.aaknopf.com

Knopf, Borzoi Books, and the colophon are registered trademarks of Penguin Random House LLC.

Library of Congress Cataloging-in-Publication Data

Names: Bennett, Roger, [date] author. | Davies, Michael, [date] author.

Title: Men in blazers present encyclopedia blazertannica : a suboptimal guide to soccer, America's "sport of the future" since 1972 / by Roger Bennett, Michael Davies.

Description: First edition. | New York : Alfred A. Knopf, 2018.

Identifiers: LCCN 2017028596 | ISBN 9781101875988 (hardcover) | ISBN 9781101875995 (ebook)

Subjects: LCSH: Soccer–Miscellanea. | Soccer–Anecdotes. | Soccer–Humor. |

BISAC: SPORTS & RECREATION / Soccer. | HUMOR / Topic / Sports. | SPORTS & RECREATION / History.

Classification: LCC GV943.2 .B44 2018 | DDC 796.352–dc23
LC record available at https://lccn.loc.gov/2017028596

Cover design by Peter Mendelsund

Manufactured in the United States of America

First Edition

ROG: To my wife, Vanessa, my kids, Samson, Ber, Zion, and Oz, and Everton Football Club. Aka the things in life that allow me to experience human emotions I am otherwise sadly numb to.

DAVO: To all my greatest mates, you know who you are, in life, love, TV, and sport. To my kids. And to my mum and Roman Abramovich. I owe you both so much.

ROG AND DAVO: To all our Great Friends of the Pod . . . Kung Fu Fighting America!

EDDY: The entire British Empire was built on cups of tea . . .

SOAP: Yeah, and look what happened to that.

EDDY: . . . And if you think I'm going to war without one, mate, you're mistaken.

—*Lock, Stock and Two Smoking Barrels*

Introduction

Hail! Unfortunate Accidental Readers and Great Friends of the Pod.

The volume you have in your hands was designed to be many things:

1. The final nail in the coffin of the long-floundering publishing industry.
2. Living proof that it is possible to write a worse book than *Does God Love Michael's Two Daddies?* by Sheila K. Butt.
3. An ill-advised attempt to journey into the inky dark, unexplored depths of the *Men in Blazers* universe, every detail of which we have created hand in hand with our masochistically loyal listeners over the past eight years, pod by pod, show by show, tweet by suboptimal tweet.

To achieve the first two objectives, we chose to focus solely on the third. This task demanded we wallow in the history and culture of football, the sport we both love. With its pantheon of heroes and villains, moments of glorious ecstasy and searing despair, dodgy haircuts and surplus neck tattoos, it has empowered us to experience emotions other people seem to feel in real life, to which we are both inured. No telenovela could provide soapier story lines to keep us hooked like football . . . a game with plot points that unfurl live without a safety net, as the whole world watches.

*   *   *

Witnessing the game we love grow and grow in America, the nation that we love, has been the thrill of our lifetimes. We both arrived on these shores as innocents, equipped with full heads of our own hair, in the early 1990s. Back then soccer had seemingly forever been cast as America's "Sport of the Future," its recent past little more than a collection of false dawns and hyperbolic predictions that it was about to become the Next Big Thing.

We well remember the day when FIFA announced its intention to host the 1994 World Cup in the US, prompting panicked former-AFL-quarterback-turned-US-representative Jack Kemp to declare on the floor of Congress: "I think it is important for all those young men out there who someday hope to play real football where you throw it and kick it and run with it and put it in your hands a distinction should be made that football is democratic capitalism whereas soccer is a European socialist sport."

Yet, slow and steady wins the race. We have watched with wonder, World Cup to World Cup, as the game's profile has inexorably risen to the point that the sport's profile has taken its place alongside seersucker, cheesesteaks, and the collected works of Raymond Carver as a symbol of American freedom and democracy.

Indeed, our obsessive love of football and *Men in Blazers'* very existence has been possible only because it was powered and reinforced by that surging rise of interest, as well as by the fact that you allow bald men on television in the United States.

The question is often asked as to why, season to season, week to week, game to game, more and more

Americans have fallen under football's poetic sway. Many theories have been advanced. Just as baseball thrived in "the Golden Age of Radio," and the NFL was the perfect televisual sport, soccer's rise has been driven by the Internet in general, and EA Sports FIFA in particular, which have enabled fans in Los Angeles or North Dakota to experience and follow their teams as closely as supporters in Leicester or Newcastle.

Also, alcohol. If a gent is in a bar drinking a beer at 7:30 in the morning, society deems him to be an alcoholic. If Liverpool are losing to Bournemouth on a television in that very same bar whilst that afore-mentioned beer is being quaffed, we consider that man an American soccer fan. If we have learned only one thing during our beer-stained *Men in Blazers* odyssey it is this: Never underestimate the extent to which Americans adore an excuse to drink during the daytime.

Ultimately, we like to believe football's American boom has been made possible by a realization that sporting audiences here have made en masse—that when they experience soccer, they might not be watching home runs, end zone dances, or tomahawk dunks. They are glimpsing life itself unfold before their eyes. The legendary Arsenal manager Arsène Wenger once articulated this best when he said, "Football is like real life but in a more condensed way, more intense. At some moments it catches you suddenly and it can be very cruel."

As two men, we could not be more different. One of us is an optimistic Londoner who believes everything is possible. The other, a negative Liverpudlian who sees Cossacks lurking behind every door. Yet we are bonded by a mutual understanding that soccer in all of its forms—men's or women's, international or club—as long as it is played by bipeds, is the key to understanding human existence. As George Eliot once said:

> Art is the nearest thing to life; it is a mode of amplifying experience and extending our contact with our fellow-men beyond the bounds of our personal lot.

If you substitute the word "football" for "art" here, it could not be better said. This book, then, is for readers who believe that, or would like to. Fans old or new, young or old, deeply knowledgeable or neophyte. An encyclopedic collection assembled at great loss of life, of the greatest games, most legendary characters, soaring moments, salty chants, and the occasional self-indulgent yet critical detour, that make up everything you need to know about the game. Reading this cover to cover might not improve the way you play the sport, but it will, we hope, make you better human beings, which is arguably, almost as important.

Courage.

Rog and Davo

Roger Bennett   Michael Davies

New York City
May 2018

P.S. The thing we are most proud of about this book are the entries shifting from Beckenbauer to Beckerman to Beckham, thus accidentally though correctly placing the great Kyle Beckerman in the pantheon where he belongs.

Men in Blazers Present

Encyclopedia Blazertannica

Accents: I have lived in the United States for over half my life. The experience has shaped the way I think, view the world, and drive my automobile. One thing it has not come close to changing is my accent. My wife has always joked that I clung on to my English accent because it is my only asset. Truth is, it is a liability rather than an asset. Fifty-seven percent of my interactions with random shopkeepers or bank tellers involve them being unable to resist uncorking their own English phrases in marbly-mouthed Dick Van Dyke–esque accents:

"Fancy a cup of tea, luv?"

"Fish 'n' chips!"

"David Beck-ham."

"Jus' let me sweep ya chimnee."

Yet, I have nothing to counter with. I can't even do a vague American impression. On the eve of my fortieth birthday, as I took stock of my life and the seventeen years I had spent in the United States, I attempted to list the phrases I could say like a true American:

"Hot Dawg"

"A million bucks!"

"The whole enchilada"

"Hooray for Hollywood!"

"Soccah"

"Ful-HAM Football Club"

"F*%k You, Pal"

Brad Evans, player for the USMNT and Seattle Sounders, challenged us over Twitter to do an entire episode in fake American accents, wondering if anyone would still watch the show if that was the case. The question touched a nerve in the American soccer-loving community—why are so many English-accented broadcasters immediately afforded respect based solely on their accents? As it turned out, NBC's research division delved into our ratings and discovered that the people who adore *Men in Blazers* are not even soccer lovers. They are bald fetishists who couldn't give a crap about our accents or our mediocre soccer expertise. **—RB**

Achilles Feet: A symbolic medical predicament ascribed by John Oliver to any player like former Liverpool legend Jamie Carragher who appears low on skill, high on passion.

Adidas: My relationship with Adidas dates from 1974. It was formed not by football but by my love of tennis and particularly a balding, mustachioed, comb-overing, gangly, but oh so elegant tennis player from Southern California—Stan Smith. The man whose face and name is emblazoned on the coolest and most understated, pure sneaker slash tennis shoe of all time.

Stan Smith before he was a sneaker

I liked everything about Stan Smith's game— the rhythm of his serve, his catlike movement, the effortless power of his crisp volley. But mostly, I was obsessed with Stan Smith's shiny white and green shoes. Stan Smiths replaced my Dunlop Green flash, my department store brand tracksuit was upgraded to a slick gray meets blue that Adidas called "Petrol," with three navy blue stripes on the sides of the arms and legs and a scarlet trefoil on the chest. I have never owned any sportswear which I have worn with more pride. —MD

Allardyce, Sam: A walking morality tale as a man who spent his life dreaming of becoming England manager only to be forced to resign within sixty-seven days after advising undercover reporters on

how to break the laws of the game in return for lucrative kickbacks. His rise and fall are even more remarkable when you consider his body consists of 73 percent ham products and resembles the bastard offspring that would result if a hippopotamus made love with a steak and kidney pie.

American Television and Soccer: In 1990, I spent one of the greatest summers of my life as a counselor at a sleepaway camp in Maine. For those of you who went to camp, I was the requisite creepy English counselor with cut-off denim shorts who spent eight glorious weeks savoring the American summer camp traditions of lanyards, Devil Dogs, and wedgies. But my overriding memory was my first encounter with America's cruel indifference to the sport I loved. This was the World Cup in which English football momentarily shed its hooligan brand on a march into the semifinals which had stoked England's hyperbolic tabloid media to jingoistic fever pitch. The day of the semifinal against West Germany was one of the most frustrating of my life. I spent an afternoon

driving frantically from one sleepy rural bar to another. All were broadcasting the local Portland minor league baseball game. Not one was able to direct their massive satellite dishes toward a signal that could pull in the World Cup semifinal. In the pre-Internet age I had to wait for the next day's *Boston Globe* to discover the bitter result. England predictably lost on penalty kicks. Perhaps it was for the best. —RB

Argentina: Not to go all Paul Krugman on you, but one of the most admirable things about Argentina's consistency as a world footballing power is that while Germany, Brazil, and Italy all rank among the world's ten biggest economies (and between them, they've won 13 of the 20 World Cups) Argentina is the economic outlier. The team that defies the correlation between a nation's GDP and their ability to win the big one.

Stylistically, Argentine football has patented a long tradition of violent beauty. Their fans crave both the *Gambetta,* a slaloming style of dribbling run described by the poet Eduardo Galeano as strumming "the ball as if it was a guitar," alongside a cunning guile and physicality that is known as *La Nuestra,* or "our style of play." Thus, Argentine players are able to undo opponents with clinical pace, or by pinging the ball around their box, but if a groin or kidney presented itself for a good punching along the way, they could be easily persuaded to give it a thunderous jab. Thus their great team of the 1950s were known as the "Angels with Dirty Faces."

This is a team who will stop at nothing to win, stooping even to handing opponents spiked water bottles during breaks to drug them in game. When England finally worked out how to beat them in 2002, thanks to a penalty won by a flopping from Michael Owen, the Argentine media merely nodded their approval at his deceit and willingness to cheat to win. "THEY'VE LEARNED!" was one headline.

Yet, Argentina have always been far more than Al Davis–era Oakland Raiders. Their team always had to be both admired and feared due to their production line of visionary, creative playmakers, *El Diez,* "The Ten": Juan Román Riquelme, and now Lionel Messi. Victory leads to sainthood. Lose, and it is all their fault.

As mighty as they have been in the past, Los Albicelestes have gone over two decades without winning a trophy. Dakota Fanning was not yet born when they lifted the 1993 Copa America. Their teams have been talent-stocked, yet their biggest problem was how to get the best out of Lionel Messi. As revered as he was, Argentines remained suspicious of the man who moved to Barcelona aged fourteen, viewing him as a foreigner, *El Catalán,* who never shone in an Argentine journey and even retired briefly from international football with tears in his eyes after misfiring in a doomed penalty shootout loss after 2016's Copa America Centenario final.

Despite their ongoing agony, the Argentinians find reason for optimism. The pope, Francis, was born in Buenos Aires and is football mad. Their fans draw solace from his support. "If one Argentine can do what he does," they say, "just imagine what twenty-three can do."

Arsenally: To dig a massive hole, raise your fans' hopes by almost climbing out of it, only to fail at the last minute. See their 2015 Champions League round of 16 exit to Monaco in which they slumped to a humiliating 3–1 home defeat in the first leg, then against the odds took a 2–0 lead in France but could not net a third and were eliminated on away goals.

This kind of noble defeat is possibly the most painful kind. It is also incredibly French. In 1863, the Foreign Legion cemented its roman-tic legend during the Defense of Camarón, where sixty-five legionnaires held 2,000 Mexican soldiers at bay until they ran out of ammunition. With six men remaining and not a bullet between then, the legionnaires swore to fight to the death, fixed bayonets, and attempted a futile charge. The wooden prosthetic hand of the deceased leader of the action, Capitaine Jean Danjou, was recovered, and every year it is solemnly sent out on parade, a reminder of his death, the nobility of defeat, and the Legion's motto, "March or Die!" This is French glory. Understand it, and you will appreciate the essence of everything that is Arsenally. A way of life in which stoic dignity in defeat is always preferred to a pragmatically won trophy.

Aston Villa: The most pleather, beige, vanilla team in English football. A once proud team who won the European Cup—the Champions League predecessor—in 1982, beating  Bayern in the final, bought to their knees by American owner Randy Lerner, who essentially turned them into English football's version of his former NFL franchise, the Cleveland Browns, before selling them on.

For new American fans, believing Aston Villa was once a European power is as hard to believe as learning Tara Reid was once a highly desirable Hollywood starlet. Despite their modern-day descent into mediocrity, the club still boast a glut of celebrity fans—Princes Edward and William, Duran Duran's Simon Le Bon, former Conservative prime minister David Cameron, Tom Hanks, Ozzy Osbourne, and the late Fred Perry. It always amazes me Davo does not support them, as this is, coincidentally, a list of his male heroes.

B

Baker, Gerry: Gerry Baker was one of our favorite interviews ever. The seventy-three-year-old former US international was the first American ever to score a hat trick in top-flight English soccer.

We were introduced to Gerry in February 2012, after Clint Dempsey, then playing for Fulham, smashed three goals past Newcastle. The British newspapers heralded this as the first American hat trick in the English top flight. Many of our listeners pointed out that a striker named Baker had actually done so fifty-one years earlier. We went to the record books and found the outline of the story—Baker had been born in New Rochelle, New York, to English parents who returned home to Britain ahead of the Second World War. We immediately put out an APB over Twitter and, thanks to a slew of GFOPs, tracked Gerry down in Scotland, where we found him, still eager to talk about his ca-

reer in which he had starred as a "compact striker with the grace of a gazelle" plying his trade for St. Mirren, Manchester City, Ipswich Town, Coventry City, and ultimately the United States during the doomed qualification process for World Cup 1970.

Our conversation began with us asking the retired pro how many hat tricks he had netted in English football. "So many I have lost count," Baker chuckled. "That was my job. Scoring goals was what I was paid to do." Gerry talked with excitement about the experiences he had after being called up for the US out of the blue. Most of his teammates had been born in Hungary or Germany and now played on semipro clubs dotted around New York and St. Louis. Despite the fact the US team played before crowds of 4,000, which was much less than the 20,000–25,000 Baker was used to entertaining at St. Mirren, the striker declared in his thick Scottish accent, "I can't tell you how proud I was to play for my country, the United States."

Rog tested Gerry's loyalty by asking him which team he would support if England played the US. Baker laughed and responded, "America! That should go without saying, because I am Scottish as well!" When asked if that was merely the Scottish contrarian in him talking, Gerry did not have to hesitate for a second. "If Scotland and America played, I would still support America," he said warmly. "Let's put it like that."

Sadly, Gerry Baker passed away in August 2013. To remember his life is to be aware of the rich and complex footballing history that, though often forgotten, flows through this nation's veins.

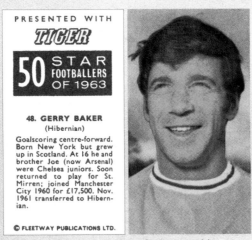

PRESENTED WITH

TIGER

50 STAR FOOTBALLERS OF 1963

48. GERRY BAKER
(Hibernian)

Goalscoring centre-forward. Born New York but grew up in Scotland. At 16 he and brother Joe (now Arsenal) were Chelsea juniors. Soon returned to play for St. Mirren; joined Manchester City 1960 for £17,500. Nov. 1961 transferred to Hibernian.

© FLEETWAY PUBLICATIONS LTD.

Gerry Baker: a lost gem of US soccer history

Bald Denier: Any man who elects to face up to thinning hair by elaborate combing, the desperate use of thickening product, a full-on hair transplant (*see* Rooney, Wayne), or the dreaded comb-over. Simply cannot be trusted in professional or personal relationships. Never rely on a person who cannot face up to the truth when it is staring right back at him in the mirror on a daily basis.

Balding Sectors: The Unicorn. The Hair Island. The Monk. The Fooling No One but Yourself. The Wayne Rooney.

British comedian and broadcaster, and fellow Chelsea fan Johnny Vaughan, was the first person I heard referring to "problems in various sectors" while he was applying hair-building fibers to his receding mop in the dressing room of *My Kind of Town,* a short-lived ABC variety series that he hosted and I produced in 2005. Over "Pops and Tops," poppadums and Lager Tops (beer with a bit of Sprite at the top), at an Indian restaurant in Hell's Kitchen, we developed the sectors theory into a very basic Dewey Decimal System for the patterns of male baldness, all of which started with the number 3:

3.1

3.3   3.1

3.4

3.2

3.5

3.1: Left high forehead
3.2: Center forehead
3.3: Right high forehead
3.4: Crown of head
3.5: Center of head, forward of
   crown

Problems in sector 3.1 always go hand in hand with problems in 3.3. Followed, almost inevitably, by 3.4. However, these same men can hang on for quite a while in 3.2 and 3.5, which is why many think Davo is "way less bald in person." Davo, however, is very worried about sectors 3.1 and 3.3 receding further to meet an expanding 3.5, which would result in a total "hair island." Some balds, like Rog actually, lose 3.1, 3.3, and 3.2 but hold on nicely to 3.4 and 3.5. A combo bald of Rog and Davo would be, therefore, hardly bald at all.

Bald Players: Wonder goals, miracle saves, visionary assists. You can keep them all. We are of the considered opinion there are few more thrilling athletic visions than the sight of an unabashedly bald man storming down a football field in search of glory. It is poetry written in human form.

Dutch winger Arjen Robben's baldness appeared to reinforce his sense of outsiderness and otherworldliness (Seth Meyers once came on our show and informed us that "when you enter the Bald and Fast Hall of Fame you pass a statue of Arjen Robben"). Zidane's baldness, which grew in proportion to his success, enhanced the sense of Zen mystery which cloaked him.

Fellow French World Cup '98 defender Frank Leboeuf's shiny pate added to his rugged menace, or teammate, jesting goalkeeper Fabien Barthez, whose teammate Laurent Blanc used to kiss his bald head before kickoff for luck.

Other balds lack the confidence to face the truth. Ivory Coast winger Gervinho obsesses about the thinning area between his headband, hair, and forehead, tending to it as if it were the Demilitarized Zone between North and South Korea. English legend and 1966 World Cup winner Bobby Charlton relied on delusion as a crutch. "When I started losing my hair in the late fifties, I was afraid it would damage my image if the public found out," he once said. "I considered making a rugging order [a wig] but our mum recommended a comb-over. To my surprise it worked and nobody noticed." By "nobody," Charlton means "everybody."

Yet by far the most famous footballing bald denier is Charlton's fellow one-time United legend, Wayne Rooney. On July 4, 2011, Wayne Rooney announced to the world by Twitter that he had undergone a hair transplant: "Just to confirm to all my followers, I have had

Best Bald Team of All Time

Gervinho

Di
Stéfano

Forwards

Yordan
Letchkov

Archie
Gemmill

Bobby
Charlton

Arjen
Robben

Midfielders

Roberto
Carlos

Frank
Leboeuf

Jaap
Staam

Maicon

Defenders

Brad
Friedel

Goalkeeper

Zidane

Manager

Subs: Thomas Gravesen, Michael Bradley, Wayne Rooney, Gerson

a hair transplant. I was going bald at 25 why not. I'm delighted with the result." His delight did not last long, as the synthetic hair failed to bed. After shaving off the new do, Rooney underwent a second transplant two years later. His subsequent career collapse serves as a cautionary tale for those who seek to cheat their baldness.

Bar Mitzvah: I once talked on the pod about how much of what I learned in life, I gleaned from listening to the bar mitzvah speeches given to my friends by their fathers. England was such a repressed place in the 1980s. Yet there was something about the transitional power of the event which empowered every bar mitzvah dad to talk with a rare dose of honesty and candor and depth.

I had the opportunity to speak at my eldest son's bar mitzvah in January 2016. The toast was entitled "Seven Lessons About Life I Wish I Had Known When I Was Thirteen." Only after giving it did I realize there were only six:

One: Every moment you have with your grandparents is a gift—they are four of the most nourishing relationships you will ever have in your life. They will ground you, offer you wisdom, and make sure you have a rich sense of who you are and where you come from. Never take them for granted.

Two: Every human being has strengths and weaknesses. Even you Samson Bennett. Know them. Play to them. And in terms of your weaknesses, work hard to decide which you can change and which you cannot. The secret to life is about knowing how to be yourself and being at ease with it all.

Three: You have been blessed with copious amounts of an emotion that is all too rare in the world: empathy. Your summer camp has a motto: "Help the Other Fellow," which I hope you will come to understand is more than a slogan they sew into the camp's socks. The ability to look at the world from different perspectives outside of your own—and to do so with compassion—is what will empower you

Rog and his grandparents at his bar mitzvah—
still light-years away from becoming a man

to achieve all that you can achieve in your lifetime.

Four: Know the difference between an acquaintance and a true friend. Make the most out of the former. Do anything for the latter because true friendships are much rarer wonders. Hold on to them dearly. They will form a spine of memory and meaning in your life.

Five: I wake up every morning and thank God I live in the United States of America and I hope you do too. I love America even more than Kid Rock loves America because this country offers more freedoms and possibilities than anywhere else in the world. Treasure that. Value it. Make the most of it. Dream big dreams. Work hard. And if you put your mind to it, anything and everything is possible.

Finally . . .

Six: Enjoy the moment. Always ask yourself: Am I making the most out of everyone and everywhere I find myself? Tonight and forever, this lesson essentially boils down to this: Whenever you get the chance to dance, do so with delight and abandon, surrounded by those you love. **—RB**

Rog at his son's bar mitzvah is peak "Other Rog." It is alternative-universe Rog. Joyous, emotional, swelling with pride, full of life, optimism, glass-half-fullness, and love. Surrounded by his adorable children, his closest friends (and oldest friends, including Jamie Glassman, his old Liverpudlian friend from birth), his absolutely charming and lovely family (his mum and dad, Valerie and Ivor, are so, so friendly and kind; his Liverpool-supporting brother, Nigel, so smart, witty, and dry; his sister, Amy, so warm and good-looking); and his beloved and so in charge wife, Mrs. B. Roger danced all night like a fool. I mean he absolutely slayed and dominated the dance floor. Like Antonio Conte dominating the sideline after a Chelsea goal. But with a bit more insane energy. —**MD**

Bata Wayfinders: The second coolest pair of shoes I have ever owned. Introduced in 1965, the Wayfinder had a secret  compass stashed in the heel, and soles that sported ten footprints of British animals. Exotic ones like badger, hedgehog, and sheep. An essential part of my Cub Scout uniform. And for my extensive tracking of badgers, hedgehogs, and sheep in South East London.

For my tenth birthday I moved up a level to the coolest shoes I ever owned, the Big Game Wayfinders, Panther edition, which left a freaking panther print whenever I stepped in mud. Which was everywhere in South East London in the mid-1970s.

The same company made one of the worst pairs of shoes I ever owned also. The Power-Points were a flimsy and excruciatingly uncomfortable football boot with three numbered target areas on the instep, outside the boot, and heel and AN INSTRUCTIONAL MANUAL that made every kid who wore them the laughingstock of the playing field he turned up wearing them on. Okay, enough. I spent years working through this in therapy. —**MD**

Sensational **POWER-POINTS** These fantastic new boots make winning football easy!

ADVERTISEMENT

Make tracks with **WAYFINDERS BIG GAME** Adventure shoes for boys

Beane, Billy: The first day we ever podded together, before the phrase "From the Crap Part of SoHo . . ." had ever been uttered, we had an on-the-fly conversation about the target audience we imagined tapping into our dreams. Two men immediately came to mind. Both were accomplished, intelligent, and rumored to be interested in football. The first was John Henry, owner of the Boston Red Sox, who, as speculation had it, in his pre-Liverpool days was said to be on the brink of investing in a Premier League team. The second was Billy Beane of Oakland Athletics–*Moneyball* fame.

Billy was reported to have become obsessed with the game and its lack of statistical usage. After the second series of our podcast wrapped, Rog received a text from a number purporting to be Billy Beane's, introducing himself and cheerily critiquing a number of comments Rog had made about Arsenal on a recent pod. We quickly called the number back and shockingly it was the man himself who answered, holding court for an hour about his love of the game, his understanding of Arsène Wenger's management style, his interest in historical fiction, and his admiration for the natural charisma of Edith Crawley. It turns out, he listens to our crap while he works out in the gym during A's games.

The first time he jumped on our Pod, Billy revealed the origin story of his football fandom thusly: "I was looking for a birthday gift for my wife years ago, and there were cheap flights to London, so the cheap flights bailed me out. I was there during the heart of Premier League season, and it was the off-season for the A's and I read all the daily newspapers and stuff and I was amazed by the passion and the emotion around it and I just thought man there must be a lot of emotional decisions going on, that was where I was first drawn." Billy has become to *Men in Blazers* what Alec Baldwin is to *Saturday Night Live*.

Beckenbauer, Franz: More Teutonic than a pair of lederhosen, nicknamed "Der Kaiser," Beckenbauer was aloof, arrogant, conservative, and efficient. It is perhaps the greatest testament to the extent he revolutionized the modern game that it is impossible to hold any of this against him. A midfielder-turned-defender—he reinvented attack as the best form of defense, in a new role called *libero,* a creative force who would carry the ball from the back, pushing up to fuse the midfield with the forward line. Before the *libero,* defenders were large, crude, and so awkward on the ball that they were unlikely to leave their own half. Beckenbauer changed the categories of the game, taking advantage of the fact that he was rarely closely checked to storm out of the defense. Technical yet graceful, rugged yet elegant, and always ruthlessly consistent, Beckenbauer appeared in five World Cup finals as a player and a coach, and never finished below third place in any of them. He remains the only man to lift the trophy as both captain and manager.

In 1974, his clinically efficient team shocked the debonair Total Footballing Dutch, led by Johan Cruyff, to win the World Cup. Beckenbauer's control of the German team at that time was total: He picked the team, shaped their tactics, handled the media, and even negotiated the squad's win bonus, quite literally becoming a German Rock God in the process. His smash hit single, "True Friends Can't Be Separated," is a hurdy-gurdy track, think Donovan meets Hasselhoff, yet its lyrics reflect the essence of the team-first ethos he so loved to marshal:

Good friends—no one can tear apart
Good friends are never alone
Because in life one can
Be there for one another

Beckerman, Kyle: The origins of dreadlocks remain unclear. Some believe they were first worn in ancient Egypt. Others believe the Indian deity

A rose between two bald thorns; Kyle Beckerman at New York's Town Hall, June 2014

Shiva first sported "jaTaa," or "twisted locks of hair." Yet, when it comes to white dreadlocks, there is little debate over who wore them best. Mr. Kyle Beckerman.

We adore KB5's story. This is a man who from the age of eight as a kid in Crofton, Maryland, signed his signature "Kyle Beckerman USA," a nod to his dream to follow his footballing heroes and experience a FIFA tournament. That dream appeared to have flamed out when he fell off the national team radar under Bob Bradley, yet Beckerman persevered, and after six years in the international wilderness, he gained a recall and a starting role against Mexico in Jürgen Klinsmann's first game as coach, going on to become a fixture in the team, and in 2014 a World Cup debutante aged thirty-two.

In Brazil, Kyle may not have scored the 65-yard wonderstrike Rog widely predicted he would unleash to win the tournament for the United States, yet his feat in just making the team is the one we marvel at—and the relentless work ethic he invested to make a childhood dream come true is the reason we revere him. In August 2013, Beckerman charged around the field against Panama, inspiring the United States to stun the hosts, eliminating them from World Cup qualification with two stoppage time goals to win a game that was otherwise meaningless for Klinsmann's team, who had already guaranteed their ticket to Brazil.

From the press box, one could see the Panamanian midfielders jawing at Beckerman throughout the game. After the final whistle, in the locker room Kyle confided to Rog what they had been saying to him. "The Panamanians were begging me to take it easy," he said. "They kept saying 'Take it easy, bro, you have already qualified for the World Cup' and I just said to them, 'My team may have qualified, but I ain't booked my place on that team yet . . . Bro.'"

Beckham, David: Before the advent of the Premier League in 1992, English football was largely a low-culture game popular amongst working-class lads who enjoyed fighting each other as much as, or more than, they cared about their own team winning.

The birth of the Premier League and the

global reach that came with it transformed the culture of the game. The players were no longer merely local heroes, they were worldwide stars, and the rise of the Internet meant the details of their lives off the field—the clothes they wore, the women they dated/cheated on, the cars they drove—were as interesting to the world as their creativity on it. And so players began to up their game.

The Premier League "lifestyle" can trace its roots to Manchester United 1960s icon George Best, who summed up his life experience with the quip "I spent a lot of money on booze, birds, and fast cars. The rest I just squandered." Best drank his way out of the game and into bankruptcy by the 1980s, when English football was kind of like a troglodyte, medieval, hooligan culture based on parochial rivalries. But Beckham was the beneficiary of better timing. His Manchester United debut coincided with the birth of the English Premier League in 1992. The league needed a face, and that face had to be English. Beckham was one of a number of stars. He was never the most talented. But always the best-looking.

Beckham's brilliance was twofold: He fused soccer and popular culture with his marriage to Posh Spice Victoria Adams, which acted like a royal marriage in the seventeenth century tying together House Bourbon and House Windsor. He and Victoria were like the English Hart to Hart and their relationship was mutually beneficial. With Beckham on her arm, Adams became more than just a candy pop star, and he, in turn, transcended football to become a style icon. His hair, until he met her, wasn't very special. She introduced the midfielder to blond streaks, and continuous makeovers, and endorsements soon followed.

His second world-class skill set was an eternal awareness of the cameras. No professional footballer has jumped on more goal scorers' backs to celebrate after a winning strike to ensure he made the back page of the next day's newspapers. Beckham's last game in MLS was the 2012 Cup final. His Los Angeles Galaxy

There are only six kinds of Premier League haircuts. This man invented them all.

comprehensively outplayed Houston Dynamo, winning the game 3–1. The third goal came in the 94th minute after the Galaxy won a penalty at the death. Beckham approached the designated penalty taker, Robbie Keane, and asked if he could take the kick. Keane brushed the request off before dispatching the ball clinically. As he did so, Beckham, now back at the halfway line, dropped to his knees and pointed to the heavens. Deprived of the glory of scoring, he still acted as if he had done, knowing that pose would lead the news reports that evening, and distort the historical memory of the role he had played in the game.

Beckham's legacy may be left on the heads of the players who have since followed in his footsteps. If you break down the haircuts and the conveyor belt of makeovers he went through, you can only marvel retrospectively at the notes he and his stylists hit. There is a taste of punk, a taste of World War II British infantryman, a note of 1960s English footballing superstar. An incredibly complex pastiche of the high notes of English cultural history—all remade into haircuts. It speaks to the rebirth of English self-confidence in music, culture, and style that he kind of became a poster boy for. It sometimes seems as if there are only six kinds of hairstyles a Premier League player is allowed—and David Beckham pioneered them all.

Bedroom: I have always loved America. I am not sure what my Ur-text was. It may have been the fact my first ever duvet cover was Scooby-Doo-themed. I cannot describe the depth of the longings I experienced to ride beside Daphne in the Mystery Machine. It may have been the incredibly close relationship I shared with my grandfather, who also adored America. We would play chess every afternoon and he would regale me with stories about his grandfather, a kosher butcher, who had left Lithuania in the 1890s, intending to head for Chicago only to disembark when the boat had docked to fuel in Liverpool, thinking he was in New York City,

fooled, no doubt, by the one tall building on the Liverpool skyline. A family tale that always made me feel America was my true destiny.

As a result, my childhood bedroom became a shrine to all things American. Though I had never been to the United States, I collected fragments of Americana, curating them like precious gems on the wall above my bed.

Rog's bedroom wall, Liverpool, 1985. Every artifact a yearning to move to America.

Opposite are some photographs from that time.

If you look carefully you will see William "Refrigerator" Perry, Ferris Bueller, Sergeant Bilko, Debbie Gibson, Gary Coleman, the Beastie Boys, and more. Totems I fused into my own DNA.

I moved to the States at the earliest opportunity right after college, heading for Chicago, largely out of my love for the movies of John Hughes. I arrived right before the 1994 World Cup and watched with wonder as that stonewashed-denim-clad squad swaggered onto the field mulleted of hair and ginger of beard.

I fell in love with the US team the second I first glimpsed them and have adored every second of their ups and downs ever since. When they take the field in World Cup play, the nerves and fear and excitement I will feel in the hour before kickoff will be excruciating. All born of a boy who grew up in a bedroom beneath posters of Matthew Broderick and Debbie Gibson. **—RB**

Being: Liverpool: An extraordinary piece of fly-on-the-wall documentary filmmaking by Fox, which lifted the lid on Liverpool's 2012–13 season.

The series became an albatross around the neck of then new Liverpool manager Brendan Rodgers, who was depicted as a megalomaniac close-talker who lived to wave his sausage fingers in the direction of the nearest camera. Rodgers was filmed at his home, revealing to the world he had a large oil painting of his own face dominating the walls.

In by far the most infamous scene, Rodgers attempted to motivate his players with a mind game he proclaimed had once been used by Sir Alex Ferguson. On the eve of the first game of the season, the manager addressed his entire squad in a hotel conference room, holding aloft three envelopes and proclaiming that each one contained the name of a player who would fail the team during the coming campaign, then

urging all in the room to ensure it would not be them. "I think there's three players who will let us down this year—the cause, the fight, everything. And I have written them down already," he declared to his nonplussed charges. "My point to you as players is to make sure you are not the one in the envelope."

I had the opportunity to travel to Liverpool and interview Rodgers a couple of months after the show aired, and asked him if he regretted his involvement. The manager grimaced as he responded, "I didn't like it. . . . I'm a very private person," he said. "Which names were in the envelopes?" I inquired about the philosophically incomprehensible scene. "There was no names," he said with a melancholic shake of his head, "There was no names." **—RB**

Best, George: An aspirational legend and cautionary tale in equal measure. The flamboyant Northern Irelander broke into Manchester United's first team as a seventeen-year-old prodigy in 1964, proceeding to win two league titles and a European Cup, and scoring once every three games along the way. On heavy mud pitches, filled with primitive defenders, Best would swirl and spin, his long Beatle-mop bouncing as he left Neanderthal opponents in his wake. "I have never seen a player who can beat a man—or men—so close, and in so many ways," marveled his manager, the legendary Matt Busby. Yet all of his sublime achievements on the field were overshadowed by the pop star antics he lived off it. Best was Hugh Hefner in cleats.

By the time we came of age, Best was a bloated parody of a playboy; appearing as a slurred drunk on English talk shows, having stomach implants to stop his drinking, but continually drinking nonetheless. His inevitable death in 2005 triggered an outpouring of national grief. A tribute to his roguish greatness, wasted talent, and tragic life was summed up by biographer Michael Parkinson, who said much of his life has been "a suicide note." Best however linked his ruthless competitive nature on the field to his self-destruction off it when he admitted, "I was born with a great gift, and sometimes with that comes a destructive streak. Just as I wanted to outdo everyone when I played, I had to outdo everyone when we were out on the town."

Best Day of the Season: The first morning of any Premier League season is among the finest days of the year. Up there in our book with Veterans Day, Memorial Day, Yom Kippur, Independence Day, Martin Luther King Day, and Churchill Day. Squads have been refreshed. New players have arrived. Everyone has a fresh new haircut. The ink on their recently acquired neck tattoos has barely dried.

Few occasions in football carry such a sense of collective anticipation and hope. Three hundred eighty games lie ahead of us over 228 days. Each an unknown voyage of discovery within which everything feels pure and possible. Rationally, the Premier League may be a set of mini leagues within a league (six teams battling for top four, four for mid-table obscurity, the rest to avoid relegation), but on the first day of the season every fan suspends disbelief and listens to their fast-beating heart which assures them that their team's newly acquired striker will hit the ground running and score 25 league goals, the injury-prone playmaker will have the season of his life, and the young loanee from Seville whose name is unpronounceable will reveal himself to be a diamond in the rough. The moment before the referee's whistle blows is one thick with prayer. A ball has not been kicked. Dreams are not yet dashed. Everything is possible.

Big Match, The: In 1970 my parents rented, yes rented, their first color television from Radio Rentals in Blackheath Village. It was a Ferguson, weighed, conservatively, a ton, and had BUTTONS THAT YOU HAD TO PUSH TO CHANGE THE CHANNEL. The three British networks, BBC1, BBC2, and ITV (why there  were six channel buttons I never understood) had started broadcasting in color for the first time in late 1969, and remarkably, my parents were early adopters of the new technology. Suddenly, a world of sports and entertainment that I had only ever experienced in black-and-white and shades of gray had arrived in our living room in slightly dull but squeal-inducing color. Our opportunities to watch television before 1970 had been limited. My father loathed the noise of any audience, crowd, or laughter, and he hated the adverts on ITV. So pretty much the only television we got to watch was the nine o'clock news on the BBC, and children's shows before he got home from work. At weekends he would occasionally go sailing so we got to watch some sport but then a remarkable thing happened. Dad moved to Zambia for a year. We were obviously sad to see him go. But then again, we were about to watch a lot of television! In color! And I was about to fall in love with one television program above all others.

Jimmy Hill, who really worked the Sheriff of Nottingham look

The Big Match started airing in 1968, and then in November 1969 it became one of the first programs to broadcast in color. It was a football highlights show which for fifteen seasons, until 1983, exclusively showed highlights of all the London teams playing each other or at home against heathens from strange towns in "the North." Arsenal, Spurs, Chelsea, and West Ham were the most regularly featured.

Along with Fulham, QPR, and Crystal Palace. Charlton Athletic, Millwall, Orient, Watford, and Wimbledon rounded out the numbers and a few matches featuring neighboring teams like Luton, Gillingham, Brighton, Hove Albion, and Oxford. And I loved all these teams really, except Arsenal, and everything about this show.

Through the powers bestowed on Brian Moore's ever expanding pate, I got to travel all over London, to Stamford Bridge, Loftus Road, and Craven Cottage in fancy West London where our rich relatives lived, to Upton Park and Easter Road in the forbidden East where we never went, to Highbury and White Hart Lane in the cool and exotic Northern suburbs to Selhurst Park in grim and twee Croydon and the desperate and dangerous Den and Valley, homes of Millwall and Charlton, from whence I could hear the roar of thousands of violent racists on the terraces from the playing fields of Blackheath on a Saturday afternoon.

Bald denier Brian Moore

The Big Match was how I fell in love with football, in color, and primarily the exotic and classy dark, dark navy blue that Chelsea wore on *The Big Match* against Manchester United in front of more than 60,000 at Stamford Bridge on March 21, 1970. This was the first football game I had ever seen on television. It was the first time I had ever seen or heard of Chelsea. And I would never be the same or willingly miss *The Big Match* and Brian Moore's comb-over ever again. **—MD**

Black Dog, The: *"I think this man might be useful to me—if my black dog returns. He seems quite away from me now—it is such a relief. All the colours come back into the picture."* So wrote Winston Churchill to his wife, Clementine, in 1911 upon hearing of a German doctor who had treated the wife of a friend for depression. For about a week during our Sirius radio years, Davo suffered from a mild and temporary case of "The Black Dog" which manifested itself in an almost complete loss of interest in football, and on one occasion a physical on-air mauling of Rog. Rog receives visits from "The Black Dog" most weekends before and after Everton games.

Blackheath: After a Joe Hart–level performance in the tunnel, I came into this world just before eight in the evening, in time for an evening kick-off, in the master bedroom of my parents' home at 9 Foxes Dale, Blackheath, South (pronounced "Saff") East London. Blackheath is just seven miles on foot from Trafalgar Square in the center of London, but it feels like a world away. If you are forced to grow up outside of America, the South of France, or the Swiss Alps, Blackheath was and is a wonderful place to do so. Bordered by the Royal Park of Greenwich to the north, the village is named after the dark color (when viewed from the Thames) of the massive heath that dominates the quaint Victorian village. It is where I learned to play football, golf, cricket, and tennis, and to avoid gang violence. Musicians Kate Bush and Jools Holland, and most of the members of his 1980s New Wave band Squeeze, come from around there, as do Dire Straits, Jude Law, and Glenda Jackson.

The most famous footballer from Blackheath is Rio Ferdinand, who attended the Blackheath Bluecoat school. But Blackheath's contribution to football is even greater than that. In October of 1863 the Football Association was formed by eleven clubs and Blackheath FC was one of the originals. In fact, three of the eleven original clubs were from Blackheath. Over six meetings at the Freemasons' Tavern on Great

Blackheath, birthplace of violence in football

Queen Street in London, these eleven clubs and schools literally invented the sport of soccer by agreeing on a set of unified rules that they could all play under. In the final meeting, held in December of the same year, Blackheath FC's representative, Mr. Francis Maule Campbell, abruptly withdrew his club from the FA over the removal of two draft rules, the first of which permitted picking up the ball with your hands and running with it, and the second, wait for it, for "obstructing such a run by hacking" (kicking an opponent in the shins), tripping, and holding him. Had Blackheath FC won the argument, how different and much more violent soccer would be. Ryan Shawcross would be the Lionel Messi of the modern game. **—MD**

Blatter, Sepp: Disgraced eighth president of FIFA. Considered by many to be the most evil man in the world. Blatter rose from his 1971 presidency of the World Society of Friends of Suspenders—a network bonding the 120 men in sixteen countries who were concerned by women's fashion ditching garter belts for pantyhose—to run FIFA, a nonprofit with a $1.4 billion cash reserve, in the style of a Chicago machine politician on a global scale.

Blatter's character was as if Scaramanga from James Bond had a bastard offspring of *All the King's Men*'s Willie Stark. While corruption scandal after scandal besmirched his organization, the Swiss displayed the perseverance of a cockroach, seemingly able to survive anything.

So craven was Blatter, we actually began to admire his ability to lie brazenly in front of the viewing world without letting out an evil smile or villainous cackle. In 2013 he told Oxford University students "Perhaps you think I am a ruthless parasite sucking the lifeblood out of the world and out of football—the Godfather of the FIFA gravy train" in a sudden lapse of momentary self-awareness. "There are those who will tell you that FIFA is just a conspiracy, a scam, accountable to nobody. . . . There are those who will tell you of the supposed sordid secrets that lie deep in our [James] Bond villain headquarters in the hills above Zurich. . . . There are not many names the media haven't thrown at me in the last few years. I would be lying to you if I said it didn't hurt. You ask yourself: 'What have I done?'"

In 2015, Blatter traveled to meet a fawning Vladimir Putin, who declared un-ironically that the Swiss warranted a Nobel Prize for his global leadership. Looking at the two dictators in the newspaper, one's mind struggled to calculate the evil captured in one photograph. In one of our favorite tweets of all time, a GFOP @Jon-Harvey911 quipped, "If Putin and Blatter were both drowning, and you only had time to save one, what kind of sandwich would you make?"

Watching US attorney general Loretta Lynch take Blatter out in May 2015 was a great American moment. As she stood up and declared, "Anyone who seeks to live in the past and to return soccer to the days of corruption and bribery, cronyism and patronage, this global response sends a clear message: You are on the wrong side of progress and do a disservice to the integrity of this wonderful sport," it felt like witnessing the Marshall Plan being gifted to the world all over again. We both teared up during the press conference, watching Lynch say what we've always felt, what we've always believed, that we've never been able to prove.

Blazer, Chuck: It is difficult to decide whether the corrupt football administrator Chuck Blazer was a Great American™ for squealing on FIFA or, as a longtime embezzler, the worst man to walk the footballing planet, but he was unquestionably one of the great Walter Mosley characters of all time.

A vast, corpulent man with a mangy beard so bushy, he was once told by Vladimir Putin that he looked like Karl Marx, Blazer claimed to have made a first fortune marketing Smiley Face buttons in the 1970s, before graduating to the barely monitored backwater of American soccer, where his penchant for collecting commissions as a regional power broker earned him the nickname "Mr. 10 Percent," and famously creamed enough money off the top of CONCACAF football to afford two apartments at Trump Tower in Manhattan, one for himself, the other for his cats.

By the time he was confronted by US authorities with charges of racketeering and wire fraud, Blazer was riddled with cancer and elected to turn informer, wearing a wire to ensnare many of his former partners in crime. The salacious details of his life spooled into the public eye when the Department of Justice announced their charges against FIFA in May 2015. Blazer was a man who would charge New York strip club nights to CONCACAF, using the code "SONY" to pass the expenses off as if he were cultivating the Japanese multinational, even though in reality, SONY stood for "Stringfellows of New York." A local neighbor told the *New York Post* Blazer's greatest delight later in life was to cruise around Central Park in a personal mobility scooter with a pet macaw named Max perched on his shoulder, cackling as passing children squealed in terror when attacked by the bird. In short, Chuck Blazer was a Coen Brothers movie character made real thanks to global football.

Blazer, Golden: The most important blazer presentation in sports that does not involve a cabin. A celebration of those who have dedicated their lives to growing the game we love in the country we love. (See next page.)

Blazers: When I first arrived in the United States, the sports coverage was mesmerizing. We had so little live sport broadcast in England on a regular basis, and there was so much on offer in the United States, yet it was the sportscasters' blazers which were like televisual catnip. They came in mustard yellows, sky blues, and reds. With detailed blazer patches attached. The winking eye of CBS. The proud peacock of NBC. The polyester-ish clip art of

2014 Bob Ley (*see* Ley, Bob)

2015 Julie Foudy (*see* Foudy, Super Julie)

2016 Loretta Lynch (*see* Lynch, Loretta)

2017 Rebecca Lowe (*see* Lowe, Rebecca)

ESPN. Their presence made the sport and the broadcasters just fall away. Only the blazers hypnotically held my eye. The quality of the coverage, and the ability of the commentators no longer mattered. The Sports Broadcaster's Blazer has a secret power, akin to Harry Potter's Cloak of Invisibility, conferring wisdom, charisma, and authority on all who don them. —**RB**

Blazers: My first blazer was a delightful dark green woolen number with faint yellow piping and the crest of my primary school, Brooklands, which fit my four-and-a-half-year-old frame perfectly when I started at the school in January 1971. It had been handed down to me by my older brother, Will, and I had been looking forward to wearing it ever since I could remember. This blazer was almost certainly responsible for my love of blazers.

When I attended "big school" at a London educational institution named Colfe's in 2011, a big reason was my affinity for their school colors—blue and yellow—and how much I like their tie and crest, worn as a blazer patch.

English schools are all about blazers and ties, and sweaters and caps, various hierarchies marked by variations in uniform and how you choose to wear them—special ties for different "houses," different-size knots and thickness of ties to mark your music and style affiliation, colorful caps and ties awarded for receiving "colors" in an individual sport, different colored blazers for "sixth formers" (eleventh and twelfth grade), and so on.

Then as a teenager I discovered the "sport-coat" aisle at the Flip Vintage American Fashion store in London's Soho, and it was like getting in the George Michael Sports Machine and taking a trip across the entire continent circa 1956. There were exotic new kinds of blazers here, unlined, cotton, plaid, linen, dogtooth, brightly colored, corduroy, golf club, white buttoned,

A blazer for every mood. A fabric for every emotion.

Why are my eyes shut? Why am I wearing bell bottoms? Why is this in soft focus? Why do I have the van Gaal–era Man United crest on my school uniform?

hockey, college football and basketball were all exotic and featured giant athletes. But I knew none of the stars and, frankly, I wasn't that interested. What caught my eye were the real giants of American sport, the mind-blowingly self-important, jocular, ever present, impeccably groomed, treacle-tongued, blazer-clad and logo-emblazoned broadcasters. They were the real stars. And they really seemed to know it. The ones with the blazers on. Emblazoned with the brands of their networks. Ping. Lightbulb. Filed away for twenty-five years.

Over the years I have worn some terrible blazers—velvet, suede, leather, four button, epaulettes, distressed, turquoise, and denim, you name it. But I have also owned my fair share of Harris Tweed, Gieves & Hawkes, and Kilgour. To this day, I never feel fully dressed without a blazer. As I age, I intend to wear a sportcoat when I'm participating in any sport, which inevitably will be mostly golf.

I will die and be buried in my favorite blazer. The dress code at my funeral will be blazers. Chuck Blazer will be the first man I look up in the afterlife. —MD

seersucker, one button, madras, narrow and wide lapelled. Every blazer seemed to have a patch on the inside pocket with the name of the store and city where it was purchased. Suddenly I was transported to exotic place names I'd never heard of, and the likes of which we had nothing in Britain—Tulsa, Sioux Falls, Omaha, Buffalo!!!, Baton Rouge, Spokane, Cincinnati, Toledo!!! Armed with a half dozen of these "sportcoats," a word I still love, I left for America for the first time in January of 1985.

At the Mercersburg Academy, in Mercersburg, Pennsylvania, I naturally became obsessed with watching American television. I had never seen anything like it before. Yes, the British networks had imported *The Rockford Files* and *Taxi* and *Rhoda* but from an early age I loved broadcasting, live television, sports, news, and entertainment. And I lapped it all up. My first exposure to *The Tonight Show*, *Saturday Night Live*, the *Today* show, and MTV influenced me for life, but it was the way that sports were covered on television that blew my mind. Yes, baseball, the NBA, the NFL, ice

My grandfather in one of his many "golf suits." That woman is not his wife.

Books, Best We Have Ever Read:
ROGER BENNETT:

Reunion by Fred Uhlman

A short young adult novel about friendship set in prewar Germany that I read obsessively when I was a kid.

Men Who March Away: Poems of the First World War by I. M. Parsons (editor)

We had to learn much of this book by heart at school when I was seven and eight years of age. It was a dark experience, but more than anything aside from being an Everton fan, it made me who I am.

The Marseilles Trilogy by Jean-Claude Izzo

A breathtaking piece of work which created the whole genre of Mediterranean noir, soaked in both a sense of place, and human doom.

The Drowned and the Saved by Primo Levi

The greatest book of all time. I read it every year. The second essay, "The Grey Zone," articulates everything you need to know about human nature.

MICHAEL DAVIES: Okay, maybe these aren't the best. But they're my favorite. And what they reveal about me is alarming.

Harold and the Purple Crayon by Crockett Johnson

I love children's books, always have, and have continued to read them my entire adult life. As a kid I devoured the Asterix series, Tintin, all the Paddington books. C. S. Lewis, the entire Ladybird collection, and an illustrated version of the Kama Sutra which I'm not telling you how I got my hands on, in order to protect the innocent. But one book has always stood above them all and captures my imagination to this day. It gives me a thrill to even think about it, it's so freaking beautiful. Honestly. The story of a young boy who wants to go for a walk in the moonlight and draws his entire adventure WITH A PURPLE CRAYON, as he tries to find his way back home to his own room, including, ultimately, his own house and bed on which he lies down and goes to sleep. It's perfect. One of only very few things ever which is better than football.

Buddenbrooks by Thomas Mann

This impressively thick 1901 tome, written when Mann was Harry Kane's age, is basically *Dallas* or *Empire* set in Northern Germany in the mid-nineteenth century. It is a soap opera about a family business written to the highest literary standard. It led to its author winning the Nobel Prize for Literature (the Swedish Academy's citation naming "his great novel *Buddenbrooks*" as the principal reason for his prize), which is basically like the Ballon d'Or with less hair gel. Somehow, and with the help of my Collins German dictionary, I read this in German at school, and have gone back and read it again and again in English since. I love German literature. When I attended the 2006 World Cup I fell in love with Germany (a little). But I will never forgive Manuel Neuer for not admitting that Frank Lampard's shot crossed the line in that World Cup round of 16 game in 2010 in South Africa. This scene, however, does not feature in the novel *Buddenbrooks*.

Ogilvy on Advertising by David Ogilvy

I have learned more about creativity, and working in a creative field, from this one book than from any other job, course, or person with the exception of my ridiculously smart and talented, but not quite as tall, older brother, William. The book is ostensibly about how to get a job in advertising, how to run an advertising agency, and how to create successful and powerful advertising. But along the way, this brilliant British émigré to the United States (he came fifty-one years before me, in 1938), tells the entire history of advertising, predicts its future, and comes as close to explaining how ideas can be communicated using words and pictures, about the power of persuasion, than anyone who has ever written on the dark art. The book includes the story of

how he created the Rolls-Royce print ad which I still think about every time I see a Roller or think about how to sell a high-end TV project.

But he also takes time to highlight the best ads ever created whether he was involved in them or not. Like this one (above, right), from Doyle Dane Bernbach for VW, which I think about every time I'm trying to think of how to sell something different.

Straight White Male by John Niven

My favorite novel by one of my favorite contemporary writers, this is a no-holds-barred tale of the hard-drinking, always insulting, hard-womanizing, Irish screenwriter Kennedy Marr. Set mainly between Los Angeles and England, Kennedy is an amalgam of many of my closest friends, and the book is at the same time familiar and shocking at every turn. Read secretly away from your wife or girlfriend. Or probably not at all. Just to be safe.

Tinker in Television by Grant Tinker

Until Barry Hearn writes his autobiography (or rather dictates it in one forty-eight-hour,

caffeine-and-lager-fueled, way-beyond-politically-incorrect ramble to his assistant, Michelle), this remains my favorite autobiography of all time and had a massive effect on me, and how I would come to view my career, when I read it in 1994. Tinker, at that time, was the only person to have ever run both a major television production company (MTM) and a major network (NBC). He had also cut his teeth as a television executive in Manhattan at two major advertising agencies just as Madison Avenue was taking over network programming. He therefore writes from a unique perspective, from every angle, on how good and bad television is made. And as one of the people primarily responsible for bringing *The Bob Newhart Show, Rhoda, Hill Street Blues,* and *Cheers* to television, four of my favorite shows ever, he knows enough about the former to have a view on the latter. But what really blew me away about the book was the relentless drive of the man through every phase of his life, whether he was flying high or struggling mightily, and that has always stayed with me.

Boyhood Dream: A phrase commonly used in football after an expensive transfer fee. "It has

been a dream of mine since boyhood to sign for
_____." Popularized by Robbie Keane, who has
uttered it with a straight face after each one of
his moves to Coventry City, Inter Milan, Leeds
United, Tottenham Hotspur, Liverpool, Celtic,
and LA Galaxy. Davo's boyhood dream was to
be the youngest tank commander in the British
Army. Rog wanted to be either a cabin boy on
the Love Boat or a Nazi Hunter in Brazil. Being
a sports broadcaster turns out to be the perfect
combination.

Brazil: Every international football fan's second favorite football team, unless you hail
from Argentina. Five World Cup victories.
And endless production line of mono-named
heroes—Garrincha! Socrates! Ronaldo!—
whom we spent countless hours aping as
schoolkids on the muddy fields of England.

Their 1970 team remains football's gold standard. Carlos Alberto, Tostão, Jairzinho, and
Pelé were part of a flamboyant, freewheeling
spectacle that defined the Cirque du Soleil style
of the Brazilian national team at a time when
it seemed as if Technicolor had been invented
solely to capture the glowing beauty of their
jersey.

Yet football changes, and once their opponents employed all physical means necessary to
kick them off the field, the Brazilians battled to
weld some muscle or *football força* onto their
beautiful game. An ugly, imbalanced tactical
mesh resulted, the nadir of which came at the
1994 World Cup. Brazil were victorious but
with a brutal, pragmatic style of football epito-
mized by the final which was won—horror of
horrors—on penalties. Coach Carlos Parreira
complained in 2006, "Why does Brazil have to
play beautifully and the others don't?"

That pressure, combined with the corruption that has plagued the game in Brazil, has
undermined the notion of Joga Bonito, or "The
Beautiful Game," which exists now only as a
myth, much as the one that projects Brazil as
a nation of samba and supermodels. In the
modern period, the team have depended almost

entirely on the roguish, cyberpunk charisma of
Neymar. The world's first Manga football star.
An overreliance that was humiliatingly exposed
on home turf by the 7–1 bare-bottom spanking
dispensed by the Germans at World Cup 2014.

The only thing Brazil now leads the football
world in is "Honey Shots." When the Seleção
take the field, television match directors are
guaranteed an endless supply of beautiful-
looking football fans to zoom in on, as opposed
to the sunburned drunks with bellies spilling
out of a football shirt when England play.

Bristol City: Though I have seen multiple
games in the home sections at Crystal Palace,
Charlton, Fulham, and Hibernian, the only
English or Scottish team that has truly captured my imagination and broken my heart,
other than my beloved Chelsea Football Club,
is Bristol City in the late 1970s and early
1980s.

I had a family connection to Bristol through
my Uncle Michael Davies, my father's good-
humored and often hilarious younger brother,
a former music hall comedian, who lived in
the village of Long Ashton just outside England's sixth largest city. But my relationship
with the Robins was forged one wet September
afternoon on the Stamford Bridge terraces in
1975 when with my Cub Scout troop (!!!) we
watched Bristol City come from behind to earn
a 1–1 draw against the Blues, led by a tower-
ing, slide-tackling, ball-possessing, defensive
master class from the best ball-playing center
back I had ever seen in my life, Geoff Merrick.

Who?

This guy:

This curly-permed, mus-
tachioed, big-nosed human
specimen was far from fa-
mous or even particularly
well regarded. But he be-
came Bristol City captain at
twenty and was Bristol City's best player for fif-
teen years. And that afternoon he blew my Cub
Scout socks off, setting off a lifelong apprecia-

BRAZILIAN LANGUAGE

We relocated to Rio de Janeiro for five weeks during the 2014 World Cup to broadcast for ESPN, who had the wisdom to lock us up in a panic room for much of our stay. We loved what we saw of Rio, quickly immersing ourselves in the opportunity to experience different cultures and learn new languages. Here is a list of the Portuguese we mastered during our stay there:

Por que essas máscaras de oxigênio caíram do teto do nosso avião?	Why have those oxygen masks descended from the ceiling of our aircraft?
Você tem mais daqueles comprimidos grandes que você deu ao Sr. Bob Ley?	Do you have any more of those large pills you gave to Mr. Bob Ley?
A sua lavanderia pode tirar esse vômito das minhas calças?	Can your dry cleaner get this sick out of my pants?
Você acredita no "movimento do oceano"?	Do you believe in the "Motion of the Ocean"?
Você sabe tocar alguma do Phil Collins?	Can you play any Phil Collins?
Sim, gostaria muito de jogar monte de três cartas.	Yes, I would very much like to play Three Card Monte.
Estou sem dinheiro. Sequestra ele ao invés de mim.	I have no money. Kidnap him instead.
Você poderia me desatar desta mula?	Can you untie me from this mule?
Meus testículos estão muito doloridos.	My testicles are very sore.
"Na cara, não!" Or, more formally: *"No rosto, não!"*	"Not in the face!"
Não sou árbitro. Por favor não me decapite.	I am not a referee. Please do not behead me.
Por que você está segurando essa serra elétrica tão perto do meu rosto?	Why are you holding that power saw so close to my face?
Por que você está rindo? Os EUA vão ganhar a Copa do Mundo.	Why are you laughing? The USA <u>will</u> win the World Cup.

tion for comfortable-in-possession, positionally astute, intelligently physical center backs. That season, Merrick led Bristol City to promotion to the vaunted elite of the pre–Premier League era First Division. While Chelsea labored in the second tier, I followed Bristol City's remarkable 1976–77 top flight season as best as I could through occasional newspaper reports, the scores coming in by vidiprinter on the Saturday afternoon sports shows (*Grandstand* and *World of Sport*) and occasional coverage in my favorite comics, *Tiger and Scorcher* and *Shoot*. It was a nail-biting season, with Bristol sitting near, or right at, the bottom of the league the entire season, including with just two games to go. But somehow they escaped.

In the 1978–79 season, Chelsea, who had come up the year before, finished dead last in the first division and were relegated again. But no worries, I still had my Robins in the top

flight, but then they did something which was more Spursy than anything the Spurs could ever dream of. They were relegated in successive seasons between 1980 and 1982, all the way from the first division to the fourth. The club almost went bankrupt, but under the leadership of Geoff Merrick, the players ripped up their contracts and took unemployment benefits, which saved the club. This, and England's desperately depressing performance at the World Cup in Spain that summer, ushered in my dark years away from football. Cricket and tennis, and, frankly, beer and girls, took over for me and occupied all of my waking and weekend thoughts. However, at the end of the 1984 season I saw Chelsea beat Leeds 5–0 at Stamford Bridge to gain promotion back up to the top flight and I never drifted or flirted with any other team again. Even when Bristol City beat Chelsea in the FA Cup in 1990. I have always

The Rockin' Robins. One of the principal reasons cheerleaders never took off in Britain.

seen football as a battle between the forces of blue and the forces of red. But in truth, during my confused adolescence I was a red as well as a blue. Or at the very least, a Robin. **—MD**

British Empire: Britain was once the world's superpower. Was it just 1763, when Englishmen believed it was their destiny to rule the world, shape it to their will, and build an empire to rival that of the Ancient Greeks and Romans? How did it come to this?

The Japanese capture of Singapore in 1942 shattered the notion of British invincibility. India was lost and the African colonies tumbled like dominoes throughout the 1950s into the 1960s. The Suez Crisis in 1956 was a public humiliation.

The peerless football historian David Goldblatt wrote in his history of English football, *The Game of Our Lives,* that in the late 1960s Sir Richard Turnbull, the last governor of Af-

rican colony Tanganyika, once told the British defense secretary that "when the British Empire finally sank beneath the waves of history, it would leave behind only two monuments—one was the game of association football, the other was the expression 'F*&k off.'" Judging by the form of the English national football team, he was half right. The lasting impact of the decline of the Empire and the national impotence that resulted was best summed up by actor Steve Coogan in an interview with the *Times*: "Americans are about success. . . . The British get more pleasure from seeing other people fail than ourselves succeed."

Broigus (Yiddish, from *broyges*, "dispute, quarrel"): A bitter dispute or unresolvable feud, often within a family. Common usage: Spurs fans are broigus with Roberto Soldado for having cost so much money and producing bupkes in front of goal. My grandfather was one of seven siblings. He fell out with almost all of them, and spent his final years burying them, and returning from funerals in tears, furious at himself for not having been part of their lives.

I once told Davo of my efforts as a six- or seven-year-old to try to console my grandfather by asking why he had never spoken to the deceased sibling. "We had a broigus and fell out" he would mutter curtly in reply.

"What was the cause of the broigus?" I always wondered.

"I can't remember," he would burble before breaking down in a new fit of tortured sobbing.

As an optimist who always sees good in other people, Davo came to a simple conclusion. "We must not hate," he declared on the pod. I learned a

different life lesson from my grandfather's misery. Hate with reason. And always write that reason down. —RB

Brokaw, Tom: I started talking about football on television on the *Morning Joe* show during the 2010 World Cup. Football did not really belong on a show which covered global and domestic politics in such serious form, yet host Joe Scarborough had fallen hard for the game and wanted to talk about his growing love of Liverpool Football Club.

The segment was typically a rapid-fire four-minute crash through the weekend soccer headlines with the table of the regular political pundits looking on in a bemused silence. This changed the third time I was on. Former ad man Donny Deutsch interrupted the flow by expressing his shock that an American show would find a place for European soccer.

Live broadcasts are an eerie experience. The need to keep talking means the mouth often engages without passing the words through the required mental filters. Instinct just takes over. Without missing a beat, I found myself asking

Deutsch if he had any grandchildren. "I do, but what has that got to do with it?" he responded. "You are an old man, Donny Deutsch," I heard myself saying. "Soccer is the fastest-growing sport for Americans under the age of thirty in America. You might have grown up playing stickball on the street in Brooklyn, but today the young audience is following Premier League football." Suitably chastised, Deutsch was suddenly silenced as if his battery pack had been ripped out.

Two weeks later I was on again. I charged into my opening with enthusiasm, only to be interrupted again. This time by Tom Brokaw. "Wait a minute, wait a minute," the veteran broadcasting legend interjected. "We are in America!" he exclaimed. "Where we care about ball sports like baseball and NFL football. Talking about *soccer* is simply anti-American." Brokaw's rant went on and on, yet he pronounced the word "soccer" with such scorn I quickly became lost inside my own head. I thought about unleashing the ageist attack I had used to ensnare Deutsch, but this was TOM BROKAW who was steamrolling me. Television royalty. Humiliating him would be like mocking the Queen. So I sat there silently for four minutes, dying inside as the man who wrote *The Greatest Generation* mocked me and the sport I loved on live television.

Utterly humiliated, and believing my broadcast career had just been ended, I somehow crawled out of the studio. To my surprise the show producer said, "Same time next week, Roger?" as I headed for the door. "I will never, EVER go on live television when Brokaw sits at the desk," I grimaced.

I did the show every week for two years without incident. Then in early January, I took to the set and to my horror Brokaw was once again in place opposite Joe Scarborough as the clock ticked down before live broadcast resumed. "I am not going on with bloody Brokaw," I hissed. "Don't worry, he is a changed man," said the producer, shoving me into my seat just in time as the last commercial ended.

My segment began. I leapt into my opening. To my horror, Brokaw leant forward and interrupted me once more. "Wait a minute . . . wait a minute," he said, using words which had populated my recurring nightmares ever since I had last heard him utter them. "I once said soccer is un-American," he began, as I sat chilled, finding myself gasping for air. "Yet, since then, I have had the opportunity to travel to England with my sons-in-law to watch Premier League games, and I have to admit, I have developed a new appreciation for the game," he said with a quiet pride whilst across the desk the blood flowed back into my face. "We even fly coach," he concluded, handing the conversation back to me so I could charge through the Manchester United–Sunderland highlights package. —RB

Brooke, Rupert: My favorite First World War poet. Ridiculously good-looking, so much so that almost everyone he met—of either sex—seemed to fall in love with him. Like an early-nineteenth-century Kyle Martino. Commissioned into the Royal Navy Volunteer Reserve, he sailed as part of the British Mediterranean Expeditionary Force and died before the Gallipoli invasion from an infected mosquito bite. A few years earlier he had journeyed to and traveled across America from where he penned a brilliant series of letters which were published to great acclaim back home in England. I read them when I was about thirteen, and one

Great Hair

of his earliest impressions has always made me laugh out loud and still rings true:

"In five things America excels modern England—fish, architecture, jokes, drinks, and children's clothes. There may be others. Of these I am certain."

From America, he took the long way home via the Pacific and fell in love with a Tahitian woman named Taatamata.

The opening lines of his most famous poem, written en route to war in 1914, one year before his death, have haunted and inspired young Englishmen for more than a hundred years:

If I should die, think only this of me:
That there's some corner of a foreign field
That is for ever England. —MD

C

Camus, Albert: Algerian novelist, philosopher, sworn enemy of Jean-Paul Sartre, and goalkeeping youth prospect, who was once purported to have said, "Everything I know about morality and the obligations of men, I owe it to football." Though Camus experts suggest this quote has been taken out of context, we, at *Men in Blazers,* would like to believe it. The game allows us to feel the kind of emotions—joy, misery, wonder, abject failure—normal people experience in real life, yet we are otherwise numb to.

Carroll, Andy: A crusader on a holy war to prove man buns are not the single worst haircut in the world for white guys. His work was a progression. First, the man bun. Then he mixed things up and  went cornrows. His pièce de résistance came a week later when he mixed them both together and voilà, presented himself to the world as English Kevin Federline. As an editorial note, it is criminal that some men go bald early in life, yet Haired People like Andy Carroll fritter away their gifts in this dangerous fashion.

Chamakh, Marouane: Marouane Chamakh's hair was an enigma that transcended English football: long yet sparse, composed of equal part thatch and flesh, both awash in wet hair gel. In different lights, it resembled a rancid tea-towel, festering carcass, or septic wound.

It was not always this way. When the striker arrived from Bordeaux in 2010, Arsenal fans giddily turned to YouTube to feast upon highlights of the fast-paced scoring phenomenon outstripping French defenses with his hair sculpted into a sharpened scimitaresque point.

Chamakh is a lot less bald in person, and on FIFA.

Chamakh adjusted quickly to life at the Emirates, plundering 10 goals in his first 21 games. Photographs of that brief English football honeymoon prove the Moroccan's hair initially appeared proud, like a battering ram, in the red and white of Arsenal.

But a goalless purgatory was to follow. From November 2010 until August 2013 when the player decamped to Crystal Palace, Chamakh scored just one Premier League goal. A woeful lack of confidence on the field, and peripheral profile off it, transformed the once prolific forward into an object of league-wide scorn.

Chamakh's confidence was not the only thing to thin. To Google Image the player is to trace his hairline evaporating like a fresh flower in bloom decomposing in fast-motion photography. Marouane attempted to stave off the inevitable, applying wet hair gel as if it was a restorative miracle elixir. That approach only served to make him look balder.

Chamakh finally turned things around during his 2015 season at Palace, which made us realize maybe we had misunderstood his hair choices. The forward may not have been obsessed with what he had lost at all, focusing instead on what was still there. Being an attacker is all about feeling potent. In his mind, he still had it.

Chanting: New American Premier League fans are always agog at the atmosphere at English football games, especially the creativity, wit, and spontaneity of the terrace chants bolted onto melodies familiar from musicals, classic rock, and nursery rhymes.

English poet Andrew Motion once attempted to explain the phenomenon as "a natural upswelling of rhythmical thinking and feeling" but the truth is, many songs are birthed after several cans of lager on long bus rides to away games. The tunes tend to take root more on the road because only the true hard core are in attendance. They can then be spread at pubs before kickoff and be widely known by kickoff.

Success is a muse but the peril of relegation often spurs a gallows humor. Regional clashes also encourage creativity, especially in games between teams from the North and the South. Newcastle fans delight in reminding Chelsea fans they are "just soft Southern Bastards." Chelsea fans will respond by bellowing "Speak F*&%$ng English! Why don't you speak F*#king English!"

OUR FAVORITE CHANTS OF ALL TIME

"You'll never make the station . . ."
The most menacing chant commonly sung to away fans by the home mob near the end of the game.

Neville Neville, your future's immense,
Neville Neville, you play in defence,
Neville Neville, like Jacko you're bad,
Neville Neville, is the name of your dad.
Sung by Manchester United fans when both Gary and Phil Neville played for the club. The brothers' father was named Neville Neville.

"Jason Puncheon, he went for a shit."
The then Southampton winger disappeared briefly down the tunnel during a game against Everton in January 2013, only to reappear minutes later and run back onto the field, causing Saints fans to break out in this improvised chant which caused the player to start laughing on the field.

"There's only two Andy Gorams."
A riff on the popular chant to a beloved player, that there is "only one" of him. Chanted by Rangers fans to the tune of "Guantanamera," after their goalkeeper was reported to have a mild form of schizophrenia.

"Podolski to the left of me, Walcott to the right, here I am, stuck in the middle Giroud!"
Arsenal fans reworking of the 1970s hit "Stuck in the Middle with You."

"You've got chlamydia!"
During a Leeds United match against Peterborough in 2008, the local health service elected to use the occasion to promote "chlamydia awareness" by dispatching two testing vans outside the stadium. Leeds manager at the time was the legendary Gary McAllister. Once the game kicked off, Leeds fans erupted with a riff on "La donna è mobile" from Verdi's *Rigoletto*, "We've got McAllister—you've got

chlamydia!" reveling in the tune for ninety minutes, then never singing it again.

Chapman, Tracy: There are few songs I fall in love with the very first time I hear them. Tracy Chapman's "Fast Car" was one of those songs when it came out in 1988, and not only because it had been about a decade since I had heard a tune without a hammering drum machine. Chapman was an anti-charismatic folk singer with a haunting voice and a propensity to write tunes about human misery, hopelessness, cracks in the social fabric, loneliness, and suffering. To this day, whenever Everton lose, I play "Fast Car" after the final whistle. Her breakout song about big teen dreams, shattering realities, parental alcoholism, deadbeat dads, and bleak futures. An instant reminder that even though the team I love have just dropped three points, nothing in life is sadder than a Tracy Chapman song. —RB

Charlie Oboe Love Dog: One of the great advantages of growing up in the Davies household was growing up bilingual. Not with any kind of useful language like Spanish, or German or Arabic, but with mastery of the joint Army/Navy phonetic alphabet which my father learned in the Royal Engineers. When it gets a bit chilly, I still find myself muttering "Charlie Oboe Love Dog" or when spring comes and the Panic Room gets a bit sweaty, "William Able Roger Mike." Rog is "Roger Oboe George" and Davo is "Dog Able Victor Oboe" and football is often "Charlie Roger Able Peter" especially "Victor Item Love Love Able." —MD

JOINT ARMY/NAVY PHONETIC ALPHABET

LETTER	PHONETIC	LETTER	PHONETIC
A	Able	J	Jig
B	Baker	K	King
C	Charlie	L	Love
D	Dog	M	Mike
E	Easy	N	Nan
F	Fox	O	Oboe
G	George	P	Peter
H	How	Q	Queen
I	Item	R	Roger
S	Sail/Sugar	1	One
T	Tare	2	Two
U	Uncle	3	Three
V	Victor	4	Four
W	William	5	Five
X	X-ray	6	Six
Y	Yoke	7	Seven
Z	Zebra	8	Eight
0	Zero	9	Nine

Chelsea: It is hard to believe just how many Chelsea fans there are in the United States. In England, the club have a complex brand that elicits conflicting "love or loathe it" emotions. Yet, after watching Roman Abramovich's team tour America repeatedly preseason, it has become impossible not to be awestruck at the sincere, rapturous American support they draw.

I once watched Chelsea play Manchester City at Yankee Stadium and found the United States Chelsea fans to be a peculiar breed of American, unabashedly and unironically sporting their John Terry and Fernando Torres jerseys whilst patiently queuing up for their light beers and pretzels. Standing in their midst, I could not resist polling a gaggle of clean-cut college student Vampire Weekend look-alikes to uncover what first drew them to support Roman Abramovich's club. "An unrivaled history of success," explained one. "Because they are 'The Good Guys!'" exclaimed another. A third suggested "Stylish football" with a broken-voiced sense of uncertainty that made it sound as if his statement ended with a question mark.

In the wake of those conversations, I set up an experiment with branding expert Noah Brier who ran a test to crowdsource consumer brand sentiment toward every Premier League team in both England and the United States.

"Money" was the most used gut response to Chelsea in both countries, yet the term appeared to mean two very different things on either side of the Atlantic. For the English, the other most used terms were "Chelski," "Scum," and a litany of derogatory phrases. (No other team had more offensive entries, and seeing as there the program uses a swear filter, the number of creative spellings employed was admirable.) Yet in America, that tenor of disapproval ("Poor Man's City," "Bought Trophies," and "Plastic Fans") was rare, paling in comparison to "Rich," "Oligarch," and "Abramovich," which were among the most dominant, suggesting that in the home of the "American Dream," the club's gilded status warrants only admiration. —RB

Chelsea Football Club: I was selected by the Premier League sorting hat for Chelsea in 1970–71 by the confluence of a sequence of unforgettable events. My parents had rented a color television right when color broadcasts had started in late 1969/early 1970. And what a time it was to be introduced to the club. Chelsea were enjoying their best period since the 1950s. They had an amazing team, the classy Peter Bonetti in goal, protected by Ron "Chopper" Harris in the heart of defense. Up front, the gifted striker Peter Osgood and marauding winger Ian

Hutchinson were supported by a midfield that included my two favorite players, the Scotsman Charlie Cooke and the tragically overlooked by England John Hollins. But I'm not really sure it was the players, the team, or even the football that I fell in love with. It was the kit.

Look at that blue. No Chelsea kit has come close to that blue. Darker than any blue in the history of football. The matching shorts with the white stripe down the sides. The stripe-less white socks. Classic and elegant and dare, I say, fashion forward. After Chelsea beat my older brother's favorite team, Leeds United, in the 1970 FA Cup final, back when the FA Cup was still a thing, I begged for a Chelsea shirt. My mum improvised. She sewed strips of white satin down the sides of a pair of blue rugby shorts and then she found the closest thing she could find to a Chelsea shirt, a Glasgow Rangers shirt.

I would like to think my mother understood the deep historical connection between "The Blue Brothers" which have bonded Chelsea and Rangers fans for more than a hundred years.

Chelsea, the most diverse team in English football in 1970

(Chelsea's first manager in 1905 was a former Rangers player who borrowed shirts from his old club for Chelsea to play in. There are also some less savory connections to do with anti-Catholicism, pro-Ulster unionism, loyalist tendencies, fascism, racism, and gang-related violence.) But my mum has never really been into any of that nonsense or history malarkey.

1970s Scottish male model Derek Johnstone

I wore those homemade Chelsea shorts, my Rangers shirt, and a pair of long white socks pretty much every day for two years. Until, inevitably, I grew out of them. In that time, in addition to the 1970 FA Cup, Chelsea won the 1971 Cup Winners' Cup against Real Madrid in a replay and lost to Stoke City in the 1972 League Cup final. The rest of the 1970s and 1980s were a turbulent period for the club. In the 16 seasons between 1973–74 and 1988–89 after which I left Britain permanently for America, Chelsea spent as many seasons in the old second division as the old first. In that time I saw them play Man United and Liverpool and Arsenal and Leeds when they were still a big club. But I also saw them play in the wind and cold on a dreadful surface against Grimsby Town, Plymouth Argyle, Shrewsbury, and Manchester City when they were awful.

My fandom and enthusiasm ebbed and flowed during my teenage years and when I moved to America in 1989, I barely followed English football at all. Apart from the World Cup in 1990, I barely watched any soccer until 1992. When the Premier League started, I watched games when I could find them on TV, and as my job at the Walt Disney Studios started allowing me to travel somewhat regularly to Britain, I started going to Stamford Bridge again. The Ruud Gullit and Gianluca Vialli eras at Chelsea (1995–98 and 1998–2000) are

my favorite ever as a Chelsea fan. I loved the football we played—buccaneering, continental, but with a nasty bite, mainly from Dennis Wise. But mainly, I loved Gianfranco Zola, my favorite footballer of all time. For the FA Cup final in 1997 against Robbie Mustoe's Middlesbrough, I got up early and went to the Kings Head in Santa Monica with my great friend and fellow Chelsea supporter George Waud. Roberto Di Matteo scored after 45 seconds, and after Mustoe had a goal disallowed for the most marginal of offsides, Eddie Newton added a second after a superb putback from Zola. I started drinking heavily and barely remember Dennis Wise lifting Chelsea's first major trophy in twenty-six years. For Ruud Gullit, this was the first major English trophy ever won by a foreign manager. The following season, the Dutchman took the team to second place in the Premier League and the quarter finals of two cup competitions before, to begin a fine Chelsea tradition, he was fired. Gianluca Vialli replaced him and won the League Cuppity Cup Cup and UEFA Cup Winners' Cuppity Cup Cup. And in truth, like most Chelsea fans, we got over the loss of Ruud Gullit pretty quickly.

However, Gullit was vital to the transformation of the club. And without his tenure, I doubt that Roman Abramovich would ever have purchased the team in June 2003. That first season under Ranieri was spectacular, the atmosphere at Stamford Bridge was the most electric I have ever experienced (I saw us hammer Wolves, Leicester, and Newcastle at home), "Kalinka Kalinka Kalinka Kakalinka" chanted by thousands of young English thugs who had previously shown little interest in nineteenth-century Russian folk music. Abramovich started fiddling around with the loose change in his pocket and buying things—121 million GBP worth of Crespo, Smertin, Glen Johnson, Geremi, Veron, Duff, Wayne Bridge, Joe Cole, Scott Parker, and Mutu (but he was obviously broken). No purchase was more important than Claude Makélélé though, who played a role we had barely seen in English football before, shielding the defense, making tackles and short accurate passes. Chelsea reached the semifinals of the Champions League that season, and finished second in the Premier League behind the unbeaten "Invincibles" of Arsenal. But the Champions League was won that year by a young Portuguese manager at Porto. And Roman Abramovich decided he wanted some of that.

Abramovich cracked open his checkbook again before the 2004–05 season for his suave, modern, self-proclaimed "special one," José Mourinho. But this time, they bought more intelligently—Ferreira, Alex, and Tiago were all unspectacular but key ingredients of the new Chelsea squad. But in Cech, Drogba, Carvalho, and Arjen Robben, Abramovich and Mourinho had unearthed four of the greatest Premier League players of all time. Chelsea cruised to the title that inaugural Mourinho season. They clinched the title on April 30 away at Bolton and when Frank Lampard rounded Jussi Jääskeläinen and slotted Chelsea's second on 76 minutes to wrap up the points and the title, I threw my head-to-toe Chelsea-clad eight-month-old daughter JJ so high in the air and so close to the ceiling, that to this day she flinches a little whenever Chelsea score. But this was the first Premier League or first division title of my lifetime. Chelsea's first league title in fifty years, and they had done it in style, earning more points than any team in Premier League history, including the unbeaten Arsenal team of the year before. By the time they won the 2005–06 title, beating Manchester United 3–0 at home with goals from William Gallas, Ricardo Carvalho, and one of my favorite Chelsea goals of all time from a still young and electric Joe Cole, I was living in a surreal blue world of excellence, dominance, and massive expectations. Chelsea's rise after being relegated to the second division in 1989 had echoed my own rise from part-time tennis coach in Central Florida to running my own television studio which two years later I would to sell to Sony. I mean for about the amount of cash that

Roman takes out for a weekend mini-break in the South of France. But still. Suddenly, after forty years of supporting a fashionable loser, I was suddenly the fan of a Russian-oligarch-fueled winner. And the people that didn't love the club, mostly hated the club. It has never much bothered me, but it is odd, especially in America, where so few people remember who Chelsea were in the early 2000s, let alone before the Premier League era. Antonio Conte has brought back some of the fashionable and continental swagger to the club that I so loved in the 1990s, but in truth, what I love about Chelsea is still no more complicated than my love of that dark shade of blue.

CHELSEA PLAYERS
DAVO'S FIVE FAVORITE, OF ALL TIME

5. CLAUDE MAKÉLÉLÉ

The Zaire-born French international defensive midfielder made just 144 appearances for the club between 2003 and 2008 but was more responsible than any other player for bringing the Premier League title to Chelsea for the first time in 2004–05. In the process, he literally redefined the defensive midfield role, and invented a new position—"the Makélélé role." In Mourinho's Chelsea formation, Makélélé was a third central midfielder, positioned deeper than the other two, adding an extra layer of protection in front of the defensive line.

Makélélé was not a physical powerhouse. He didn't have great technical ability nor a brilliant passing range and he rarely scored. What he did have was immense intelligence, seeing attacks before

Makélélé about to make his 400th less-than-ten-foot pass of the game

they happened and sniffing them out in the most efficient manner possible. His tackling and positional sense were a joy to behold as he routinely stopped players who were stronger, quicker, and/or flashier than him.

The Makélélé role is appallingly misapplied by youth coaches all over America who stick a player who can neither defend nor attack in front of the back four and tell him or her to do both. His teammate at Real and for France, Zinedine Zidane, on hearing that Real were letting him go to Ranieri's Chelsea (the year before Mourinho arrived) and bringing in Beckham, reportedly commented: "Why put another layer of gold paint on the Bentley when you are losing the entire engine?"

4. DENNIS WISE

Dennis Wise sporting a bald-denying front comb-over on Setanta Sports

An original, card-carrying member of the Wimbledon "Crazy Gang" (so dubbed by the media because of their boisterous antics and rampant enthusiasm for playing practical jokes on their manager, Dave Bassett) that reached the FA Cup final in 1988, Dennis Wise joined Chelsea in 1990 and is arguably the most aggressive midfielder in the club's history. In his eleven years at the club he made 332 appearances and won two FA Cups, a League Cup, and a UEFA Cup Winners' Cup, making him the club's most successful captain before John Terry. Since his playing career ended, Wise has been a successful manager and sporter of very poor haircuts in television punditry roles.

3. IAN HUTCHINSON

With the greatest respect to Jimmy Greaves, Bobby Tambling, Peter Osgood, Charlie Cooke, Kerry Dixon, Mark Hughes, Jimmy Floyd Hasselbaink, and Didier Drogba, my favorite forward player in the history of Chelsea Football Club is the first player I ever idolized. In an era when tackles flew, pitches were made mostly of mud, and the ball was as hard as a rock, Ian Hutchinson ran the wings and attacked

Ian Hutchinson prepares to throw the ball the entire width of the pitch.

the ball with his head harder than any player I have ever seen in football. "If you got a ball down the line, he was so brave. He used to go where other players feared to go. He was a 110 percent player," said his captain Ron "Chopper" Harris. He was once described as a "one man panzer division" and frequently lauded for his "muscular optimism," evidenced in particular by his staggering ability with the long throw-in. Watch the one in the 1970 Cup final replay against Leeds at Old Trafford that basically won Chelsea the FA Cup for the first time in front of the second-biggest TV audience in the history of British TV, behind only the 1966 World Cup final. He threw it a mile, at speed, from the left wing, and it basically ricocheted in off David Webb's shoulder. Hutchinson played 144 times for Chelsea and scored 58 goals. He also had amazing sideburns.

2. FRANK LAMPARD

Love or hate Chelsea, it is hard not to admire Lampard's outstanding and unprecedented contribution to the club: 648 appearances, 211 goals, 13 trophies. He holds the record for most goals ever scored in the Premier League by a midfielder and the most continuous Premier League appearances for an outfield player, 164 (are you reading this, Daniel Sturridge?). His work ethic as a professional footballer has been widely lauded, both on and off the field, as

Do I look fat in this blazer?

has his brain. In fact, he may be one of only a handful of Premier League footballers to ever have one. Rog is convinced that he is fat. But I'd like to see them both take their shirts off so we could compare.

1. GIANFRANCO ZOLA

It is not the 309 appearances made, or the 80 goals scored that make Zola Chelsea's greatest-ever player, or my favorite-ever player, it's that almost every time he played, the Magic Box made in Sardinia was by far the best player on the pitch, capable of humiliating opponents, with a smile on his face, and doing things with his feet that took your breath away. He brought trophies to the club the minute he arrived. He won the football writers Player of the Year in 1996–97 having played only A PARTIAL SEASON. He made the players around him stars. And he taught a young Frank Lampard and John Terry and every other Chelsea player how to train, eat, and play like professionals.

This man just did something ridiculous.

More than anything else, though, Zola played the game with irrepressible joy, electricity, and such a clear love of the game. He's like the grown-up one-man version of both Italian kids in *Kicking and Screaming*. When he left the club for Cagliari on his native Sardinia in 2003, it is reported that Roman Abramovich tried to buy Cagliari just to get him back. His number 25 has virtually been retired at Chelsea. Who would ever dare to wear it anyway? Just You-Tube a collection of his goals for Chelsea. And him turning Jamie Carragher inside out. And what he did to Manchester United that had Alex Ferguson describe him as "a crafty little bugger." Chelsea will never see another player like him. And I doubt the Premier League will either. **—MD**

Cherophobia: An aversion to happiness based on the fact something tragic is around the corner. Rog probably suffers from it.

Cherundolo, To: Inspired by once buccaneering USMNT right back Steve Cherundolo, who first caught our eye in Kaiserslautern, Germany, at the 2006 World Cup during an against-all-odds 1–1 draw against the eventual winners of that tournament, Italy.

The definition of the full verb is to charge both forward and backward, playing both offense and defense, usually in the right back position: *Micah Richards used to Cherundolo more when he was younger and played at right back.*

However, the larger verb can be, and usually is broken into two separate verbs.

- *To Cherun:* To run up the pitch in an attacking manner. *Remember when Ivanovic used to Cherun all the way from his penalty box into the other team's penalty box to try to get his head on a cross?*
- *To Dolo:* To sprint back from the attacking third into the defensive third of the pitch to play defense. *Glen Johnson has always been an attacking threat, but at Stoke he seems to*

Rog would like to have this photograph of him and Cherundolo tattooed as a tramp stamp.

have added a new dimension to his game, he always Dolos to get back in position.

Some fullbacks Cherun more than they Dolo. Others only Dolo and almost never Cherun. The greatest fullbacks do both.

Rog is fairly sure that "Azpilicueta" is Spanish for "Cherundolo."

Children: One of the greatest parenting challenges I have ever faced is the year my oldest son, Samson, decided he was a Liverpool fan. He was five at the time and under the sway of my charismatic, new-to-our-family brother-in-law whose parents' home happened to back onto that of real-life professional footballer Fernando Torres. I took the news about as badly as if my son had told me he was off to volunteer for ISIS.

The love of Everton has run in our family's blood for three generations. From an identity perspective, that support outstrips football. It is a character-building way of looking at the harsh reality of humanity. A worldview. An awareness that life is unforgiving, and happy moments are fleeting.

Samson spent a year in the football wilderness before miraculously coming back to Everton and me of his own accord. Liverpool captain Steven Gerrard infamously beat up a local DJ who had the temerity to ignore his requests to play a Phil Collins track. This sensational incident, captured on security cam, was replayed on a nightly basis on FOX Soccer News. The brutality and omnipresence of the images traumatized my young son, and thanks to DVR technology, I made sure he was exposed to them on a twice-daily basis.

It took three weeks for my son to crack. One morning over breakfast, he approached me with an offer: if I purchased him a Tonka pickup truck and an England jersey with Jack Rodwell's name and number on the back (such innocence) he would return to the Everton fold. A bribe I had to beg for my wife's permission to invest in, which I received on a one-time emergency basis, along with a pledge from my son this return was irrevocable.

I am not proud of my behavior as a father over this period, but it worked. —RB

Choosing a Team: In England, the choice of team you support is traditionally dictated by local geography over multi-generations, but in the United States (indeed throughout the new global world order in which the English Premier League is growing like a weed) that relationship is not always forged in blood. Lacking deep roots, team allegiance can quickly shift.

Gareth Bale's leap into La Liga highlighted this peculiar phenomenon. The Welshman's 2012–13 Player of the Year season, in which he blasted home a European best 11 goals from outside the box, and earned his team an extra 24 points with his 21 Premier League goals, served as footballing catnip for a contingent of American fans who were new to the game and quickly became hooked on Tottenham's plight.

Yet, the combination of Clint Dempsey's sudden exit, and Bale's cash-soaked transfer to Real Madrid exerted an unsettling emotional pull away from White Hart Lane, in the Welshman's case, toward the Bernabéu.

This may prove to be more than an American problem. In an age in which football's transcendent players have sidestepped the strict control of their clubs' public relations machines by taking to social media and building a following that outstrips that of their clubs—Lionel Messi has 47,698,018 Facebook likes to Barcelona's 44,209,738; Ronaldo has 20,858,107 Twitter followers, compared to Real Madrid's combined 10,901,573—it's possible to foresee a future in which global fans, freed from the confines of local geography, follow individual superstars more than they do individual teams.

Despite that, our advice to new American fans remains the same. There is an old footballing adage we believe in: "You can change your husband or wife, you can change your underpants, but you can never, ever change your team."

Churchill Day: April 9. One of the most sacred days of the year, which is oddly yet to catch on in America. This does not feel fair to us, especially as the British have now adopted both Thanksgiving and Halloween.

Churchill, Winston: Wartime leader, soldier, bon viveur, wit. Every English schoolboy's childhood hero. Two things we love most about him? He was reputed to have spent $1,672 a year on wine—$150,492 in today's money—and his last words, which were so perfectly timed: ". . . I am bored with it all . . ."

Clarks Shoes: The shoe of our youth. I have owned at least one pair each of Clarks Polyveldts and Desert Boots since I was three. The Desert Boot was based on that worn by Britain's Eighth Army during the North African campaign of the Second World War. They were originally the school shoe of choice chosen by mothers across England for their functional, durable qualities. Yet once the Jamaican reggae dancehall scene claimed them in the 1980s and stars like Eek-A-Mouse and Yellowman were pictured in pairs of Wallabees, Clarks became willful staples of every gent's wardrobe. **—RB**

CONCACAF Thunder!: A frenzied emotion experienced in the loin area whilst watching the 2014 World Cup and witnessing Costa Rica, Mexico, and United States charge forward fearlessly. The feelings it conjured were part regional pride, part total shock. For a moment, the footballing world was Biff Tannen and little, unfashionable CONCACAF was George McFly, in a tuxedo, landing a miracle punch.

"Concacaffy": An adjective that means "subpar," "shoddy," or "suboptimal." Born of World Cup qualifying in the CONCACAF region, where teams struggle less against their opponents and more with waterlogged fields, threadbare turf, and generally crap play, broadcast mostly in Standard Definition. Usage: "The *Men in Blazers* show is so CONCACAFFY."

Conveyor Belt, The: A man usually becomes aware of "The Conveyor Belt" upon the occurrence of one of two events—the death of a father or the birth of a son. When both have occurred, its presence, and your journey upon said conveyor belt, following your father, proceeded by your son, becomes impossible to ignore. Often accompanied by the purchase of a red sports car, the sudden appearance of an inappropriately young girlfriend, or the acquisition of a favorite team in Serie A. In extreme cases can result in looming and unshakable appearance of "The Black Dog" (*see* Black Dog, The).

Cooper, Tommy: Tommy Cooper was a staple of British TV in the 1970s and the man who virtually invented the crap-on-purpose comedy routine. A brilliant magician and member of the prestigious Magic Circle, Cooper returned from seven years of service in North Africa (where he

The pioneer of Suboptimal in his trademark fez

first picked up a fez from a passing waiter while performing his act in a Cairo nightclub) and Europe during World War Two and quickly realized that when he messed up his tricks he was always able to get laughs. Quickly he developed a routine of big illusions that always went wrong, completely crap illusions (search for "spoon, jar, jar spoon" on YouTube) that were barely illusions at all, lame jokes which cracked him up, and the occasional mind-blowing illusion or sleight-of-hand which he threw in when you were least expecting it. Career highlights included appearing four times on *The Ed Sullivan Show,* headlining in Vegas with the Rat Pack at the Flamingo, almost killing Britain's most famous talk show host, Michael Parkinson, with a guillotine illusion in 1979, and most dramatically, collapsing from a heart attack on stage during a *Live from Her Majesty's,* a live TV variety show broadcast to millions of viewers across the UK, from which he tragically died on the way to Westminster Hospital. I have heard from a reliable source that ten years later,

in the mid-1990s, after David Letterman's staff had found clips of Cooper performing on *Sullivan*, Letterman tried to book him on *The Late Show*. He would have killed. Suboptimally.

Corduroy: One of the most evocative and emotional fabrics ever fashioned. To wear it is to synapse back in time to a world of memory: English teachers, childhood suits, student days, and lost loves. A corduroy blazer exists more in the subconscious than it does in reality. Its name comes from eighteenth-century Corde Du Roi—the cloth of the king—though it dates back to the early Egyptians and thus predates Wes Anderson by roughly twenty-one centuries.

Cosmos (New York): It is hard to describe what it was like to watch the pre-MLS American pro soccer league, NASL, live out its boom and bust from the grim perspective of England in the late 1970s. English football was in the midst of a numbing decline. The national team had failed to qualify for the 1978 World Cup. The domestic game was plagued by brutal play on the field and hooliganism off it.

The English media bought the razzle-dazzled shiny-new-thing hype of the NASL, hook, line, and sinker. The moment the league's glamorous flagship team, the New York Cosmos, signed such legends as Pelé, Franz Beckenbauer, and Carlos Alberto, we truly believed, for a moment, the United States was poised to take over the world's game. My bible back then was the kid's magazine *Football Handbook,* which would report breathlessly on the development of the league in the United States, which they referred to frequently as "The Land of Opportunity."

I still own the magazines, which I used to bind faithfully into a green plastic binder on a weekly basis. One of their features kicks off with a startling quote from Memphis Rogues coach (and ex-Scottish international) Eddie McCreadie, who said, "Before long an American club will suddenly turn up at Chelsea with a fistful of dollars and simply say—'Now let's have [then star] Ray Wilkins' . . . and there won't be much anyone will be able to do about it." The same article had a quip from Cosmos coach Eddie Firmani, who boasted he had "the money available to buy the whole England squad if I wanted." I remember as a kid reading that statement and asking my father, "No one would be that mad would they?"

Yet, it was not the star power and money apparently swilling around the league that were most startling to the English eye. Back then, British football was a savage Lord of the Flies affair pockmarked by tribalism and regional pride. *Football Handbook* remarked with astonishment that American soccer culture contained none of this. Instead, it noted disdainfully, "The American sports fan . . . expects comfortable seats, clean, uncrowded facilities, and entertainment for all the family: including short-skirted cheerleaders, autographed footballs and instant replays on flashing electronic scoreboards. Even if his team loses, he can leave the stadium feeling that at least someone was trying hard to entertain him." My mind could not conceive of football thriving in such a positive, safe atmosphere. I knew then, the Cosmos were doomed, and football in America would take more to catch on. —RB

Cossacks: A fear of Roger's. He lives by the learned familial wisdom "The Cossacks are always coming" and "There is a Cossack behind every door." Like many Jewish families who hail from Ukraine, Rog's family tree includes a great-great-uncle who was known as "the Cossack Killer." Like many Jewish families who hail from Ukraine, the roots of that nickname are 100 percent purely mythical.

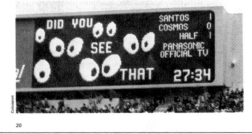

A spread from *Football Handbook* proclaiming America to be football's future.
Just read that opening quote . . .

The first time Alex Morgan graced our show was on the eve of the 2012 Ballon d'Or Female Player of the Year ceremony for which she was nominated. After remarking that she had not yet written an acceptance speech, Davo advised her to just lean into the microphone and say one word, "Courage." Sadly, Abby Wambach was voted Player of the Year, so we were deprived of the opportunity to discover if Alex took our advice. If you ever win an Oscar, Tony, Daytime Emmy, or award for Akron's Dental Hygienist of the Millennia, the speech is yours.

Courage: March 9, 2005, was a sad day for me, both as an American soccer fan and a lover of the great traditions of American television. Earlier that evening, in Germany, Landon Donovan was substituted in the 56th minute of Bayer Leverkusen's 3–1 loss to Liverpool in the Champions League, eliminating his team and marking his last appearance in the competition. And a little later, shortly before 7 p.m., 4,000 miles away in New York, Dan Rather signed off from the anchor chair after twenty-four years on the *CBS Evening News* with a beautiful and poetic farewell:

"To our soldiers in dangerous places. To those who have endured the tsunami and to all who have suffered natural disasters, and who must find the will to rebuild. To the oppressed and to those whose lot it is to struggle, in financial hardship or in failing health. To my fellow journalists in places where reporting the truth means risking all. And to each of you: 'Courage.'"

I like to think that Landon Donovan heard those words. I certainly did. I love a sign-off. As a kid, one of my favorite TV comedy duos, the Two Ronnies, made me laugh every time with their signoff "It's good night from me" "And it's good night from him." Edward R. Murrow's "Good Night and Good Luck" is so good it became a movie title. And the NPR *Car Talk* guys, Tom and Ray Magliozzi, managed to enthusiastically squeal, "Remember, don't drive like my brother" or "Don't drive like my brother" at the end of hundreds and hundreds of broadcasts. Rog and I go a little overboard with the sign-offs at the end of our podcast. Most of it is comical and absurd. But "Courage" I really mean. It's a tribute to a great man and broadcaster. And nothing means more to me and Rog when we hear from our GFOPs that during difficult times we've been able to bring a little bit of joy or escape into some people's lives. So once again, Courage. And a bit of War Pig also. **—MD**

Cruyff, Johan: Known as "Pythagoras in boots," the gaunt Ajax, Barcelona, and Netherlander was one of the most stylish footballers to ever grace the game. His career was synonymous with the avant-garde tactical vision known as "Total Football," a versatile system in which all outfield players consistently changed roles to take advantage of open space and bamboozle their opponents. Cruyff was listed as a striker, but a truer description of his role would be fulcrum as he found a way to drop to the flanks, or pull deep to find the ball. His balletic ability, free-flowing pace, and ability to switch direction like a Jedi Knight, leaving queasy defenders in his wake.

Fig. 1   Fig. 2   Fig. 3

How to Cruyff Turn in 3 dance moves

This grace is best exemplified in the move known as the "Cruyff Turn." Unveiled against Sweden at the 1974 World Cup, the Dutchman held up the ball with his back to goal as an opposing defender, Jan Olsson, chaperoned him toward a seemingly harmless position near the corner flag. Cruyff somehow pretzeled his upper and lower torso into two different directions, flicking the ball away in a third, causing his opponent's brain to short-circuit as his legs gave way, leaving the Dutchman free to whip in a lethal cross. The measure of Cruyff's greatness was best captured later by Olsson, the poor Swede whom he posterized with that move. "[That moment] was the proudest of my career," he said. "I thought I'd win the football for sure but he tricked me. I was not humiliated. I had no chance. Cruyff was a genius."

A god we can all believe in

As great as he was, Cruyff's true strength lay not in the way he played football, but in the way he thought about it. In retirement, his work as a coach changed modern football. Eschewing traditional footballing orthodoxy with Ajax and Barcelona, he developed a brand of football which emphasized control of possession and a smothering defensive press. "There is no medal better than being acclaimed for your style," the man who netted 33 goals in 48 fleeting international games once proclaimed.

Crying: The noblest of emotions. Especially when in reaction to John Anthony Brooks scoring a late, great, American World Cup goal, or at the end of an Arthur Miller play; and never more so than when watching a deeply mediocre movie on an airplane. Virgin Atlantic once uncovered that 55 percent of their travelers admit they experienced "heightened emotions while flying." Forty-one percent of men have "buried themselves in blankets to hide tears in their eyes from other passengers." Count us both amongst that number. Rog has been turned into

a weeping wreck by scenes in *13 Going on 30* and *In the Name of the Father*. Davo once started sobbing the second Mike lollopped onto the screen in *The Blind Side*, ultimately needing to be consoled by the Japanese businessman flying alongside him. The man spoke no English, but knew that a hug was necessary, because to cry is the most human of emotions.

Cuff Bus, The: We do not fight often, but one of the most wounding, and to this day still unresolved, arguments we have ever experienced came in the run-up to World Cup 2014, while shooting a series of preview videos for Grantland in Los Angeles. When I arrived, I realized I had neglected to pack a blazer. A battery of frantic phone calls ensued, and with great relief a local tailor delivered one directly to the set, moments before the shoot began.

We filmed exhausting back-to-back full days, beginning early and ending late. The atmosphere on the set was amazing, our research thorough, and the shoot felt like it really clicked as we shot twenty-two short films over the course of forty-eight hours. Yet, when the first video found its way online, to my horror, it presented me sitting opposite Davo with the sleeves on my newly acquired jacket glaringly three inches too short, leaving my shirt cuffs cruelly and humiliatingly exposed.

Desperate to assess the extent of my humiliation, I called my wife into the room for a second opinion. She is far more rational and good-natured than me, slower both to either anger or falsely accuse. After watching silently for four minutes with a poker face I was unable to decipher, she slammed the top of my laptop shut, then spoke with a barely containable fury. "Davo is your friend, yet he looked on knowingly at your cuffs just hanging out there and did not say a word," she said, pausing for a beat before completing her sentence in the staccato of disgust, "He threw you under the Cuff Bus!"

We happened to be taping a pod the next day. Unable to contain myself, I broached the issue of his silence at the top of the show in accusa-

The man on the left is under "The Cuff Bus." The man on the right threw him there.

tory style with the subtlety of a banshee. To his credit, Davo listened to my lengthy tale of Cuff Bus suffering without interruption, waiting for me to punch myself out before responding with a withering, clinical brevity. "There are few rules of etiquette I believe in more religiously than this: Every man is responsible for the lengths of his own cuffs."

Our argument was never settled. It has remained *Men in Blazers*' most festering of wounds. As a curious coda, the Cuff Bus became "a thing." Hundreds of our listeners adopted it as a symbol of pride. We have received countless images over Twitter of lawyers about to make an important presentation to court, or grooms about to head to the altar with cuffs hideously overextended, as if they would bring luck or cloak them in confidence like some magical juju totem. **—RB**

The correct cuff length, according to Kent Kilroe, tailor at Freemans Sporting Club:

"The length of the jacket sleeve is the key to looking well dressed. With the arm at rest, the jacket sleeve should end where your hand meets your wrist. Make sure your tailor measures from the thumb on each hand because your arms are asymmetrical. If you have the right sleeve length on the jacket, your shirt cuff should fall between ¼" and ½" inch below your jacket sleeve."

Cuppity Cup Cup: The Football League Cup, the fifteenth or sixteenth most important trophy that Premier League, Championship, League One, and League Two teams play for, has had multiple sponsors over the years. In our lifetime (and it has only been in existence since 1960), it has been known as the Milk Cup, the Littlewoods Challenge Cup, the Rumbelows Cup, the Coca-Cola Cup, the Worthington Cup, the Carling Cup, the Capital One Cup, and the Carabao Cup. We just call it the Cuppity Cup Cup. Because everyone knows what we're talking about.

FA Cup: Oldest football competition in the world

EFL Cup: No one cares if you win this one.

Champions League: Best theme music in the world of sports

Europa League: The "Randy Quaid" of European trophies

MLS Cup: Even Messi has *never* won this.

World Cup: American property in 2022

Cylon: Increasingly, I am becoming convinced that Rog is a Cylon. If you don't know what a Cylon is, either you are a Cylon programmed to not know what a Cylon is or you have never watched the reimagining of *Battlestar Galactica* on what was then the SciFi Channel between 2003 and 2009. The Cylons are a form of highly evolved robot, sentient machines that look like humans, but contain both organic and bio mechatronic body parts—including nuclear warheads. Bearing a Rog to the power of José Mourinho to the power of Arsène Wenger–sized grudge against the humans who developed them and enslaved them, the Cylons return, forty years after signing a peace treaty, to destroy the twelve humanoid colonies. They then chase the *Battlestar Galactica*, led by Edward James Olmos, all over the universe as the real humans try to find the fabled thirteenth colony of Earth. There are several types of Cylons—regular robot-looking ones, all shiny and silver who walk like Per Mertesacker. The leaders are the Final Five, humanoid descendants of the thirteenth tribe, an ancient humanoid life-form created by humans. Then there are the Significant Seven, humanoid robots created by the Final Five, OF WHICH THERE ARE MULTIPLE COPIES. These are the ones that contain the nuclear warheads. Rog is almost certainly one of these. He bears a grudge like no man I have ever met. He always says his head is going to explode. And he loathes most humans. Also, I could easily imagine multiple Rogers. Thousands of them. Like Minions. Let's keep our eye on this. **—MD**

D

Dare to Jozy: To persevere. To struggle and overcome. To suffer and find redemption.

While making my behind-the-scenes film for the US 2014 World Campaign, I visited Jozy in Sunderland, where he was then playing in the midst of a one-league-goal-in-42-Premier-League-games slump. Sunderland is a proud city yet inescapably grim. It was only while driving around it with Altidore that I realized how hard it can be for an American to grind out a career in foreign top-flight football. US internationals may harbor romantic dreams of playing in England—but those dreams undoubtedly do not involve the boarded-up storefronts and burned-out lots of Sunderland. I asked Jozy what he missed about life in America. He laughed and said, "The candy," in a tone which suggested candy was a euphemism for "everything." —RB

Darke, Sir Ian (b. 1950): Poet laureate of American soccer forever beloved for his poetic reaction to Landon Donovan's 2010 last-minute World Cup stunner, "Oh, can you believe this? Go, go, USA! Certainly through! Oh, it's incredible! You could not write a script like this!" Ninety-six percent of American soccer fans believe his knighthood is actually real.

Davies, Rebecca: Before my sister, Rebecca de Pont Davies, became an internationally renowned opera star, but long after she used to routinely nail left-footed penalties into the corner of the chalk-painted goal on the wall at the end of the courtyard of garages behind our childhood home, she attended music college in London. Her great friend Sverir, a brilliant violinist, used to take me to see Fulham, and sometimes Chelsea, on Saturday afternoons in the early 1980s. The 1982–83 and 1983–84 seasons were my most formative years watching football. I attended more

Davo with talent and hair

games those seasons than at any time in my life. Bear in mind that this was mostly crap football. This was the second division, long before the French revolution by the Thames at Fulham or the Gullit, Vialli, Zola era at Chelsea. But standing there in the terraces at Craven Cottage and Stamford Bridge with my new, older, Icelandic violinist friend, football was sinking in and I was intoxicated by all of it. The smell, the noise, the ebb and flow, the individual tussles, and the tactical, team-on-team primitive warfare practiced by unsophisticated British footballers in the second tier of English football in the Spandau Ballet era. But it was sinking in way deeper with Sverir. Ten years later, he and his wife, Gudbjorg, also a classical musician, gave birth to a daughter, Rebekka, named after my sister. Earlier this season, Rebekka Sverrisdóttir, after a terrific four-year career at the University of Massachusetts, was named to the All Mid-Atlantic Second Team as announced by the NSCAA. She is one of eight players representing the Atlantic 10 to earn a spot on one of the three all-region teams representing the A-10, the Ivy League, the Patriot League, and the Colonial Athletic Association.

I have watched several videos of her games and I am convinced that Rebekka would have made it in the English second division, at Craven Cottage or Stamford Bridge in the early 1980s. And that's partly where I like to think she was created. But apparently it doesn't work like that. —MD

Rebekka
Sverrisdóttir

Davies, Robert (no relation): Artist responsible for my three favorite football photographs in my collection. Shot off television images, these stills of iconic World Cup moments evoke the most powerful sense of memory. Even though I don't remember watching these matches at all. Of course I have seen all these clips, but these frozen frames make you feel like you are transported back to the '66, '70, and '74 World Cups and are watching live as your breath is taken away with the rest of the world by the magic and magnificence of what you are watching.

Geoff Hurst blasts his third goal, England's fourth, to leave German keeper Hans Tilkowski motionless. Hurst is still the only man to have scored a hat trick in a World Cup final.

Pelé, in his pomp, dummies the Uruguayan goalkeeper, Mazurkiewicz, before running behind him to collect Tostão's through ball. One of the most elegant and breathtaking World Cup goals ever, so creative, so simple, so perfect. Brazil won the game 3–1.

Johan Cruyff dummies to cross and with perfect balance executes what becomes known as the "Cruyff Turn." Swedish defender Jan Olsson was completely and utterly posterized, but the match finished 0–0. —MD

World Cup final, 1966, Wembley, England

World Cup group stage, 1974,
Dortmund, West Germany

World Cup semifinal, 1970, Guadalajara, Mexico

"Dead to Me": A phrase often muttered by Roger the moment an Everton player he worships leaves to sign for a bigger club. For example, "Marouane Fellaini's move to Manchester United means he is dead to me." Yes, Rog once loved Fellaini in a way he has never loved outside of the confines of his own family, but the combination of betrayal and impotence he experiences is overpowering. Proof of a truth articulated by late-seventeenth-century restoration playwright William Congreve, who once wrote, "There's nothing in this world so sweet as love and next to love the sweetest thing is hate."

Derby, Pronunciation of: One of United States soccer's most critical questions: How should an American pronounce the word "Derby"? Should consistency rule the day, and be sounded "Durby" as in Kentucky Derby? Or should British idiom be aped, a "Madonna-in-London" English accent temporarily adopted and the word "Darby" conjured?

Roger's advice was to go English, in the same way he has unconsciously adapted to speak of "garbage" in place of "rubbish," "skedules" not "shedules," and pryvacy in place of "prih-vacy." The only two words Rog cannot pronounce in American English are "water" (which he still enunciates like a Northern Englishman as "war-uh" to every waiter's chagrin) and his own name Roger, which every Starbucks barista interprets via the Indian restaurant spelling, "Raja" (*see* Accents).

Derby, The: A game against a local rival which matters too much. Arsenal against Chelsea, Manchester City versus Manchester United, or the one I have lived, and died with, the most, Liverpool's clash with Everton.

To the outside world, the Merseyside Derby may just be a regional scuffle between the Blues and the Reds, but growing up in Liverpool in the 1970s and 1980s, it always felt like something more. The game was nothing less than a savage battle with good and bad, truth and injustice, reward and punishment all hanging in the balance.

At the core of the agony is that the two teams' histories and fan bases are so intertwined. Liverpool emerged as a splinter of Everton fourteen years after its founding back in 1878.

Their home grounds, Goodison Park and Anfield, sit at opposite ends of a park, less than a mile apart. Extended families contain both blue and red factions. Witnessing the game is like watching a boxer trot into the ring solo and proceed to punch himself in the head.

The first Derby I remember was Everton's 1–0 win in 1978. Liverpool swaggered into the game as league leaders who had not lost a Derby since 1971. A sumptuous 58th minute volley by Andy King changed that. Bereft in defeat, Liverpool defender Phil Thompson could only say that he was "as sick as a parrot." With his thick Scouse accent, the word "parrot" dragged on as if it contained multi-syllables, supplying Everton fans with the perfect sound bite to torture their rivals in offices and schoolyards until the next game.

The roles were often reversed in excruciating fashion. In 1982, Kenny Dalglish propelled his pass-and-move Liverpool side to a 5–0 rout at Goodison Park. Liverpool attacked with an unrelenting fury that could not be repelled. To make matters worse, mustachioed marksman Ian Rush, who knocked home four goals, had been a boyhood Evertonian. *Et tu, Rushie?*

Mercifully, I had been unable to secure tickets for the game and was forced to listen to the action unfold on the radio in the privacy of my bedroom. Back then, I believed quite literally in the footballing cliché "it only takes a second to score a goal." Until there were five seconds left in the game, I clung on to a naive belief that Everton would somehow turn the game around. By the final whistle, I was lying on the floor in prone position, groaning softly, as if I had just been kicked in the kidneys. My heroes had been humbled. A harsh and early life lesson about idols and clay feet.

In the 1980s, Liverpool was a bleak, economically scarred backdrop with one of the highest unemployment rates in the country. Social unrest simmered. Margaret Thatcher's cabinet debated the possibility of allowing the city to sink into a "managed decline." Football was a respite and when both teams battled their way into the 1984 League Cup final, one out of every four Liverpudlian males invaded London to savor the first ever Wembley Derby. The event was less a game of football, more a delirious celebration of the city itself.

The final, which ended goalless, which in those days necessitated a replay, was best remembered for both sets of fans uniting to bellow the name of their beloved county in unison. Cries of "Merseyside, Merseyside, Merseyside" rang out across North London.

Despite these emotional scenes, I seethed in silence on the long journey home with my father. The referee had inexplicably allowed Liverpool defender Alan Hansen to use his hand and save a goal-bound Everton shot. The rematch, which Liverpool won 1–0, told us what we already sensed. Everton were doomed.

We were right, as it turned out, but in a way we could never have foreseen. In the mid-1980s, Everton finally managed to assemble a squad to rival the gold standard set by their neighbors. Their 1985 team plundered both the league title and the (now defunct) European Cup Winners' Cup and was poised to become one of the best sides on the continent. Yet the 1980s were the peak of the English game's hooligan years, culminating in the tragedy of the Heysel Disaster, a fatal confrontation between Liverpool and Juventus fans ahead of the 1985 European Cup final, which led to the death of thirty-two Italians. A blanket five-year ban resulted, expelling all English clubs from European competition. Everton never recovered.

The Blues failed to adjust to the new financial realities of the game and the Derby entered a dark age in which it felt as if Evertonians had no choice but to line up for the inevitable humiliation of a bare-bottom spanking. The nadir came during 1999's 3–2 loss. Robbie Fowler controversially dropped to the Goodison turf after scoring a penalty and celebrated by "snorting" the white line along Everton's penalty box, mocking Evertonians who had long sung of his rumored drug habit. As Fowler ridiculed us, we howled in derision. The cries, a thin attempt to mask our powerlessness.

When I talked about the pain I experience around Derby Day with my Liverpool supporter and noted philosopher Simon Critchley, he admitted he feels a similar sense of Derby Day doom, even as a Red. "The game," he explained, "matters too much." His final words that day have stayed with me because I believe any fan, even Arsenal or Tottenham supporters, can relate to them. "The worst part about football in general and the Derby in particular is not the disappointment, it's the endlessly renewed hope," he explained. "It's the hope that kills you." —RB

The pain of the Derby is best represented by this photograph, which captures how I inevitably end up feeling like an Everton fan by the time the final whistle is blown. A blur of black eyes, beige wallpaper, and shattered hope. Perhaps only Munch's *The Scream* or Hopper's *Nighthawks* can rival it as an image of human despair.

The photograph was taken at the final whistle of Derby Day, November 6, 1983. On the back, my dad has marked the date and carefully noted "Rog with black eye watches Liverpool 3 Everton 0." —RB

Dodgy Flapper: A move pioneered by Dutch winger (and bald hair hero) Arjen Robben, a player with one move: The left-footer receives the ball on the right wing, and as defenders swarm around to shut him down, he flaps his left arm up and down frantically, accelerates, then cuts inside at pace, working a way to slam the ball at goal.

Never stare into the eye of the vortex.

Great mystery surrounds the maneuver. When Robben receives the ball, every viewer watching at home, and every fan in the stadium, knows exactly what he intends to do next. "He is going to cut inside! He is going to cut inside!" we all shout in one voice. One imagines his opponents have watched hours of game film detailing this signature move and that they too know what is about to happen. Yet they are always powerless to stop him.

Robben came on *Men in Blazers* and suggested the strength of what he called his "special move" lies in his "intuition and timing." We do not believe him, clinging to the most logical explanation, which is that the undulating maneuver with the arm, or "Dodgy Flapper," has a hypnotizing effect on defenders, lulling them to sleep. Our solemn advice to Robben's opponents is always this: Never, ever stare into the eye of the Vortex.

Dominate!: The email sign-off of Warrior Sports founder David Morrow. Rog once had the pleasure of setting up an interview with the then Liverpool jersey supplier, and no matter what the email message was, Morrow would sign off "Dominate." Rog realized this philosophy was sadly antithetical to the way he approached his own life.

Donovan, Landon: The Vincent van Gogh of American soccer. A man whose achievement may truly be appreciated only when he is gone (if he ever retires).

Compare Donovan's first retirement to the season-long feting of Yankee legend Derek Jeter. One finely choreographed and legacy-defining with its *New Yorker* cover and Nike Re2pect video. The other sudden, slightly awkward, and barely reflective of the athletic smorgasbord of records to which his name is connected: The 57 national team goals and 58 assists he has notched. The five World Cup goals he netted in 12 tournament games, or the MLS goal-scoring categories led: 144 regular season, 22 playoff, and 6 All-Star Game goals.

Yet those numbers do not capture the immensity of Donovan's achievements, because such a large percentage of America's football-loving audience is relatively new. They have seen so few of the gilded moments that littered his career.

A great American

The majority savored his fairy-tale 91st-minute World Cup strike against Algeria, an emotion-soaked moment which could be considered "The Goal" in the same way as Dwight Clark's 1981 NFC Championship–winning reception is "The Catch" or Michael Jordan's 1998 Game 6 jumper against the Jazz is "The Last Shot."

But how many can summon memories of his breakthrough as a bleached-blond phenomenon who scooped up the Golden Ball at the U-17 World Cup in 1999? The crucial, brassy 2001 strike he thrashed home as a fresh-faced youth in his first MLS Cup final? Or even the speeding, stooping header with which he killed off Mexico in the 2002 World Cup round of 16?

Donovan's career straddled a time of radical transition for US Soccer. When the Californian entered MLS in 2001, it boasted just twelve teams, two of which soon folded as the league appeared on the brink of collapse. Serving as the nation's best outfield talent back then was on par with being the country's greatest yodeler or didgeridoo player. He retired with America in full thrall as the sport has ventured from the shadowed periphery toward the center of the nation's sporting radar.

In the early 2000s, a boyish Donovan racked up goal after goal when soccer's profile could be classified as "tree falling in empty forest." Yet the era in which football edged toward the mainstream has coincided with a time in which Landon has suffered. The 2010 Algeria goal was a Susan Boyle–ish moment that thrust the player blinking into the cultural spotlight, forcing him to adapt to sudden national fame, and crowning him as the only footballer every American knew by name (and perhaps the nation's most prominent Landon, bar Michael Landon).

A loss of motivation ensued. A candid Donovan publicly wrestled with his mental fatigue, embarking on a controversial sabbatical to try to restore his passion for the game. In interviews during this period he sounded like someone who had lost his love for their job. It was impossible not to be impressed by both his self-awareness and willingness to brave the derision of those who refused to sympathize with his predicament.

Unfortunately for Donovan, Jürgen Klinsmann was amongst those who lacked patience, ultimately axing the national team talisman from the squad on the eve of World Cup 2014. A humiliating, dramatic departure on par with Eddard Stark's.

This World Cup rejection was not the only bruise to pockmark Donovan's career. The Califonian's early, fleeting attempts to establish himself in the Bundesliga always came with a scent of failure—a product, perhaps, of the hint of self-loathing, frustration, and inferiority laced into American soccer culture in the 2000s.

Oddly the one set of fans who adore Landon unequivocally are those of Everton FC, the Premier League side with whom he savored a brace of intriguing loan cameos in 2010 and 2012. Football's equivalent of painting a miniature work of art on a grain of rice. Everton had been a one-sided team, raiding opponents down the left flank. Donovan's fleeting presence gave them a genuine right-sided threat, providing balance and forcing opponents to play them honestly. The loanee embraced the opportunity with gusto, lancing the accusation he could not play abroad in the process. To this day, Everton fans praise Donovan full-throatedly in a way we believe all Americans will in time.

Donovan's is a career that will be reappraised the more MLS improves, and the greater the United States' global standing becomes. Like Jimmy Carter, whose approval rating grows the further removed we become from his presidency, he will be seen for what he is. A human, complex, always intelligent, often breathtaking footballer. A genuine US goal threat in an era in which American goalkeepers were more the norm. A home-loving player who suffered for his decision to remain in MLS, a reality which is now standard. An inventive spark on national teams built to persevere. A divisive figure in the United States who is admired in England, and both feared and respected in Mexico. A human being in an image-dominated age who knew exactly when he needed to take a break. —RB

Drakkar Noir: What cool smells like to the mind of a fourteen-year-old boy trying to slip into English pubs for the first time in the early 1990s. Created in 1982 by aroma-master Guy Laroche, its overwhelming bouquet of fresh pine and crude chemicals make it de rigueur everywhere from singles bars to the bar mitzvah circuit of Long Island. Named for the Viking word for "flat-bottomed ship." Ronaldo is the closest thing to a bottle of Drakkar made human. At Euro 2012, Rog moved into a hotel room the

Portuguese National Team had just evacuated in Donetsk, Ukraine. His clothing reeked of "The Noir" for the rest of the tournament.

Draw: A tie occurring when the final whistle blows and the scores are level, with both teams departing honors even. A feature that many American broadcasters feared would hold the sport's development back in the United States where sporting sensibilities traditionally demand a clear-cut way of determining a winner to be lauded and a loser on which to pour scorn. Englishmen feel differently. Not losing is what is important. Even more than winning. Not losing is winning.

Dreams of American Glory: This is a recurrent dream Rog experienced in the run-up to the 2014 World Cup. The first time he had it, he woke up, grabbed his laptop, and recorded every detail:

"A beaming, shirtless Michael Bradley is the first to reach the staircase. The American midfielder drapes his shoulders in a Stars and Stripes flag, gives a television camera the thumbs-up, and shakes his head in disbelief as Landon Donovan puts his arm around him. The man who has become known to the world as 'St. Landon' has just propelled the US to victory with his inspired play. Unable to mask his joy, he pulls on a comically oversized Uncle Sam hat, and moonwalks up the first three steps.

"Brazilian fans reach over the handrail desperate to slap the weary Steve Cherundolo, and an animated Stu Holden on the back. Halfway up the stairs, supersub Kyle Beckerman, whose late wondergoal proved the difference in the final, soaks in the moment, turning round as a fan deposits a red, white, and blue rasta wig on his head. Facing out toward the vaunted Maracana, he holds his arms aloft. His face

The last act of the Qatar World Cup will look eerily like this.

appears on the scoreboard in close-up causing the legendary stadium to ignite in cheers. The Marylander stands in exhausted triumph, part clown, part victorious gladiator.

"At the top of the long, narrow staircase stands Sepp Blatter with the grimace of a man desperate to look as if America's darling run to glory had been his idea all along. Standing between him and an ebullient Sunil Gulati is the World Cup trophy. The only thing preventing the ambitious US Soccer honcho from pushing the Swiss off the balcony and defenestrating the FIFA president live on television. Before them, Clint Dempsey mounts the stairs with a grave look on his face, aware of the historical weight of the task that lies ahead of him.

"In this moment, the man who grew up dirt-poor in Nacogdoches, Texas, is an American Trailblazer. A man who knows his next act will forever change his nation like George Washington, the Wright brothers, or Neil Armstrong before him. As confetti swirls all around, sticking to his sweat-soaked temples, the thirty-one-year-old wipes his palms on his jersey, and approaches the World Cup trophy once won by Pelé, Beckenbauer, Ronaldo, and Zidane.

"A giddy Tim Howard begins to jump up and down beside him, causing the rest of the squad to do the same. Dempsey reaches out to grab the trophy from Blatter's hands. As he cradles then kisses it, he is overcome by the memory of the days he first learned to play the game, kicking a deflated basketball around a dirt scrub on a Texan trailer park. A single tear rolls down his cheek but that does not deter him. With a sudden roar, the Texan arches his back, thrusting the trophy upward, over his head as dry ice and columns of fire erupt all around him. The US have won the 2014 World Cup. America will never be the same again."

Dressing Room Music: "Dancing Queen" is Roger's eighth favorite ABBA track of all time (after "Voulez-Vous," "Super Trouper," "Take a Chance on Me," "The Winner Takes It All," "SOS," "Gimme! Gimme! Gimme!," and

"Chiquitita"). It is also the subject of his favorite detail from Roy Keane's autobiography. The former Manchester United hardman-turned-ineffective Premier League manager realized he was doomed during his coaching spell at Sunderland because of the tunes his team listened to before taking the field. The Irishman wrote: "The last song before the players went on to the pitch was 'Dancing Queen' by ABBA. What really worried me was that none of the players—not one—said: 'Get that shit off.' They were going out to play a match, men versus men, testosterone levels were high. You've got to hit people at pace. Fuckin' 'Dancing Queen.' It worried me. I didn't have as many leaders as I thought."

Anyone reading that statement will realize Roy Keane did not properly understand the alchemy of "Dancing Queen." ABBA's lyric "Anyone could be that guy, Night is young and the music's high" is just about the most positive message any Premier League player could have front of mind before taking the field.

Below is the music we would play if we were Premier League managers before our team played the game of their lives:

Davo:
"Rock the Casbah" by The Clash
"Let's Groove Tonight" by Kool and the Gang
"Highway to Hell" AC/DC

Rog:
"Block Rockin' Beats" by The Chemical
    Brothers
"Fisherman's Blues" by The Waterboys
"Father and Son" by Cat Stevens

Duhamel, Josh: The actor Josh Duhamel kissed Rog on the mouth on the *Men in Blazers* show. It was our Murphy Brown moment. Rog likes to tell people his tongue was strangely reptilian and that it was like being kissed by one of the visitors from *V* hell-bent on destroying earth. The honest truth was, Josh was just showing how daytime soap opera stars lock

Rog's first ever kiss went a little like this. He still can't feel his legs.

lips. It was a mixture of angle and proximity, but what he really did was nuzzle against Rog's neck. It was worth it, because Josh smelled so good—a mix of single malt and sugar-free gum—and the whole experience reminded Rog of his favorite-ever Lord Grantham quote from *Downton Abbey:* "If I would have screamed blue murder at everyone that tried to kiss me at Eton, I would've gone hoarse in a month!"

Duos: When we started *Men in Blazers,* we self-consciously modeled our relationship on the tandems we admired. And there are many, for as well as being the land of the free, home of the brave, and epicenter for great barbecue sauce, the United States overfloweth with remarkable duos. Here are our role models:

Roger:

Starsky and Hutch: In life, you are either a Starsky or a Hutch. Starsky was freewheeling. A man who ran on emotion. No doubt, an Everton fan. Hutch was rational, process-oriented, and methodical and able to freeze his body the second he landed on the hood of a car. Proper Chelsea.

Kathy Lee and Hoda: The amount of wine they can imbibe at 10 a.m. every morning is what sets them apart. They make it look easy. It is not. Trust us. We have tried.

Alexi Lalas and Marcelo Balboa: The United States' starting center back pairing at the 1994 World Cup. Just like us, apart from haired and supremely athletic.

Hall and Oates: The bestselling duo in musical history. One is recognized as creative genius who is never satisfied. The other had a mustache but shaved it off after becoming divorced in the 1980s. We are both Oateses.

Davo:

Cagney and Lacey: Fictional, regrettably, NYPD cop partnership featured in eponymous television series that originally aired on the CBS television network for seven seasons from 1982 to 1988 and on BBC1 in the UK. A police procedural, the show stars Tyne Daly and Sharon Gless, detectives who lead very different lives: Christine Cagney (Gless) was a single, career-minded woman, while Mary Beth Lacey (Daly) was a married working mother. The series was set in a fictionalized version of Manhattan's 14th Precinct (known as "Midtown South"), which we like to think was actually the crap part of SoHo.

Laurel and Hardy: Laurel and Hardy were a comedy double act during the early Hollywood era of American cinema. The team was composed of thin Englishman (from the North) Stan Laurel and heavyset American (from Down South) Oliver Hardy. They became well known during the late 1920s through the mid-1940s for their slapstick comedy, with Laurel playing the clumsy and childlike friend of the pompous Hardy. When we were kids growing up in England in the 1970s, they were always on television. Their humor was mainly composed of physical arguments with each other, which were quite complex and involved cartoon violence, which prevented them making any real progress in the task at hand. Much of their comedy involved milking a joke, where a simple idea provides a basis from which to build multiple gags without following a defined narrative. Sound at all familiar?

Wham!: Though not strictly American, well actually not at all American, the UK pop duo from Watford sold more than 25 million records worldwide between 1982 and 1986 in what Rog and I like to refer to as "The Cagney and Lacey Era." The most astonishing thing about their partnership is that George Michael did everything, and Andrew Ridgeley did virtually nothing, other than occasionally dance in the background with the band's backup singers/dancers Pepsi and Shirlie. After disbanding in 1986, Ridgeley briefly attempted becoming a race car driver and released truly one of the worst albums in the history of pop music, *Son of Albert,* in 1990. George Michael went on to win two Grammys and sell 80 million more records albeit while getting into a few scrapes with the law for his enthusiasm for Class A and Class C drugs and certain illicit activities in public bathrooms. When George Michael died on Christmas Day 2016, it hit me harder than any celebrity death ever. It was like losing a long-lost teenage friend. Thank God Andrew Ridgeley is still with us.

E

El Blazérico: The twice annual Men in Blazers Derby in which Davo's Chelsea play Rog's Everton. A lesser-known version of El Clásico. A game that feels less like football and more like fratricide. Typically, a game Davo looks forward to, but for Rog the clash is a major cause of cherophobia (*see* Cherophobia).

England, National Team: I can pinpoint the exact moment when my relationship with the English team was severed beyond repair. Ahead of the 1982 World Cup, the team released a World Cup single "This Time (We'll Get It Right)." A chirpy yet bold number which dominated the radio airwaves and fired up my imagination with images of glory conjured by the chorus: "This time, more than any other time, this time, we're going to find a way . . . To win them all."

That summer, I spent a solid month in my bedroom playing that single endlessly on repeat to kill the boredom until the tournament kicked off. I would stare at the players on the record cover as I did so, realizing these men were warrior-heroes whose words I should treat as prophecy.

From today's perspective it will come as no surprise to the reader what ensued. England crashed out in second group stage without scoring a goal. To this day, that single is sadder to me than Eric Clapton's "Tears in Heaven." I have never trusted the team again.

England are now a small dog that thinks it's a big dog. We invented the game. We host the Premier League, where many of the world's best players ply their trade, but the vast majority are foreign, robbing homegrown players of the playing time they need to compete at the elite level. The English jersey has become heavier than chain mail. Whereas Uruguayan, Costa Rican, or Egyptian players seem propelled to collective heights when pulling on their national team jersey in World Cup play, the English shirt bleeds the confidence out of even our most talented athletes.

As a result, England have become a mediocre also-ran. Their World Cup record over the past forty years roughly akin to that of a Sweden or Mexico. The only attributes that set the team apart are their spectacular self-loathing and the cruelty of the tabloid media, who bait them for sport.

When I tried to tell my children the story of how England once won the World Cup in 1966, my boys screwed up their eyes in disbelief and suspicion before walking away. I was left alone at the breakfast table, wracked with the same self-doubt I would experience if I had just tried to persuade them Tara Reid had once been considered a desirable movie lead. **—RB**

English Breakfast: The full English breakfast is one of life's under-discussed pleasures. A full fry-up: eggs, Irish bacon, sausage, mushrooms, tomato, beans, and toast. Best consumed in an English greasy spoon cafe, but any American soccer bar will do just as well. It is less a meal. More a validation of life. The secret is in the brown sauce. Preferably HP. A condiment only in name. A bedrock British institution in reality.

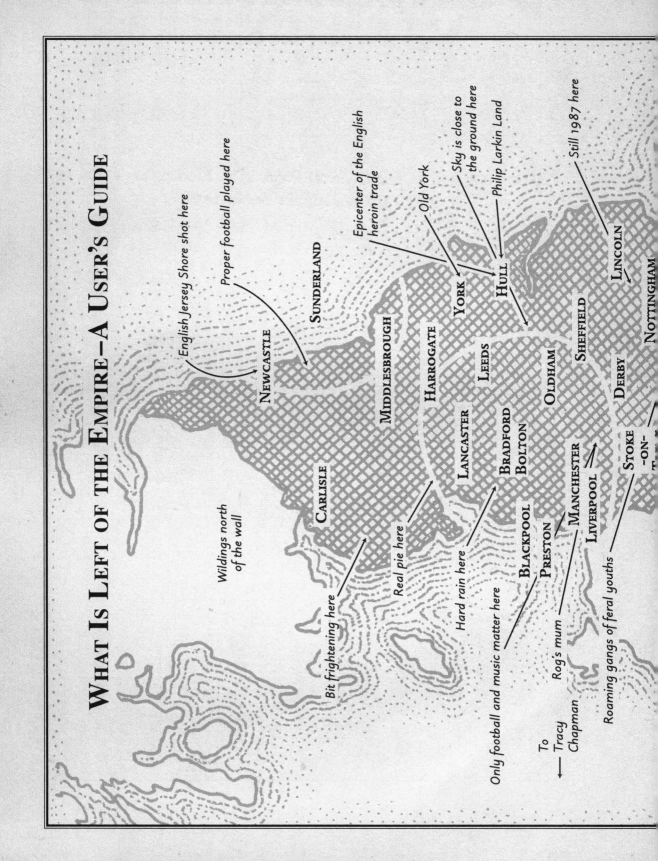

What Is Left of the Empire—A User's Guide

Wildings north of the wall

English Jersey Shore shot here

Proper football played here

Epicenter of the English heroin trade

Old York

Sky is close to the ground here

Philip Larkin Land

Still 1987 here

CARLISLE

NEWCASTLE

SUNDERLAND

MIDDLESBROUGH

HARROGATE

YORK

HULL

LEEDS

LANCASTER

BRADFORD

BOLTON

OLDHAM

SHEFFIELD

LINCOLN

DERBY

NOTTINGHAM

STOKE -ON-

LIVERPOOL

MANCHESTER

PRESTON

BLACKPOOL

Bit frightening here

Real pie here

Hard rain here

Only football and music matter here

To Tracy Chapman

Rog's mum

Roaming gangs of feral youths

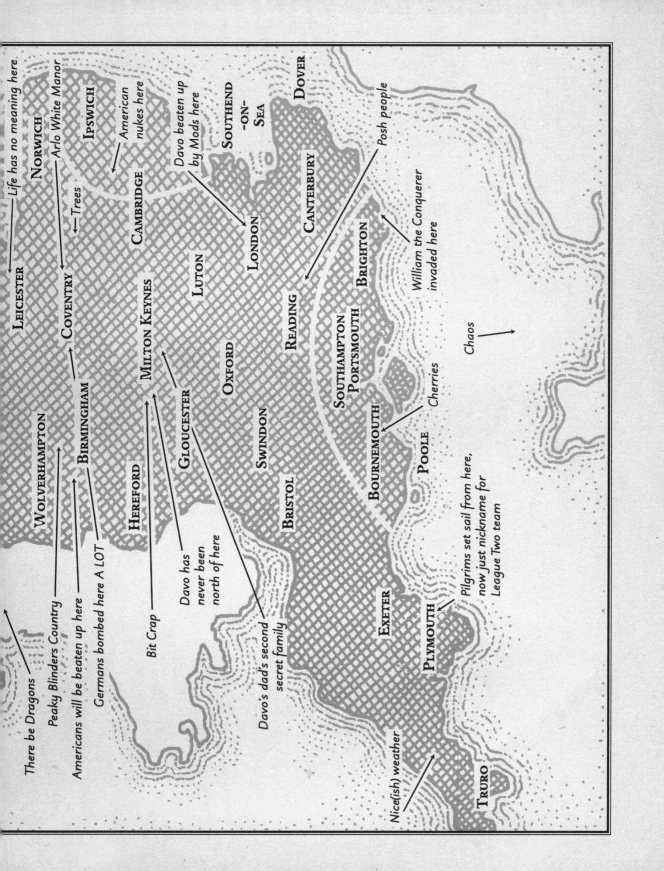

Life has no meaning here

Arlo White Manor

American nukes here

Davo beaten up by Mods here

Posh people

William the Conquerer invaded here

Chaos

Cherries

Pilgrims set sail from here, now just nickname for League Two team

Nice(ish) weather

Davo's dad's second secret family

Davo has never been north of here

Bit Crap

Germans bombed here A LOT

Americans will be beaten up here

Peaky Blinders Country

There be Dragons

Trees

LEICESTER

NORWICH

IPSWICH

SOUTHEND -ON- SEA

DOVER

CAMBRIDGE

LONDON

CANTERBURY

COVENTRY

LUTON

READING

BRIGHTON

BIRMINGHAM

MILTON KEYNES

OXFORD

SOUTHAMPTON

PORTSMOUTH

HEREFORD

GLOUCESTER

SWINDON

WOLVERHAMPTON

BRISTOL

BOURNEMOUTH

POOLE

EXETER

PLYMOUTH

TRURO

A Complete List of the English National Football Team's World Cup Songs and Their Most False-Hope-Inducing Lyric

1966, "World Cup Willie,"
Lonnie Donegan
He's tough as a lion and never will give up
Outcome: Victory. England 4, West Germany 2 in the final

1970, "Back Home," England Squad
Back home, they'll be watching and waiting / And cheering every move
Outcome: England eliminated by Germany 3–2 in quarter finals

1974, England failed to qualify

1978, England failed to qualify

1982, "This Time (We'll Get It Right)," England Squad
This time, more than any other time, this time, / We're going to find a way
Outcome: England eliminated in second group stage after failing to score a goal

1986, "We've Got the Whole World at Our Feet," England Squad
We've got the whole world at our feet, / There ain't a single team that we can't beat
Outcome: England eliminated by Argentina and Diego Maradona's Hand of God 2–1 in quarter finals

1990, "World in Motion," England Squad with New Order
We ain't no hooligans, this ain't no football song / Three lions on my chest, I know we can't go wrong
Outcome: England lose to Italy 2–1 in third-place game

1998 "(How Does it Feel to Be) On Top of the World," Ian McCulloch and Spice Girls
*How does it feel, to be on top of the world, / Now it's for real, you're
on top of the world / We're on the top of the world*
Outcome: England eliminated by Argentina 4–3 on penalties in round of 16

2002, "We're on the Ball," Ant and Dec
*White will be the colors, the whole world in our hands, / The time
has come to kick it—can we kick it? / Yes we can!*
Outcome: England eliminated by Brazil 2–1 in quarter finals

2006, "World at Your Feet," Embrace
With the world at your feet, / There's no one you can't beat, / Yes it can be done
Outcome: England eliminated by Portugal 3–1 on penalties in quarter finals

2010, No song
Outcome: England eliminated by Germany 4–1 in the round of 16

2014, "Greatest Day," Gary Barlow
Today this could be, the greatest day of our lives / Before it all ends, before we run out of time
Outcome: England fail to emerge from the opening group stage

Eredivisie: The Dutch league. A footballing mystery grab bag into which the world's elite teams put in their hands to pluck out a supposed goal machine, knowing the legal term "Buyer Beware" applies.

Some—Dennis Bergkamp, Ruud van Nistelrooy, or Luis Suarez—retain their sharpened edge and thrive in the big leagues. Others—Mateja Kezman, Afonso Alves, and (sigh) Jozy Altidore—flounder like a blobfish yanked from the ocean depths, humiliating themselves in one game after another until being dumped onto the transfer market in a move that feels like a mercy killing.

Alves is a case in point. Middlesbrough signed the Brazilian striker for club record $24 million in 2008 after watching him lash home 48 goals in 48 games for Dutch side Heerenveen. Boro fans hoped the big goal scorer would save them from relegation, but the only thing he attacked with relish during his eighteen months in England was the local pie shop. Overhyped and overweight, Alves scored just four times in 31 games in his first full season as the team were relegated, leaving loyal fans to channel their suffering into "The Alves Song" (sung to the tune of "You Are My Sunshine").

You aren't my Alves, Afonso Alves,
you make me sa-ad when skies are blue,
*and Georgie Best, cost f*****g less,*
so please take my Alves away.

Ethnic Nosh: How my father, Trevor de Pont Davies, describes all foreign food and something he abhors. Actually, the concept of "ethnic nosh" applies a fairly liberal definition to "ethnic," encompassing, in addition to any form of curry or spicy cuisine, any kind of pasta, rice dish, meat, or vegetable with any kind of sauce on it. Or anything that smells vaguely unfamiliar or of any foreign country real or imagined. The appearance of any kind of bean or lentil immediately renders a dish "ethnic." Any dessert not in the prewar or postwar English cooking lexicon is definitely "ethnic." And frankly, most desserts are "vulgar" anyway. Any ice cream flavor other than vanilla is "ethnic." Most fruits, including pineapple, watermelon (actually, any kind of melon), and certainly anything as exotic as a kiwi or a pomegranate (yeuch)—"ethnic." Italian lunch meats, soft cheeses, anything yellow or orange other than lemons or carrots, cold soups, iced drinks, anything with a foreign-sounding name, anything sold on the street or eaten standing up, wraps, smoothies, anything stuffed with anything else, pizza, quiche, any meat more adventurous than rabbit, chips, crisps, and any snack in a bag other than Twiglets. All "ethnic nosh." **—MD**

Europa League: A UEFA continent-wide tournament rebranded in 2009, pitching a motley crew of Europe's second-tier teams into battle against each other. In England, the teams that come fifth and sixth (and often seventh) in the Premier League qualify.

The tournament, a marathon slog, is overshadowed by the Champions League in terms of profile, brand exposure, and financial reward. Powerhouse teams that qualify feel like they are slumming it. Aspirational underdog teams have their small squads stretched and run ragged by the cruel "Thursday and Sunday" game schedule and grueling travel demands which often drag them to parts of Moldova and Albania previously known only to white slave traders, and international arms dealers.

Qualifying for the tournament can actually feel more a punishment than a reward for an ambitious team looking to build on a strong season. Like catching a dose of herpes after a one-night stand with a supermodel. **—RB**

Europa League: As a Chelsea fan, it was really fun winning this in 2013. We beat Benfica 2–1. It was really the only thing I enjoyed about Rafa's (Benítez) spell as manager. Torres scored. Not as fun as winning the Champions League in 2012. But still, really fun. Much more fun than not winning anything since 1995. **—MD**

Everton: The English adage that soccer's history is a story of fathers and sons (and in the slightly less patriarchal modern period, mothers and daughters) proved true in our house. My support of Everton was born of a sense of filial duty. They were my dad's team. But I truly fell in love with the club the first time he took me to a match. It was an achingly cold April morning in 1978 and Derby County was the visitor. Goodison Park heaved with sound as we arrived. The stench of beer, cigarettes, and police horse turd hovered over the ground.

I was seven years old and had feverishly dreamed of this game for weeks, but little had prepared me for the reality. Our seats were tucked away at the back of the main stand. With rows of full-grown, beer-bellied men between me and the field, I could not see a thing.

My neighbor, though a stranger, instantly recognized my plight. Defying the cold, he stripped off his full-length sheepskin coat in theatrical fashion, folded it neatly into a square with one hand whilst scooping me up with the other. The coat was dumped onto my seat and I was deposited atop of it, elevating my sight line considerably. Problem solved. Now clad in just a T-shirt, my savior spent the next 90 minutes plying me with the local delicacy, Everton Mints, that was gratefully received, and a flask of Scotch that was declined by virtue of the fact that I was still in first grade. When iconic 30-goal-in-a-season striker Bob Latchford slapped home the winner, the stadium rocked deliriously, and my neighbor cloaked us in a cloud of whisky mist as he hugged me and bellowed, "We're all one big family here at Goodison, son."

True as that may have been, in the money-driven modern game, goodwill, spirit, and a concealed flask of cheap whisky will get you only so far. In a game dictated by financial muscle despite Farhad Moshiri's recent investment, it is predetermined Everton are doomed to be second tier. Goodison Park, the first purpose-built soccer stadium when opened in 1892, has become an albatross, rich in tradition but perilously low on match day revenue until a new stadium is built, win or lose, the club falls ever further behind the Manchester Uniteds and Arsenals with every game they play.

Yet, that reality is too rational for fandom which is all about the emotional experience. The club's highs have provided me with some of the richest, most meaningful memories of my life. In the mid-1980s Everton were poised to be one of the best clubs in the world. Their triumph in the 1985 European Cup Winners' Cup was one of the most important nights of my youth. The miraculous season they qualified for the Champions League under David Moyes in 2005 was akin to an out-of-body experience in which everything blue felt joyful and soaked, all too briefly, in optimism.

Being a lifelong Evertonian has been a lesson in suffering. A life of despair born of years in the wilderness during the early Premier League

The match program from my first ever Everton game is the one object I would rescue from a fire!

era, when it felt that if we played against opponents who had Johnny Cash, Leonard Cohen up front, Lou Reed patrolling the middle, and Edith Piaf and Tracy Chapman shoring up the back, Everton still would have been the more depressing team.

The pain of the club's 2012 FA Cup semifinal defeat to Liverpool is still searing. I had taken my two older boys—one then aged nine, the other six. Everton scored first, only to concede twice in predictable, self-sabotaging fashion. By the time the final whistle blew at Wembley, both my kids were sobbing. I hurriedly dragged them to the exit in case the television cameras noticed their pain and broadcast their anguish in close-up, making them an instant Internet meme. As we scurried through the gate, we passed a fat, drunk Evertonian with a plumber's crack venting his anger by urinating against Wembley's walls. Despite his disarray and anguish, the fan posed a profound question whilst relieving himself, "Why do we always play like crap against the Red Shite?" As we scurried past, I noticed the tubby urinator was wearing a T-shirt emblazoned with the legend "Bitter Twisted and Proud," and forced my kids to memorize the moment so they could soak up those values.

It is those values which the club embodies that make me proudest to be an Evertonian. Those of collective endeavor, loyalty, tenacity, and passion, all of which transcend football. For me, Everton are less a club, more a way of viewing life and the world in which honor counts more than glory. —RB

Everton in Davo's eyes: I have been asked by our editors to write something about Everton Football Club. Here are the positives:

1. They play in blue
2. They're not Arsenal
3. They are completely and utterly harmless

Other than that I don't have a lot. I could probably summon more words on the taste of the water or my favorite Nickelback lyrics or reasons I want to go to the North Pole. Rog believes that Chelsea are evil, but the worst I could say about Everton is just that they're mostly irrelevant. They are the Finland of the Premier League. —MD

EVERTON PLAYERS, ROG'S FIVE FAVORITE OF ALL TIME

This was hard for me. A Sophie's Choice. As a rule, I have loved nearly every man who has pulled on the Everton blue jersey and tried his hardest for the team. There are many legends—Neville Southall, Duncan Ferguson, Steven Naismith—who have been enshrined by more articulate writers than me. The five I chose were selected on the basis of the feeling they conjure deep in my gut. Though scattered across different squads, in different times, together they create a rainbow—all of it colored blue—capturing the culture and value of the club: Commitment. Passion, collectivity, and tenacity in the face of mediocrity:

LEIGHTON BAINES
(*see* Greatest Footballers of All Time [according to Rog])

THOMAS GRAVESEN, 2000–05
With his jagged, bald cranium and wild, bulging eyes, if the Orks had an international football team, Thomas Gravesen would have captained it. The Danish attacking midfielder took the field as if hell-bent on taking the "attack" part of his role literally. He played like a man whom if given the choice between putting in a bloodcurdling tackle or scoring a jaw-dropping goal, would choose the tackle every time. Hence his nickname "Mad Dog," which was easily attached to a gent who stumbled around Goodison Park like a rabid, lunatic ogre.

The Everton faithful grew to love "Tommy G." His giddiness, physicality, and surplus passion matched our own and he became a cult hero at a remarkable time. In 2004 he propelled an Everton squad which had narrowly avoided relegation the year before, then suffered the defection of then young stud Wayne Rooney, to romp deliriously to a fourth-place finish.

The tightly bonded squad of such misfits, reclamation projects, and bargain basement scrubs as Tim Cahill, Mikel Arteta, and Tony Hibbert charged wide-eyed into Champions League football. Yet, Tommy G would not fight alongside them. After his apex season, Real Madrid came calling, seducing our Dane and making him as random an Everyman signing as if Kyle Beckerman had been summoned to the Bernabéu. A Galáctico squad alongside the likes of Raúl, Robinho, and Beckham was no place for a pub brawler with heart and desire but little in the way of technical ability. The minutes Gravesen racked up for Real could actually be better counted in seconds. Always the maverick, Tommy G exited stage left and reinvented himself, socking his career earnings into tech investments and reemerging, according to Danish tabloid reports, as a millionaire VC based in Las Vegas, which if true suggests a savvy he successfully repressed throughout his playing career. For me, Thomas Gravesen will always be coiled in the center circle, spending the last seconds before kickoff slapping team-mate, and fellow bald, Lee Carsley repeatedly across the face, to prepare for the battle which lay ahead.

BOB LATCHFORD

(*see* Greatest Footballers of All Time [according to Rog])

DAVE THOMAS

A pacey, right-footed left winger with a cross as a true as a galloping archer in the Mongolian cavalry, capable of firing an arrow with unnerving accuracy whilst mounted on horseback. When my schoolboy hero, Bob Latchford, netted 30 goals in the 1977–78 season, it was Thomas who delivered assist after assist, the John Stockton to Latchford's Karl Malone. Though Thomas was a player of vision, skill, and humility, what young Rog admired most about him was his bravery. In an era in which lumpen defenders lived to perform in-game surgery on their opponents' ankles, Thomas defiantly took the field without shin pads and with his socks rolled down around his ankles. A look I sported on the schoolyard until my teens, with my gray school socks permanently rolled down around my sandals. A silent tribute to an otherwise all-too-forgotten hero. —RB

F

Facial Hair: In an era in which image and charisma on the field almost trump the quality of play per 90 minutes, facial hair can be a footballer's best friend—and not only for the weak of chin.

Even in the 1970s and 1980s, decades in which facial hair was a societal norm, footballers knew how to utilize the beard as a branding tool. Brazilian midfield poet Socrates, snug of short, brilliant of brain, and clipped of beard, pioneered the rasping curls to reinforce his sense of suave. Fallen hero George Best wore a perfectly weighted thick mane and beard which encircled his face as if a halo of potency was emanating from his very libido. Spanish midfielder Xabi Alonso's stubble was that of a corduroy-loving intellectual who could have written novels if he had not elected to dedicate his life to undoing opposition defenses. Diminutive Italian Andrea Pirlo's late-career romantic bush became a defining symbol of his professional renaissance.

A beard can also be proof you belong. The sweaty red wisps of USA 1994 star Alexi Lalas were indicative of his endeavor and tenacity, even as an English tabloid cruelly joked the Michigan-born defender "looked as if Jesus and Carrot Top had birthed a son." Young coaching phenom André Villas-Boas grew a beard during his doomed tenure at Chelsea as if

Nicolas Anelka

Djibril Cissé

George Best

Andrea Pirlo

Ricky Villa

Xabi Alonso

Tim Howard

Adam Clayton

to exclaim, "I am a man, not a boy. As evidence I have grown this . . ." Yet for Tim Howard, a beard was not an accessory. It was the source. After his 16-saves-against-Belgium World Cup night of legend, the American lumbersexual-goalkeeper marveled, "I think I gained most of my strength from the beard."

Fake Injuries: The first thing Americans marvel about when they are new to world football is the extent professional soccer players both feel pain and experience gravity. Shin pad molecules need merely to be grazed before the athletes plummet, often at physics-defying trajectories, in paroxysms of agony, as if every bone in their body is on the brink of shattering.

In such circumstances, many of our listeners wonder about the training football team's physios have undergone. Their abilities seem to border on that of faith healers. Recovery is most often instantaneous, even in the most dire-looking of cases.

Many cynics have dared to suggest footballers do not feel pain more exquisitely than other Homo sapiens but are in fact faking the injuries in order to gain a competitive advantage for their team. Such a scenario would mean the medical staffs are complicit in medical deceit, playing along with fake injury, and perhaps even receiving a wink from the "injured" party to ensure he is not removed from the field of play. We prefer to think of each occurrence as an everyday miracle. Ronaldo rolling around in near-feverish torment one minute and trotting around without apparent long-lasting effect the next being just an updated version of the old biblical proverb "Physician heal thyself" (Luke 4.23), "Cristiano, heal thyself."

Fandom, The Essence of: Why do we watch? Experiencing Everton struggle through a mid-table campaign can be sufficiently nerve-numbing to make me wonder what else in my life I experience like football. Something that can be bereft of pleasure, or borderline unbearable, over which I have no control, yet I voluntarily put myself through week after week, and indeed would be miserable without.

Willful delusion and cognitive dissonance may play their parts. The exquisite intangibles of belonging, commitment, life narrative, and familial bonding provide others. Yet a Cambridge University neuroscientist, Wolfram Schultz, discovered that the neurotransmitter that controls the brain's pleasure centers and the quantity of dopamine released—the chemical which enables the feeling of happiness—is inversely related to how much an event was expected to occur. Schultz's research suggests fans who are deeply connected to a team that rarely expects to win are those who experience the greatest dopamine rush. Dopamine trumps silverware, and it is for that reason football is, as Italian coach Arrigo Sacchi once said, "the most important of the unimportant things in life." **—RB**

Fears That Are All Too Real:
Pentheraphobia: fear of your mother-in-law
Geniophobia: fear of chins
Peladophobia: fear of bald men
Peladophobia is real. Marouane Chamakh has it (*see* Chamakh, Marouane).

FIFA: The governing body of global football. Under the leadership of now-disgraced President Sepp Blatter the organization ran like a cross between an Albanian show trial and the annual SPECTRE board meeting. The United Nations has 193 members. FIFA saw fit to recognize 209 nations, empowering such micronations as the Solomon Islands and New Caledonia. The South Pacific's Cook Islands, population 10,900, wielded as much voting power as Germany, Argentina, or the United States.

Only Franz Kafka, or perhaps Roger Goodell, could appreciate the brazenness of FIFA's culture of graft and corruption, operating in plain light of day, as the organization's "development program" doled out millions in patronage to far-flung territories, a strategy ripped straight from the Chicago political machine's playbook.

Rumors of gross malfeasance always circulated. Yet even photographs of cash being handed around in manila envelopes in hotel conference rooms did not dent the organization's reputation. Nor did the selection of Qatar as a venue to host a World Cup. Even Harvey Keitel in *Bad Lieutenant* would admit that decision seemed a little corrupt.

It took an American to transform the organization: Attorney General Loretta Lynch (*see* Lynch, Loretta), whose forty-seven-count indictment uncovered racketeering, money laundering, bribery, wire fraud, and obstruction of justice. One hundred sixty-two pages' worth of glory with the stamp of US District Courts Office and the legend of the United States on the top. America's greatest contribution to world football since Alexi Lalas (*see* Lalas, Alexi).

Fighting: English footballers are high-performance sportsmen who excel in every athletic pursuit except for one: They are terrible at fighting. Whilst Argentinian football players are sufficiently brazen to fire tear gas canisters at their opponents, and Brazilian football is replete with referee beheadings, Premier League violence has a ritualized choreography, part chaste Victorian courtship, part Thracian War

dance in which anger must be channeled into six customary steps of erotic rutting:

Step one: Two players, most commonly one English hardman and one fancy foreigner from Spain or Italy who "does not like it up 'em."

Step two: After the initial clash, Johnny Foreigner elects to "leave a foot in."

Step three: Both players are now deprived of free will. Footballing lore dictates they must confront each other, height differential or weight class be damned.

Step four: Foreheads must be placed in the general vicinity of opponents like bull elks rutting to prove their dominance in front of the herd.

Step five: Both players pray for the slightest contact, mere molecule grazing satisfactory.

Step six: Contact or imagined contact is sufficient cause for player to fling himself backward in the style of Capa's "Falling Soldier." NB: If the player toppling backward is Johnny Foreigner, cue color commentator to declare "We need to stamp that behavior out of the game." If the player is English hardman, expect color commentary to the effect of "He must have felt something, because he is not that type of player."

Step two   Step four   Steps five to six

Figurine Panini: Before the Internet. Before EA Sports invented the FIFA game. In the days before European football was globally broadcast, stickers reigned supreme. Before every major tournament of my schoolboy years, vast amounts of pocket money would be squandered on Figurine Panini stickers. The stickers would come in packets of five, which would be immediately ripped open, emitting a faint whiff of print and adhesive which signaled the giddy discovery of which random players, coaches, and team crests you had just obtained. These would be stuck into the appropriate blank space in an accompanying official staple-bound pamphlet.

The ultimate aim of every football-crazed kid was to collect the entire set by the time the tournament kicked off. This would necessitate the frantic schoolyard swapping of stickers and overcoming the myth that certain players were put into scarce supply by the cruel Italian printers, ensuring we would all amass waste mountains of duplicate players as we approached completion.

Filling a sticker book offered the traditional thrill of any form of collecting but it also played a more crucial role in an era in which global information flow was limited. British football was insulated from the rest of the world. Every English schoolboy knew the Germans, Italians, and Brazilians were footballing powerhouses, but their players were unknown to us tournament to tournament until we glimpsed their permed hair and intimidatingly suave mustaches. My first encounters with World Cup stars Zico, Michel Platini, and Paolo Rossi were all via sticker. They never appeared more menacing, nor many of their Eastern European counterparts more terrifying than via their Panini selves.

In presenting this gallery of the finest stickers of our youth, we do so under the proviso that it is impossible to convey the nostalgia and urge to swap they will provoke in any European male reader over the age of thirty-five. **—RB**

First Jersey: I came of age in Liverpool, a city in which soccer is exalted like high school football in Central Texas or Kabaddi in the Punjab. As I approached my seventh birthday, I became convinced nothing could empower me to have friends and influence people like an Everton jersey with a large number 9 seared on its back. A replica of the one sported by Bob Latchford, a goal machine of a striker, and local hero.

After seven months of crude, repetitive hinting, the day of reckoning came and I ripped open my birthday presents like a bald man tearing open a FedEx from the Hair Club. To my horror, my parents had forgone the opportunity to invest in an officially licensed product, in the hope they could pass off a 100 percent polyester phys-ed shirt on which a felt number 9 had been crudely Krazy Glued as the real deal.

The rest of my gifts were opened in a seething silence. Even the two tickets my grandparents gifted me to the upcoming Everton–Aston Villa game barely registered. I tried on my new shirt in the mirror, looking on morosely as the felt 9 peeled halfway down, dangling limply off my back while my mother enthusiastically chirped "You will look so handsome when you wear it to the game."

I barely spoke to my parents until game day, and only then because I needed a ride. Clad in a fake shirt, my father and I witnessed our beloved Everton triumph with Latchford lashing in two goals. Aston Villa lost the battle but their fans still hoped to win the war. This was the height of the hooligan years, when watching the game was really just an opportunity to maim anyone in the opposition's colors before and after. As we headed back to the parking lot, I was separated from my old man when the crowd split as if attacked by a phalanx of pillaging Vikings.

Frozen in terror, I fell to the floor while a dozen spotty, malnourished Villa fans descended upon me. Time froze. I was surrounded. Fists were raised by the gang as their leader loomed over me. Yet while I curled in a ball and prepared to meet my fate, his demeanor changed. Pointing at my shirt, the skinhead muttered to his spittle-

ARGENTINA 78 — OSVALDO CARLOS ARDILES — ARG

ARGENTINA 78 — ROBERT SARA — AUT

ARGENTINA 78 — RIVELINO — BRA

ARGENTINA 78 — DOMINIQUE ROCHETEAU — FRA

ARGENTINA 78 — BAHARAM MAVEDAT — IRN

ARGENTINA 78 — PAOLO CONTI — ITA

ARGENTINA 78 — LEONARDO CUELLAR — MEX

Players rarely looked more menacing than
in their Panini photographs.

ARGENTINA 78 — JAN PETERS — NED

ARGENTINA 78 — TEOFILO CUBILLAS — PER

ARGENTINA 78 — KAZIMIERZ DEYNA — POL

ARGENTINA 78 — ALAN ROUGH — SCO

ARGENTINA 78 — FERENC MESZAROS — MAG

ESPAÑA 82
PAOLO ROSSI
ITALIA

ESPAÑA 82
HARALD SCHUMACHER
DEUTSCHLAND-BRD

ESPAÑA 82
RENE VALENZUELA
CHILE

ESPAÑA 82
DIEGO ARMANDO MARADONA
ARGENTINA

ESPAÑA 82
KEVIN KEEGAN
ENGLAND

ESPAÑA 82
MICHEL PLATINI
FRANCE

ESPAÑA 82
NOEL BROTHERSTON
NORTHERN IRELAND

ESPAÑA 82
FERNANDO BULNES
HONDURAS

ESPAÑA 82
FALCÃO
BRASIL

ESPAÑA 82
OLEG BLOCHIN
SSSR

ESPAÑA 82
STEVE ARCHIBALD
SCOTLAND

ESPAÑA 82 WORLD CUP

FIGURINE PANINI

Jail mug shots are more flattering.

THEOPHILE ABEGA

CAM

EMMANUEL KUNDE

ESPAÑA 82

lipped followers, "Leave this one alone, lads. He's disabled." And so I escaped, losing only one soiled pair of underpants, and my ability to appreciate a gift, which to this day I lack, like others are deprived of a sense of taste or smell. **—RB**

Football Books, the Five Best We Have Ever Read:

ROGER BENNETT:

Ajax, the Dutch, the War: The Strange Tale of Soccer During Europe's Darkest Hour
by Simon Kuper

My favorite football writer, who understood first how to write about the world when writing about the game. The greatest work of football storytelling I have encountered.

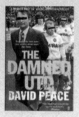

The Damned Utd
by David Peace

The book, not the movie. The best novel I have read about the sport, rife with detail about 1970s football, England at that time, and human motivation.

The Ball Is Round
by David Goldblatt

More a monumental achievement than a book. A precisely written, 992-page cultural history of soccer, a little bit like Bill Simmons's colossus *The Book of Basketball* but without the sense of humor. Reading it is like running a marathon—a test of human stamina and endurance that is uniquely rewarding at the finish.

The Glory Game
by Hunter Davies

The *Ball Four* of soccer. A classic fly-on-the-dressing-room-wall piece of reportage in which the English journalist was granted all-areas access to a season with Tottenham Hotspur. Radical in its day, the book is savagely dated, yet that is its delight. It offers an opportunity to appreciate just how fast the sport has changed in a relatively short time.

Soccer in Sun and Shadow
by Eduardo Galeano

The Uruguayan who was hailed by *The Atlantic* as "one of Latin America's fiercest voices of social conscience" may seem an unlikely candidate to author one of the most animated, concise histories of the evolution of football, World Cup to World Cup. Yet Galeano claimed, as a self-described "beggar for good soccer," he had felt compelled to craft a volume which would enable "fans of reading to lose their fear of soccer and fans of soccer to lose their fear of books."

MICHAEL DAVIES:

Among the Thugs
by Bill Buford

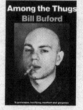

This book would also make my top five in books about England, books about men, books about violence, books written by Americans, and books written in the English language. Buford's memoir about his infiltration of some of the hardest soccer "firms" in late 1980s England and the awful things he witnessed and participated in while in their thrall is hilarious, gruesome, and, well, deep. It is a must-read for any Premier League fan who wants to understand the tribalism of football fans, and the hooligan culture which always lurks in the background, or at least the foundation story of English football.

Hero and Villain
by Paul Merson, with Ian Ridley

There have been flashier and splashier football autobiographies, and a few have been more widely lauded by the sportswriters, but 1990s Arsenal legend Paul Merson's simple and honest diary about his attempts to maintain a domestic and international career at the elite level while battling a massive relapse into gambling, drugs, and alcohol addiction is beyond refreshing. No player of Merson's ability has  ever written more honestly and in such a less self-aggrandizing manner about being a deeply flawed professional. Reading about the mundane details of his daily reality, even at its most shocking, reminds us fans that we never see the monotonous training sessions, and we really have no idea about what goes on behind the scenes. Or how bored these guys are most of the time.

A Life Too Short: The Tragedy of Robert Enke, by Ronald Reng

The sort of book I would normally never read, nor enjoy, has moved me more than any sports book ever. From the outset, you know how it's going to end. Tragically. But long before the elite German goalkeeper's suicide, you start to understand Enke's anxiety, his pain, and even the elements of his unspeakable depression. Louis van Gaal makes a cameo, and does not come off well. Nor do many in the young keeper's football life. For months after reading this book, I found it impossible to say anything remotely negative about any football player or athlete in case they heard about it. It just felt wrong. I should read it again. Quickly.

Pelé by Edson Arantes do Nascimento (aka Pelé)

The large format limited edition of this book is one of my favorite things, let alone my favorite football books. Owning it, and even reading it, is quite a commitment. It is massive—720 gold leaf pages, measuring 18 by 14 inches and weighing in at 23 pounds—a healthy toddler! Each copy is signed by Pelé, and contains 1,700

images and articles collated from a variety of sources. It is a simply beautiful book about a beautiful player and if you don't like it, you can always use it as a beautiful doorstop.

Scorcher Annual 1979

When I was twelve, I devoured this annual, the end-of-year edition of my favorite comic book, cover to cover and again and again until every page fell out. There were extended versions of my favorite comic strips, *Billy's Boots* (about a kid, Billy Dane, who finds a pair of old soccer cleats at a flea market and when he puts them on, instantly becomes inhabited by the pro "Dead Shot" Keen, who used to wear them in the 1950s, and suddenly BILLY IS AMAZING AT FOOTBALL) and *Hot Shot Hamish* (about a Highland Scottish pro for lowly Princes Park FC who is so meaty that he breaks the nets with every goal). But the features were also memorable. This is the first time I ever read about an exotic new league in America named the NASL, where 76,000 fans

Still basically my reading level

and celebrities had just bid goodbye to Pelé at Giants Stadium, "a famous baseball stadium in New Jersey."

Foudy, Super Julie: As a player, she was an artful mix of skill and thunder. A 272 capped midfielder, former captain of the national team, twice World Cup winner, twice Olympic gold victor, one of the most successful national team players this country has ever birthed, she is competitive drive personified. As a broadcaster, she has become one of the most human analysts in the soccer field. What you do not see at home is how she acts as glue on the set, binding the odd characters around her—and believe us, they are plenty odd—making everyone look good. Winner of the 2015 Golden Blazer.

Julie is the one in the middle.

France: Hard as it may seem to believe, when we were growing up France, was a footballing backwater. Gallic football was slow to professionalize, and as a result the French were honestly much easier to like. The nation had an inferiority complex, "Petite France," which made them approach every international tournament as if they were a small yet gallant fighting force for whom defeat was inevitable. Losing nobly was always the goal and much preferred to winning without style.

The 1982 French World Cup campaign was the most French thing ever witnessed. Like Amelie in cleats, ending as it did in a plucky

semifinal loss to a great foe in football, and war, West Germany. France had played some of the most beautiful football in the tournament, led by the effortlessly elegant Michel Platini. The game lived up to its billing as a battle between the "artistes" and the "automatons." The game was defined by a moment of thuggish brutality in which German goalkeeper Harald Schumacher demolished French defender Patrick Battiston as he advanced on a one-on-one. The French recovered to go 3–1 ahead in extra time only to wilt, leaking two goals in the last six minutes and exiting via penalties. They had been mugged.

Schumacher later beat Adolf Hitler in a national French poll of the country's most hated historical figure but the dramatic loss to the physical Germans thrilled the nation. In the words of French commentator Georges de Caunes, it revived "memories of emotions felt during the Second World War," reinforcing the sense that the French loved tragic heroes who come up short but always delight.

The 1998 World Cup, held in France, shattered that myth. The triumphant multiracial "Black, Blanc, and Beur" (Black, White, and Arab) squad led by Zinedine Zidane, forced the nation to remake itself as *"France qui Gagne,"* a France that wins. To an Englishman, there are few sights more grating than a self-confident Frenchman, and so we were delighted and relieved that one of the most emotional victories in modern World Cup history was followed by one of the most humiliating defenses as France crashed out in the opening round, losing to former colony Senegal, and failing to score a single goal. The French still do not mind losing, but lack of effort, loyalty, and honor fills them with self-loathing, forcing them to seek the solace of an Edith Piaf Greatest Hits CD, which is just how we like them.

Free Kicks: Every team has an elite free kick master, for whom any foul awarded within 90 feet of the opposing net is as good of a chance on goal as a penalty. The likes of Dimitri Payet of France, Gylfi Sigurðsson of Iceland, or Cristiano Ronaldo of Portugal are overcome by the Thickening as soon as the referee blows his whistle and the ritual choreography of the free kick commences. The goalkeeper frantically attempts to shield his goal, constructing a human wall with his defenders, placing them in the line of fire, a mere ten yards from a ball about to be driven at speeds of up to 90 kilometers an hour. The defenders grab their undercarriages while the goalkeeper works out how to cover 75 percent of his goal face, protecting the far post while leaving himself a clear sight line on the shot.

All the while, the kicker stands Jedi-like under pressure while his brain computes a complex set of equations involving spin (impart too much and the ball won't clear the wall; too little and it will sail over the bar) and atmospheric drag (which accounts for the aerobatic dips and curves of the most spectacular blasts). The margin for error is infinitesimal. The striker is attempting to slot the ball through a letter box of extraordinarily small dimensions just above the wall. Physicist Ken Bray calculated that for a kick from 75 feet, the target is a mere six ball widths across, causing physicists to marvel at the act, particularly because players, not typically known for their intellectual prowess, can process the information quicker than even the most powerful computer. David Beckham was the quantum scientist's poster boy. In the same way many came to admire his "goldenballs" persona, engineering researchers like Keith Hanna lust after his mind. "The man can carry out a multi-variable physics calculation in his head to compute the exact kick trajectory required, and then execute it perfectly," he once said. "That is why the man is a football physics genius."

Friedel, Old Man: An American legend who played in the English top flight for the best part of six decades until he retired aged eighty-seven. Famed for his unique broadcasting brogue which is equal parts Irish, Middle English, pre-Revolution Colonial-era American, and High Valyrian, Friedel has become a coach and an astute color commentator. We would love to hear his recital of *Angela's Ashes* recorded as a book on tape.

Funeral Music: Nobody likes to think about death, but everyone should spend some quality time thinking about the music they would like to accompany their remains as they descend into their final resting place. A recent BBC report uncovered the most popular tunes played at funerals in the United Kingdom. Two of the top four were traditional hymns, "The Lord Is My Shepherd" and "Abide with Me." Yet number four was the "Match of the Day" theme—the opening music to the nation's weekly Premier League football highlight show. The most popular track at British funerals is currently "Always Look on the Bright Side of Life," which suggests there are batches of Monty Python fans now at dying age.

For the record, Rog would like Sting's "Russians" to be sung morosely and a cappella by a bass-voiced chorister, followed by "Tears of a Clown" by Smokey Robinson and the Miracles, and then "I Am a Rock" by Simon and Garfunkel as the handful of mourners return to their cars in the rain. Davo has requested "Today Was a Good Day" by Ice Cube.

G

G., Stevie: One of the greatest English players of his generation. After his 2014 Greek Tragedy of a slip against Chelsea derailed his dream of bringing title glory back to Liverpool, the team he had dedicated his life to there became something late-career Matthew Brodericky about him. Here was a man who once had it all, but suddenly knows you know that he is not what he once was and he knows it too. His career ended in Los Angeles, somewhat defeated, and cloaked in the gray pallor of self-awareness, as he came on our show and admitted his highlight had been his discovery of the "Animal Style" option at In-N-Out Burger. John Oliver talked to us about the melancholy he experienced as a lifelong Liverpool fan watching Gerrard transition from the Reds to LA Galaxy:

"It's so heartbreaking—this is not the way for it to end. Find someone to put a pillow over your face because that is the dignified way out. I don't mind seeing Frank Lampard do whatever Frank Lampard is going to do out here, I really mind seeing Stevie G. do it. The Los Angeles Galaxy! It's so sad. Beckham, it made sense, you think, oh, he's going to thrive in Hollywood. Stevie G. is going to be walking around like, 'Sushi, what's sushi? Why aren't you going to cook it?'"

Game of Thrones: Everything I know about ancient history I learned from *Game of Thrones*.

Some analysts believe Brazil 1970 to be the greatest team of all time.
To that, we say the same thing as we do to death: "Not today."

And I know I am not alone. The HBO series is so painstakingly realistic; it runs like a Ken Burns documentary, except more interesting.

Those of us who love soccer—America's Sport of the Future since 1972—can only look with envy at the millions of fans the book series has garnered in the United States. I am among them. Finishing the five-book series certainly ranks as the greatest accomplishment of my life (marriage, witnessing Everton become league champions in 1986–87, becoming a father, and "winning" Dana Plato's autographed headshot off eBay round out the Top Five).

I read the books the summer before the series debuted. I was on the way to the MLS All-Star Game with an enormous Liverpool fan who recommended them to me. "I don't read that kind of fantasy crap," I replied closed-mindedly. "Have you ever tried to read that kind of fantasy crap?" he countered enigmatically enough to silence me. Within a chapter of the first volume, I was hooked. Retrospectively, I realized the true attraction for me was

that the shifting geopolitical balance of power in Westeros is identical to the narrative, goals, dives, and feigned injuries of Premier League football. A world in which the ruthless, brutal flayers at Chelsea are House Bolton of the Dreadfort, cash-soaked Manchester United, the Lannisters, the faded Northern glories of Liverpool, House Stark, and Everton, with their rich heroic history, and collective commitment to be "the sword in the darkness," forever doomed to be the Night's Watch. —**RB**

George Michael Sports Machine, The: The first thing we did upon signing a deal with NBC Sports was to work out a way to acquire the original signage from *The George Michael Sports Machine*. Both of us had shared the same experience as Englishmen new to this country in the early 1990s: To cast eyes upon George Michael was to glimpse the mechanics of everything that made America the world's sole superpower. If you never glimpsed the late-Sunday-night sports highlight show, it pulsated

This sign belongs in the Smithsonian; until they call, it resides in our Panic Room.

with promise from the very opening. Scenes of baseball, the NFL, rodeo, surfing, and a Carl Lewis victory culminated in stock footage of a satellite zapping highlights directly into the studio.

And what a studio. One in which a bronzed George Michael presided over proceedings like an American Julio Iglesias. All tan of skin and white of teeth, with slacks stay-pressed and hair greased back. A clipboard permanently in his grasp to reinforce the truth that this ship had only one captain.

After a brief background on a clip, be it from a baseball game, an NFL playoff game, sky diving, or dwarf wrestling, George would smack a single button—most often the one with his name on it—sending the reel tapes into a blur of motion. And when those reels sparked to life, he would declare, "Let's go to Cleveland Municipal Stadium!" creating the sense he could propel the viewers from one geographical location to another with a wink at the camera and a push of the button.

Having grown up in 1980s England, where restrictive television rights made sports highlights a rarity and where soccer was perceived too déclassé to make the evening news, this weekly half hour was a revelation. Athletic pursuit was out in the open. Sports was entertainment. Elite human achievement could be improved with a coat of schmaltz.

The man was completely at ease, both selling the fiction and being in on the joke. He was the man Rog wanted to grow into. Being a balding Englishman made that dream regrettably impossible, but when *Men in Blazers* signed with NBC, it was George we both thought about—and in fact emulated by building a "Sports Machine" of sorts in our studio from which our show would be controlled. The man was a master of concept, polish, packaging, illusion, and above all, narrative, to whom we still genuflect today.

Germany: When I think of Germany I think of Castles Schlosses, "99 Luftballons," and Basil

Fawlty screaming "Don't mention the war." Yet when it comes to football, Germany have been like Walmart if Walmart developed enough world-class footballers to not only fill the German national team but half the American one too.

Determined, prepared, organized, German football was best summed up by British television pundit Gary Lineker's famous quip that "football is a simple game in which 22 men chase a ball for 90 minutes and at the end the Germans win." In the 1970s and 1980s they played grim, consistent, pragmatic football. Almost every game against a European team felt like a seismically massive, historic rivalry in which resistance was futile.

Spitting on a German player won this Dutchman the vote in "Israel's sportsman of the century."

As an Englishman watching those German teams it was like seeing Darth Vader run around the field in cleats. My favorite memory from that period came from World Cup 1990 when the Netherlands' Frank Rikjaard, in a fit of pique, spat on the perm-haired Rudi Völler not once but twice. I distinctly remember the phlegm just seeming to fly end over end in slow motion before lodging in the German's curls. Both men were somehow sent off. Rikjaard was later voted Israel's sportsman of the century.

Yet, Jürgen Klinsmann, Völler's strike partner on that '90 World Cup winning side, became coach in 2006 and oversaw the Nationalmannschaft's transition into a young, bold, attack-minded free-flowing squad—something the world never thought was possible: a German team the rest of the world could admire and root for.

Klinsmann's successor, Joachim Löw, a manager who seemed to devote his most creative tactical thinking to the way he shamelessly picked at his extremities in-game, tweaked that philosophy and led the 2014 squad to glory at Brazil 2014. By that time, there were so many admirers clad in German jerseys visible on the streets of Manhattan before that World Cup final, the city felt like Philip Roth's *Plot Against America* made real. —RB

Germany: Country I unexpectedly fell in love with, or almost fell in love with, during the World Cup finals in 2006, when I was covering the tournament for espn.com. I saw more than a dozen games in eight cities—Munich and Köln my favorites, Nürnberg was a head trip, Kaiserslautern and Gelsenkirchen the most charming—and drove all around the country in my rented Mercedes-Benz CLK 350. From the way they played football—fast, expansive, electrifying—to the wonder of their autobahns, the efficient professionalism of their service employees, the unexpected beauty of the countryside, and the surprising quality of their food and drink (I spent days consuming nothing but wurst, cheese, and wine on the German Wine Route—Die Weinstrasse), Germany is light-years ahead of the rest of Europe in almost every aspect of work, life, and football, except for humor (they have little sense of it, Jürgen Klopp notwithstanding), pop music (they really have an unhealthy enthusiasm for death metal), and the width of their toilet paper (just impractically and astonishingly narrow). The problem is, every time you think you were loving the people, a group of several thousand of them would march around the corner carrying flags and yelling "Deutschland, Deutschland" and it would send a shiver down your spine. —MD

GFOP—Great Friend of the Pod: As with so much that is good in world football, we have

Sepp Blatter to thank for this phrase's invention. Its origin dates back to the earliest days of the pod. Back when we began podcasting on a daily basis during World Cup 2010 on ESPN, our producers asked us what we wanted to be called. We suggested "The Martin Tyler Experience." They thought it might be smarter to call us *Off the Ball*. And so we became roughly the 143rd football podcast in the world to be named *Off the Ball*.

Our offerings were an acquired taste. We like to remember that time fondly and refer to our show as a "cult favorite." Cult here being a euphemism for fringe ramblings. Most of our content revolved around one of three subjects: We were mesmerized by the bombastic yet empty authority of "Don Fabio," then England manager, Fabio Capello, the "Cherunning" and "Dolo-ing" of US right back Steve Cherundolo, and a random Danish band named Nephew, who released an awesomely cheesy yet official Danish World Cup song, "The Danish Way to Rock."

Early on, we had to introduce the notion of Sepp Blatter to our American audience, most of whom were new to the game. Even back then, the FIFA president was such a nefarious, overt, and craven figure in my mind, I did not know where to begin. So, before launching in, I took a deep breath, waited a beat, and muttered, "This is the one man in the world who is not a Great Friend of the Pod."

The phrase struck a chord. We had only seven listeners back then, and two of them were my parents-in-law, but they were a die-hard bunch who took to the term immediately, using it as an email sign-off or a social media hashtag. We spent the rest of the World Cup pretending that everyone in the world was listening to our random crap. Whether we talked about Bill Clinton, Henry Kissinger, or Diana Ross, we would add with a boast, ". . . and he's a Good Friend of the Pod." The legend of the GFOP was born to stand alongside AWOL, LMAO, and AARP as a great American four-letter acronym. —RB

"We stand with Gingers!"

Gingers: At *Men in Blazers,* we stand up for the rights of Gingers, the last group in America it remains socially permissible to be biased against. Our concern is propelled by a slightly bastardized reading of the classic Pastor Niemöller quote, "First they came for the Gingies, and I did not speak out—

"Because I was not a Gingie."

As a result, we cannot stand idly by when academics at Université de Bretagne Sud, in France, declare that redhead women are the last to be approached by men who prefer blondes and brunettes. We feel compelled to speak truth to power, and have probably, over the past five years, spent more time talking about Apple's persistent and pernicious disregard of our Gingie Friends through their failure to produce Ginga emoticons than we have about actual football.

Get on it, Apple.

In the name of Gingie Self-Love, we proudly present our Greatest Ginger Footballers of All Time (see following page), each one a Ginger Ninja.

GINGIE HISTORY, TOP FIVE MOMENTS

1492: Christopher Columbus discovers the New World. The ginger explorer was probably trying to put as much distance as possible between himself and the hair haters.

1533: Birth of Queen Elizabeth, who beat the Spanish Armada and then convinced everyone she was a virgin for more than sixty-nine years.

1874: Churchill's birth. A redhead as a child. School bullies gave him the nickname "Copperknob."

1986: Molly Ringwald delivers the line "I just want them to know that they didn't break me" in *Pretty in Pink.*

2011: Carrot Top's career disintegrates.

Great Crap Players: A classification of Premier League players who have not been blessed with terrific speed, strength, deathblow power, or any type of identifiable skill yet are revered because of the mental strength, endeavor, determination, and will they have employed to gut out a career in professional football. Steven

BEST GINGER TEAM OF ALL TIME

David
Fairclough

Louis
Saha

Forwards

Paul "Ginger
Prince" Scholes

Jack "Ginger Pirlo"
Colback

Alan "Ball of
Fire" Ball

Gordon
Strachan

Midfielders

Alexi "Big Red"
Lalas

Wes
Brown

Gary "Ginger Pelé"
Doherty

John Arne "Ginge"
Riise

Defenders

Adam "Wolf"
Bogdan

Goalkeeper

Sean Dyche aka
Ginger Mourinho

Manager

Naismith was one such player in his Everton days. He came on the pod and admitted he was a "a wee bit in awe of the other players," when he first arrived in the Premier League locker room. Others include George Boyd of Burnley, Southampton's Shane Long, and West Brom's entire starting eleven.

Greatest Footballers of All Time (according to Rog):

BOB LATCHFORD

The first man I ever loved. Long before Adam Ant, Hervé Villechaize, and Jim Mc-Mahon, his poster was over my bed from the moment he arrived at Everton in 1974. In the early sentient years of my Everton fandom, most of which were lived with the club cloaked in Liverpool's shadow, the romance of his 1978 30-goal season had to be, in Arsène Wenger's words, "like a trophy." Back then, the club was big on characters, low on success. Latch was physically unremarkable and would appear stocky by the standards of today's athletes. But to my seven-year-old self he was cut like a god able to thunder home any cross delivered within the vicinity of his head in the opponent's penalty area.

That season, the race to 30 goals had become a particular "thing" because an English newspaper, the *Daily Express,* had offered a $16,000 bounty—a huge sum back in the economically depressed England of the 1970s. By the last day of the season, Latch had headed, kicked, and shinned in 28 goals. Beleaguered Chelsea came to Goodison Park and I was among the sellout crowd of 40,000 who went in hope of witnessing history. Everton stormed to a 3–0 lead, yet Latch was not among the goal scorers. As the game clock ticked to 70 minutes, it seemed as if his odyssey, and our dreams, as so many Everton dreams before them, would be shattered by cruel reality.

But in the 72nd minute, Latchford rose up to head home, sending pulses racing. Defensive warhorse Mick Lyons then broke through—a simple pass would have left Latchford with an open goal—yet inexplicably the defender chose to finish the chance himself. The stadium became thick with anxiety. The release came with ten minutes remaining. Everton won a penalty, and although Latchford was not traditionally the man to step up from the spot, he converted to score the holy 30th and send us into heavenly raptures. I was about four foot two back then, and because the crowd stood the last twenty minutes of the game I was able to see nothing of this moment, yet the image I could not glimpse was so powerful, it is still etched on my eyelids.

ROGER MILLA

Out of loyalty, I have always been drawn to Rogers. Rogers Clemens and Goodell may have done their best to sully the name but I draw vicarious pleasure from Roger Moore, who remains my favorite James Bond. In my opinion, drummer Roger Taylor was the coolest member of Duran. Mimi Rogers is still my favorite Tom Cruise ex-wife. So, when thirty-eight-year-old Roger Milla stumbled out of retirement to burst onto the World Cup stage in 1990, the Cameroonian had me at first name.

Yet, that was just the beginning. Milla had lived out an unspectacular career, stumbling around the French Leagues before decamping to the part-time world of football on the remote Indian Ocean island of Réunion. A call from the Cameroonian president himself had been necessary to coax him out of paradise. Rumors have long abounded the player was older than his reported thirty-eight, but he arrived in Italy with muscles coiled, ready to spring onto the field with 20 minutes to go and changed the way African football was perceived around the globe.

Before Cameroon, Africa's representatives had largely been comical character actors contributing a brief slapstick cameo to World Cup lore. The continent lacked a single direct qualifying spot until 1970. That looked like a commonsense decision when the Mighty

Leopards of Zaire arrived at World Cup 1974. President Mobuto's team proceeded to leak 14 goals in three games—a hapless performance best remembered by panic-struck defender Mwepu Ilunga's desperate attempt to protect his team from a Brazilian free kick by breaking from the wall to blast the stationary ball downfield before his opponents had a chance to take the set piece.

The laughter stopped when Cameroon bullied Argentina in the opening games, battering the defending champions, and leaving the field with nine men and a 1–0 victory. From that point on, it was Milla time. He scored twice, against both Romania and Colombia. In that game, he humiliated the great yet risk-taking goalkeeper René Higuita, who was attempting to sweep the ball up near midfield, only to be dispossessed by the Cameroonian, who then strolled toward the open goal.

For all of his potency and clinical finishing, I remember Milla best for the unbridled joy of his trademark goal celebration in which he sauntered toward the corner flag and proceeded to dry hump it in the manner of an excitable Scottish Terrier. English football was dour at the time and to witness such unabashed giddiness on the football field was to glimpse the game played as it should be—with full-throated joy, bordering on delirious abandon.

LEIGHTON BAINES

Cuter than a baby platypus, the Everton defender may look more like a hopeful who has just auditioned for the lead role in a local amateur dramatic society's production of *Oliver!* but there are few Englishmen who can tear up the flank with such nonchalance and menace. Pass and move. Nip and tuck. Run, run, run. That is his game. Anchored by a bottom so large you could rest a pint glass on it, the England international is a blur of artfully constructed sideburn that stops only to take set pieces.

The true measure of the man was captured one off-season when he appeared in a club promotional film, personally delivering a season ticket to the home of an Everton fan who had just lost his wife to a brain tumor. Clad as if he was a roadie for the Style Council, Baines knocked calmly on the family's door. The grieving fan was taken aback when he saw the England left back standing on his doorstep, but he instinctively found the words anyone would when faced by the most cuddly man in football. "Can I get a man hug?" he asked tentatively, before sliding into the player's arms and holding on as the defender cuddled him back. And that is Baines. Whether you are an Everton fan, England diehard, or grieving human being. Leighton Baines is more than a football player. He is hope incarnate.

ALEXI LALAS

Alexi Lalas is such an omnipresent broadcaster, it is often forgotten just how good a player he was. Perhaps that is fitting. Lalas never dreamed of becoming a professional soccer player as a kid growing up in Michigan. He played the guitar. He loved Van Halen. His sport of choice was ice hockey. But with ginger goatee bouncing, and red hair flowing, he became an American pioneer: the first US-born player to join the 1990s greatest league: Italy's Serie A.

Ahead of the World Cup, no American would have been able to pick him out of a police lineup. Before the tournament kicked off he had never played professional club soccer. But his physical ability and endurance won him a place on the US team and through the course of the World Cup campaign, Lalas, in the words of *Sports Illustrated,* became "the rock-and-roll American face of the game."

As an Englishman watching him play in 1994, that seemed true. Lalas was America itself taking the field. All hustle, idiosyncratic style, and can-do spirit wrapped up in that frosted denim jersey I could not help but admire. Both shirt and athlete unlike anything I had seen on the world stage before. There was something else that was so completely American about Alexi.

His ability to make it on his own terms. By the time the World Cup ended, he had been elected to the All-Tournament team, had a sneaker deal, a European agent, and offers to play in every major league in the world. After signing for Italian team Padua, Lalas reveled in his guitar-strumming maverick persona, jamming on Italian television and supporting Hootie & the Blowfish on their European tour. What could be more American than that?

MICHEL PLATINI

What people are is not what they always were. Long before Michel Platini jumped aboard the football bureaucrat gravy train known as the Sepp Blatter Express, and became a disgraced administrator, he was one of the most beautiful visionaries ever to play the game. Stubbled of cheek and mussed of hair, Platini was a visual sensation. Not merely because he could elegantly dismantle all comers with his artistic use of space and time, but because he rarely seemed to run. The ball always seemed to come to him. It was as if a couch potato had jumped into the television onto the World Cup field, yet was somehow able to control the tempo of the game and bend professional athletes to his will.

L'Équipe wrote, "You can find three million French people who run faster than him, who can jump higher than him, but you could not find a man who can play football better than him." The entire globe came round to this point of view at World Cup 1982, when Platini led an inexperienced French team into the semifinal against the mechanical West Germans. France was not yet perceived as a sporting powerhouse. Germany was a fearsome machine. Alongside Alain Giresse and Jean Tigana, Platini composed a midfield known as the "Three Musketeers." The game ended 3–3, with the Germans predictably proceeding via penalties. But the game was remembered for a moment of thuggish brutality when West German goalkeeper Harald Schumacher used a bona fide Kung Fu Kick to demolish French defender Patrick Battiston as he advanced on goal one-on-one.

The moment reinforced everything we felt about the Germans and the ruthless use of power against the French. Yet the moment I remember best as a kid was watching how Platini held the hand of his unconscious teammate Battiston as he was stretchered off the field. A gesture of nobility and fearlessness when facing doom.

That summer, my family drove around Normandy and Brittany. Every small French town we drove into had a small sports store, and every small sports store had the exact same window display. A tiny television set alongside a French national team jersey with Platini's number, and the clip of him accompanying his battered teammate off the field playing over and over again on an infinite loop. The essence of Gallic pride in which the nobility of heroic defeat is always preferable to a victory won "by all means necessary." **—RB**

PEP GUARDIOLA

Equal parts philosopher, innovator, football manager, and Power Bald. I interviewed Pep halfway through his first season at Manchester City. Our meeting came days after City had been crushed 3–1 by eventual champions Chelsea. Guardiola, always reluctant to talk on camera, was in an edgy, reluctant mood. While responding to my first two questions, he never once looked up from his shoe, letting me know he was an interview partner in body but not in spirit.

Yet Pep is a polemicist to his core. When I asked whether Premier League football is more like an orchestra in which he is the conductor, or like John Coltrane–level free jazz, in which the players constantly improvise, he could not help himself, suddenly sitting up erectly and snapping into life, before barking at me passionately in Spanglish for the next half hour. We talked about football theory, his insistence that the team's quality of play is more important than their results, and his declaration that he would not coach much longer, instead retiring to the golf courses of the world where

Have two balds ever been more different?

"you will not find me." So intense was Pep's energy and concentration, that the second he left the interview room, I had to lie down on the floor to recuperate, as he had drained all of my strength. I have rarely met a gent like Guardiola. A mix of intelligence, creative thinking, leadership, and athletic ability that I crave yet lack. The only thing we have in common, sadly, is hairstyles. —**RB**

Guilty Pleasures in Football:
1. Goalkeepers heading up field in the dying moments of a game to try to get their head on the end of a corner or set piece and summon a last-second equalizer. The closest football comes to the glory of two goaltenders fighting in the NHL, Patrick Roy–Mike Vernon style.
2. When the referee is in the process of sending a player off and one of the guilty party's teammates tries to hold on to the official's hand and prevent him from brandishing the red card, in the desperate belief that if the card is not shown, the dismissal cannot

occur. A cop once told me someone who is about to be shot will instinctively hold whatever they have in their hands—even a piece of paper—in front of them to try and stop the bullet. The police call it a "Phantom Shield." I think about that every time I see a player like Branislav Ivanović grab a referee in the act of sending off Diego Costa.
3. Fans giving cameras a double-fisted wanker sign. Grown men. Lost in football.
4. A shot so poorly struck that it not only misses the goal but goes out for a throw-in.

Guinness: When the Premier League season starts, this Beverage of the Gods is Breakfast in a Can.

Gullit, Ruud: One of the many surreal joys of the 2014 World Cup, right up there with the tiny bananas, sharing a closet-sized studio with Rog, and the quality of the Brazilian militarized police vehicles and body armor, was meeting one of my favorite players and managers of all time, Ruud Gullit. As a player, Ruud had joined

Davo's selfie of a double-fisted wanker sign didn't make it past the lawyers.

Chelsea before the 1995–96 season as the final stop in his outstanding playing career, which had included multiple titles in Holland and Italy and the Ballon d'Or in 1987. Manager Glenn Hoddle immediately employed Gullit, who had mainly played attacking midfield and forward in his playing career, as a sweeper. I traveled a lot to England that year, and saw Chelsea several times that season. Gullit was by far our best player, probably the best we'd ever had at that point. We'd also brought in Mark Hughes that season, and before he became, arguably, the dullest manager in the history of the Premier League, he was a lightning bolt of a center forward. But it was Gullit's transition to player-manager at the end of that season that really helped transform the club. In his time in charge his massive continental reputation helped Chelsea sign the brilliant Italians Roberto Di Matteo, Gianfranco Zola, and Gianluca Vialli, the Dutch goalkeeper and porn star look-alike Ed de Goey, insane Uruguayan Gustavo Poyet, and the superbly named and prematurely bald French defender Frank Leboeuf. I really don't

believe we would ever have started winning anything, had he not become the manager.

Anyway, one night toward the end of our prison term/time in Rio, during a night of moderate Malbec consumption at the JW Marriott bar on Copacabana, beIN Sports' Kay Murray (one of the nicest and most fun people in football or television) introduced us to Ruud. He could not have been more charming, amusing, or enthusiastic to meet us. He loves British comedy, he explained to me and Rog, though we weren't quite sure how that applied to our suboptimal crap. In fact, he had learned English by watching *Monty Python* and classic British sitcoms of the 1970s, *Dad's Army* and *Are You Being Served?* on Dutch television. He then blew us away by launching into full-on reenactments of all his favorite scenes from his very favorite English comedy, *It Ain't Half Hot Mum*, a mildly xenophobic, moderately racist, and wildly homophobic sitcom about a troop of British soldiers and entertainers serving with British forces in the jungles of India and Burma during the last months of the Second World War. —**MD**

PANIC ROOM PRESENTS

We take Polaroids of every guest who has ever come into the Panic Room. Most look like "proof of life" hostage images. Here's a handful of our favorites.

Blue Steel. Mugatu (left).
Zoolander. Hansel (right).

Lewis Hamilton told us the Panic Room felt like a toilet.

Terry Crews's nipples. Scientific proof Arsenal jerseys are made of steel.

Diplo with two bald heads and a microphone

General Hux consults Rog about his Starkiller Base weapon.

John Oliver, blink twice if you need help.

Carmelo Anthony. Not as tall in person.

Mike Myers dressed as Davo's dad for Halloween

The moment Kevin Bacon became six
degrees away from Robbie Mustoe

Phoenix wish they had never left France.

Natural Police, Jimmy McNulty does
it the Western District Way.

Mumford & Sons's first talk show
appearance (seriously)

Downton Abbey's Lady Edith Crawley.
That's our queen.

Laura Linney. That's our president.

Alexander Ovechkin, second
toughest guest in Panic Room

Toughest guest ever in Panic Room

H

Hair Island: *See* Balding Sectors. Hair in sector 3.2, stranded in center of forehead after major problems in sectors 3.1, 3.3, 3.4, and 3.5. Also known as "The Unicorn."

Steve McClaren. "I am a rock, I am a hair island."

Happiness: When my daughter was five, she had a school assignment in which she had to draw her family in their most natural settings. In crude crayon, she etched my three sons playing HORSE, my wife running through Central Park on a sunny day, and me sitting on a couch, red-faced, screaming at a big screen television on which Everton were playing.

The depiction was eerily accurate. I find watching football an all-consuming experience. Frequent emotional outbursts make it hard for me to watch games in bars in public. Yet, being an Everton fan, as my English teacher would sob whilst discussing Thomas Hardy's *Tess of the d'Urbervilles,* "Happiness is but a fleeting emotion."

Indeed, happiness is an all too elusive long-term emotion for fans of most teams outside of the top four or five. There will be the rare wondergoal, struck often in a losing cause, or an occasional shock win against a Champions League contender to savor. But mostly there are a mix of numbing draws, blown leads, and insipid losses. Hope, in the shape of homegrown young talent, is fleeting. They will soon be lured away by a team higher up football's food chain.

There are few things which create such misery and disappointment in my life over which I have no control, but to which I voluntarily return, and actually elevate to a core part of my identity. The question is, why?

Science has a raft of studies attempting to probe this issue. Many point to the physiological arousal supporters experience whilst watching games. We feel alive. More than that, we experience communion and community with others, which feeds our sense of self. None more than the few occasions when the team muster a win to be savored when we "BIRG," the psychological shorthand for "basking in reflected glory." BIRG-ing is great for you. That goal you neither assisted on nor scored does wonders for your self-esteem.

As it turns out, the significant difference between fans of traditionally successful teams and cellar dwellers may be physical, not mental. French researchers at INSEAD Business School discovered fans of losing teams immediately consume more pizza, cake, and cookies than those of winners. Better to be on the Arsenal diet than the Sunderland one. **—RB**

Hate: English football in the 1980s was pockmarked by this emotion. The sport was brutally tribal. Allegiances were black-and-white. Hometown players were heroes, visiting teams were despised. These opinions were defended not only on the field, but off it, with fists, bricks, and flick knives.

Spurs fans loathe Arsenal supporters. Sunderland fans despise Newcastle. When footballer-turned-broadcaster Gary Neville was asked if he "hated Liverpool," he responded, "When I was younger there was no doubt about it. . . . It came from jealousy through my childhood—jealousy, hatred, passion for your own club. You don't want them [Liverpool] to win anything, and you don't like the people who are winning, just like I've seen in the last fifteen or sixteen years, from a good side, everybody is now 'we all hate Man United'—and they hate Man United because we are winning."

Americans who are new to football quickly develop deep attachments to players and teams, yet the hatred and animosity baked into the English game is the hardest emotion for them to conjure, be it because of a lack of historical experience or sense of geography. We receive so many letters from new Norwich City fans expressing a vague embarrassment that they cannot yet summon disgust when they meet a fellow American wearing an Ipswich Town jersey.

The issue is a fascinating one. It forces you to think how global fandom is changing the game of football. When I came of age in the 1980s, you followed your local team through thick and thin. Today, fandom is more fickle. Even in England, kids gravitate toward the winning teams they see play Champions League football on television, irrespective of where they live.

In the United States, thousands of newly minted fans are picking teams shorn of geographical constraint and the regional animosity that often comes with it. As a result, we may see the development of fandom shorn of the hatred which can pockmark and besmirch the English game. As Martin Luther King Jr. once said, "Darkness cannot drive out darkness: only light can do that. Hate cannot drive out hate: only love can do that."

Having said that, if you are a new Everton fan, stare at vintage clips of Brendan Rodgers marching pompously up and down the Liverpool sideline with his new teeth and fake tan long enough—I would prescribe five minutes every morning when you first get up—the hatred should soon overfloweth in your veins. —RB

Hearn, Barry: Ten Lessons of Life: The legendary London-born accountant turned sports promoter, and occasional football team owner, is one of our favorite guests. Our listeners found him to be like Brick Top from *Snatch,* yet real. In February 2014, he unfurled his "Ten Lessons of Life" live onstage in New York City. It remains one of our most listened-to pods of all time. Here are Barry Hearn's rules to live by:

Rule #1: It is better to be born lucky than good-looking
    "When you talk about being born lucky, the principle is we are all great at something. The sadness is a lot of us don't discover in our lifetime what that is. Everyone in this world is a unique person. The principle is this, if you find out what you're good at, it doesn't matter what academic qualifications you've got, they're useful but they're not fundamental."

Rule #2: Tell the truth, it is easier than telling lies
    Barry: "The secret about this of course is it's something you acquire as you get older. When I'm young I told lies all the time; in fact I only stopped telling lies in 1982. As you get on in age you've got to tell the truth because you can't remember the lies. Life's about living, enjoying yourself, feeling relaxed, being relaxed and if people don't like it, sod 'em."

Rule #3: Sheer work ethic can make you look like a genius
    "This is so underestimated, what have we all got in common with every other human being? The answer: There's a certain amount of hours in every day. What we are talking about here is the ability to focus and achieve your goals. Let's be serious, we all would like to be successful but so many of us pay lip service to the essence of being successful that we don't make the sacrifices that are needed to be successful and then we moan that we're not successful."

Rule #4: Pressure is felt only by those who fail
"We all get beat, pressure is an excuse, pressure is nerves, nerves is something we all get every day of our life. Deal with them."

Rule #5: You will run a better business and a better life if you think poor
"Complacency is the biggest killer in any business. . . . There's always better, there's always more."

Rule #6: Unusual things happen every day of your life, it's how you deal with them that makes you unusual

Rule #7: Life ends in tears
"We know who we are, we know that one day we are not going to be here. . . . Our obligation is to enjoy every single second while we're here."

Rule #8: Your life does not change by sitting on the sofa

Rule #9: Avoid being a secret, if you are good admit it, and if you are great shout it from the rooftops
"If there's no passion there's no point. If you really think you're good at something don't wait for someone to identify you because they maybe never will."

Rule #10: When you need a hand you're more likely to get a kick in the nuts; when you need no help there will be a queue of people waiting to give you things
"Your real friends, of which there are very, very few, will stick with you."

Heroes: My late grandfather was a meat wholesaler, and through a friend of a friend down at the stockyards he arranged for the two of us to go to Everton's training ground and meet my childhood heroes. We reported at the assigned time on a cruel winter day. He, a frail, well-mannered Englishman. I, a seven-year-old innocent. My adrenaline was flowing so hard that the plastic "Wembley" football I had bought for my heroes to sign kept squeezing out from under my arm because I was gripping it so tightly.

A secretary greeted us at the front gate and calmly pointed to a door we should walk through to meet the players. "The lads are in that room," she said, as I gripped the handle. We walked in and found ourselves in the players' locker room post-training. All of my heroes were there for sure. Stark bollock naked. I remember seeing my grandfather take one step into the room, catch his first glimpse of pubic hair and testicle and abort mission, pulling a speedy U-turn right out of the door we had walked through. I was alone. A child and his heroes, left to discover they had feet of clay.

Slack-jawed, my body felt weak. The soccer ball escaped from under my arm, bouncing awkwardly on the floor before rolling to a stop. Chirpy Scottish midfielder Asa Hartford picked it up and walked it back to me. "Who are you here to see?" he asked. I must have been able to get the words "Bob" and "Latchford" out, as my hero was quickly summoned from the shower, soon strolling toward me with hand outstretched, naked as the day he was born. He was shy and not much of a conversationalist. I could not get words out, as my tongue felt like it was being sucked back toward my throat. We did not need to communicate, he grabbed a pen from somewhere and signed my ball. As he did so, Asa Hartford thought it would be a good idea to show me how he could make his genitalia look like a seal, proceeding to walk round the room while making a screeching sound.

I was soon out on the street. The wicked Liverpool winter rain revived me. I drove home in silence with my grandfather, running straight to my room to throw myself on the bed. The poster of Bob Latchford stared down at me, and even when I covered my face with a pillow to block it from my line of sight, Asa Hartford's seal bark echoed in my ears, and continued to torture me until I fell asleep. **—RB**

Herrera, Miguel: As anyone who has bellowed "Dos a Cero" during a United States World Cup qualifying victory against Mexico in Columbus will tell you, "El Tri" are the sworn enemy of the US national team.

If only . . .

Yet during their daring run into round of 16 at World Cup 2014, we found ourselves strangely and irresistibly falling in love with the Mexico team, all because of the sideline antics of one man, manager Miguel Herrera. The former player turned coach, who looked as if Pete Rose and John Candy had sired a bastard offspring, had inherited a team in turmoil deep into the qualifying process. He transformed them into one of the most thrilling stories of the Brazil World Cup.

Whenever his team scored, Herrera celebrated each single goal with more joy than a generation of English football fans have experienced in their entire lifetimes. We first marveled at "Wet Herrera," the figure who leapt into the air maniacally amidst a Natal rainstorm to celebrate his team's winning streak. While celebrating a creditable goalless draw against hosts Brazil in a sweltering Fortaleza, the coach sweated through his suit and showed us "Dry Herrera."

By the time Mexico beat Croatia to secure their passage into the elimination round, and Miguel celebrated on the sideline by wrestling one of his players to the ground, then lifting

goalkeeper Guillermo Ochoa off the ground and constricting him in a bear hug ("Barfight Herrera"), he had become a global Internet meme. A coach whose emotions mirrored those

We created this series of images as part of our "Herrera for England" campaign, which became all too real.

This has not been Photoshopped.

of fans watching around the world. After England sluggishly failed to emerge from the group stage, we launched the "Herrera for England" campaign which sparked enough traction on the Internet, Herrera later had to deny he was

With Marouane Fellaini

angling for the job in a press conference. Yet we remain convinced we had found the only man who could give the English national team what they have lacked for the past twenty-five years: the unadulterated passion we experience as we watch the team we adore play the game we love.

Hill, Benny: English physical comedian whose *Benny Hill Show* was one of England's greatest television exports in the 1970s and 1980s, as the world thrilled to his singular brand of vaudeville-and-burlesque-tinged sketch "comedy," which involved old men fondling and ogling nubile young women. Despite that, Benny Hill gave *Men in Blazers* its only truly good joke: No man understood better than Hill that there are fewer funnier things in the world than bald men being slapped hard on the top of their foreheads.

Hotspur: The second half of Tottenham's club name. Coined in honor of Sir Henry Percy, the fourteenth-century peer whose family owned a massive amount of land around Tottenham rough-ly around the time they were last a good football team. Though Sir Henry earned the nickname "Hotspur" on account of his temper, he lived the kind of life we can only aspire to. Knighted at the age of twelve, he experienced battle at age fourteen at the Siege of Berwick. His family were active in King Richard II's downfall and subsequent replacement with Henry IV—a monarch they proceeded to fall out with to such an extent that when Hotspur died in combat at the Battle of Shrewsbury in 1403, aged just thirty-seven, his body was beheaded, quartered, and displayed across the country. The four separate pieces were dispatched to London, Newcastle, Bristol, and Chester, while his head remained on a pole at York's gates until the king eventually sent the body back to his widow. What a life. What a way to go.

Iceland: A nation of just 325,000—a population on par with Corpus Christi, Texas—whose twenty-year strategic youth development plan paid off in Euro 2016 as they shocked England 2–1 in the round of 16. Rog had traveled to Reykjavik before the tournament to make a film about their unprecedented investment in coaching and facilities and to meet their charming head coach Heimir Hallgrímsson, a part-time dentist. Hallgrímsson attributed their success to the Icelandic mentality. In particular, their tenacity. Hallgrímsson underlined that concept by introducing Rog to the word *Duglegur* (DOOG-leg-uhr), which roughly translates to "work harder." "In America, when your toddler takes his first steps, you praise him and say good job," he explained. "In Iceland, our reaction to the same act is to say *'Duglegur'* and demand he keep working harder." As in infant care, so in football.

Iglesias, Julio: Spanish songster and expert lovemaker in eleven of the world's languages. Our greatest memory from broadcasting the Running of the Bulls in 2015 were two sayings the Spanish commonly use in regard to Iglesias and his potent image:

"He is *all* of our fathers."

"Women, be careful, if you look at Iglesias you will become pregnant."

Instagram: We joined Instagram the day we arrived in Brazil for the 2014 World Cup.

Our first post (above right) was taken back when people still used filters, from the roof of our hotel, as we watched the menacing, milita-

rized police helicopters fly sorties out across the hillside favelas that frame Rio.

Opposite and overleaf are seventeen more Instagram shots that we love. And are emblematic. And that we can clear for publication.

International Breaks: A weekend in which FIFA schedules international games such as World Cup or Euro Championship qualifiers. Hence there is no Premier League football to be televised, making the two days feel like they last longer than the Hundred Years War (which actually lasted for 116 years). We encourage all GFOPs to use this time to work on their relationships. Make your partner breakfast in bed. Step out for a long brunch. Be the master of token gestures. And if you feel blue, buck up. The International Break serves a purpose. It is a stark reminder of what America used to be like before it fell in love with soccer.

(1) Rog would be able to talk about this World Cup game for three hours straight at a microphone. Staying awake for it was another matter. **(2)** This was early days at the World Cup while Michael Ballack was still talking to us. **(3)** Hero. Also, Rog's talent for making faces which speak a thousand words. Often the same face, or a variation on the same face, always implying he doesn't really want to be in the picture or wants to remain somewhat separate from it. **(4)** One of our first shots in our Panic Room in the crap part of SoHo. This was a photo shoot for *Eight by Eight* magazine and is a perfect illustration of Davo's stealth height. **(5)** Halloween 2014. How far we will go for our art. **(6)** When producer Lexi took over our Instagram it instantly got more creative. This was how she styled our holiday shot for 2014. Perfect Rog face. **(7)** And then she made us do things like this fake tan and fake hair (aka proper American sports broadcasters). **(8)** She got this great shot in Austin surrounded by GFOPs. Davo signed a baby that night. **(9)** This was an angry, tired Rog arriving in Austin after being heavily delayed by snow in the UK. Mini were delighted with this product shot.

(10) (11) (12)

(13) (14) (15)

(16) (17)

(10) Lexi knows how to do things on her computer. It's really useful, because we never would have got Louis van Gaal to pose for this photograph. **(11)** When she had us shoot this we had no idea what she was going to do with the image. But we're afraid of Lexi, so we always say yes. **(12)** This was genius. Davo likes the way he looks in this one. **(13)** This is what Davo would look like if he won the Masters. Rog actually owns that blazer/shirt/tie combination. **(14)** Rebecca Lowe sent us this selfie after we sent her a pair of Crystal Palace gnomes as a housewarming gift. Fortunately, she has really long arms. **(15)** Our bulbous hair and tie knot hero Kyle. **(16)** Our favorite shot from Blazercon. The final night. We're basically holding each other up. **(17)** Rog has never sweat more than when we shot this episode with his teenage crush (ongoing), Andie Walsh.

Internet: Al Gore may have received a Nobel Prize for his environmental activism, but he deserves a second one for the role he played in empowering America's dizzying love affair with soccer. After all, it is his Internet which made it possible to live in the United States and be a die-hard Premier League football fan.

Many factors have contributed to this revolution. The serious investment in the quality of football broadcasting and the explosive popularity of EA Sports FIFA key amongst them. Yet the Internet has empowered American fans to follow breaking news from the teams they love as closely and quickly as supporters who live right next to that club's home stadium.

Consider this: Exhibit A of how football was lived before the Internet. In 1995, Everton played Tottenham in the FA Cup semifinal. The game was not televised in the United States. To follow the action, Rog had to call his father from his apartment in Chicago and have him hold the receiver against a radio broadcasting game commentary for ninety minutes. In those days, transatlantic phone calls were a prohibitive luxury. Though Rog had to take a second job to pay off that phone bill, Everton's 4–1 victory made it worth every cent.

Is That Your Analysis?: On December 1, 2013, I attended Chelsea's home game against Southampton with my nephews at Stamford Bridge. Our seats are right on the halfway line, just above Roman Abramovich's box, where, according to Rog, the Russian oligarch routinely tortures and sacrifices young children. The stadium was packed and buzzing at kickoff. It was Mourinho's first season back at Stamford Bridge, it was John Terry's 400th Premier League appearance, and with a win Chelsea could keep the pressure on the leaders Arsenal. However, Mauricio Pochettino's young Southampton squad had started the season *en fuego* and were sitting fourth in the table, just two points behind Chelsea in second.

Thirteen seconds after kickoff. Let me repeat that. Thirteen seconds after kickoff, Michael Essien, the Ghanaian international formerly known as "the bison," in his first league start under Mourinho since the Portuguese manager's return, played a deft, volleyed lob over his own back line to set up Jay Rodriguez for a simple finish past Petr Čech. The stadium fell nine-tenths quiet, except for the section of red-and-white-clad Scummer fans who were going bananas in what used to be the shed end. My nephews both groaned and put their heads in their hands. All around us, grown men were swearing and bemoaning Essien, "He's past it!," "Typical Chelsea," "F&%king Scummers!" and the posh idiot in front of me, in the most grating, high-pitched, I've-eaten-a bag-of-lemons, upper-class accent ever—"Well, I think Peter Čech might reasonably have been expected to do a little better there, don't you think? Typical bloody Chelsea. What a flipping disaster!"

Clearly I needed to lift the spirits of my nephews and all around me. It was also abundantly clear to me that what Southampton had just done was going to cost them dearly—away, at Stamford Bridge, against old Chelsea. I turned to my nephews and loudly proclaimed, "They've scored far too early." My nephews immediately took in and accepted the universal and irrevocable truth of my statement. The idiot in front of me turned around to face me, with a look of disdain and disgust on his ratlike and entitled face, a face which I assume and trust has been thumped a thousand times by the righteous, and squawked: "Is that your analysis?!" He was attempting to mock me, to call into question my almost psychic-level ability to analyze football through analysis, to predict the football future unaided by either octopus or pie.

Chelsea went on to win 3–1. Each Chelsea goal was punctuated by a loud scream from a forty-eight-year-old man, six foot two (rounding up), way less bald in person, in section 5, row 2, seat 114 of the Upper West Stand—"THIS IS IN LINE WITH MY ANALYSIS!!!!!" —MD

Italy: Tight of jersey, flowing of hair, beard, and with a heavy hand on the hair gel. Before their

A Collection of Rog Pulling Awkward Faces
with Premier League Managers

Two men who know suffering

Twins

Jose not happy with club's new signing

Mauricio Pochettino photobomb

Hold me closer, Tiny Dancer

Pound for pound, football's biggest head

Rog with Rog's crush

This man is everything Rog is not.

shocking failure to qualify for the 2018 World Cup, we Englishmen only marveled at both Italy's big tournament track record and their looks. In the 1970s and 1980s, their glory was built on a negative, defensive style of soccer born of a deep insecurity. Fear of losing was their prime motivation, and the team became masters of the black arts of the dive and the professional foul. Italy is, after all, a nation where un-penalized cheating is not just tolerated, but celebrated, to the extent they have even coined a word for it— *furbo,* gamesmanship.

Yet, Italian football is far more than that. Few nations have such tactical discipline embedded in their DNA. Italian soccer at its finest is like watching a team of unbelievably good-looking chess grandmasters playing moves ahead of their opponents to force them off their game plan. After witnessing AC Milan and Juventus dissect each other in the 2003 Champions League Final, their expertise forced even *The Times* of London to concede, "Football is an Italian game that just happens to have been invented in England."

Our favorite Italian archetype is the unpredictable genius. Sandro Mazzola and Gianni Rivera in the 1960s, Roberto Baggio in the 1990s, and Francesco Totti in the 2000s. The waifish Baggio struggled in particular. Perhaps the most un-Italian of Italian superstars, known, thanks to his signature ponytail and conversion to Buddhism, as *The Divine Ponytail.* Few players were more beloved than he at the domestic level. A pop song written about him described his inimitable style with the line "When you watch Baggio play / You hear children." Fans of his club team Fiorentina rioted when he left them, but for much of his international career he was a jigsaw piece that did not fit. This changed in 1994, when he stubbornly used his sublime skills to transform Italy from laggards to world beaters (after equalizing in the round of 16, he famously stormed toward the television camera, screaming "God exists! God exists!"), dragging the team into the 1994 World Cup final, although he remains best remembered as the forlorn figure who blasted the final penalty kick of the shootout over the bar to hand victory to the Brazilians. Traumatized, he later retired, becoming the Bono of soccer, finding serenity by blogging about world peace and eradicating global poverty.

In a regionally splintered country, torn between its north and south, the Italian national team is one of the few truly cohesive symbols beloved by all. During the 2006 World Cup, the Italian press corps became horrified that the players were not singing the pregame national anthem. The team had to send out a representative to admit with embarrassment that the tune is sung so rarely in Italy that they just did not know the words.

J

Japan: Country with which I became truly obsessed after basing myself there for thirty-one straight days at the 2002 World Cup. Based out of the near-perfect Pan Pacific Hotel in Yokohama, I visited eight of the ten venues, from Sapporo on Hokkaido in the north, to Oita on Kyushu in the south. The joy of witnessing the young Japanese fans chanting elaborate Scott Joplin tunes, singing their beautiful and haunting national anthem, and embracing their outstanding team and the concept of nationalism for the first time, moved me beyond words. There were some outstanding matches (England versus Argentina in Sapporo is a game I will never forget). Nor will I ever forget traveling with the Irish fans and seeing how they lifted their boys in green, and seeing players like Brazilian Ronaldo, Ronaldinho, and Oliver Kahn perform at levels I had never seen. I even saw Emile Heskey score a World Cup goal. I loved the rice balls, the lace covers on the seats in the back of the taxis, the karaoke bars, and the vending machines. My goodness, the vending machines. But the enduring memory of Japan and its millenniums-old culture is the ceremony, beauty, and ritual that is introduced into every aspect of daily life. The simple act of purchasing chewing gum at a station kiosk is imbued with grace and meaning—the way the purchase is wrapped and presented, the ceremonial exchange of paper money and change, the appropriate depth of bow from each of you as you part. Upon boarding my Delta Airlines flight from Narita back home to JFK, after seeing Brazil conquer Germany in the final in Yokohama (most notable for the peerless refereeing performance by Pierluigi Collina), I have never been more shocked by the rudeness of an American airline cabin crew. You get snapped back into real life real fast. But Japan is a dream. You must, must go there. —**MD**

JC Is Awesome: On more than one occasion, the words used to greet Davo by GFOPs convinced that as the gentile component of the *Men in Blazers* partnership, Davo is therefore really into Jesus Christ. The truth is, Davo thinks Jesus Christ possesses a great left foot, looks useful with or without the ball, and has a lot to contribute. In the right formation. Also, he'd be really good at running FIFA. Rog always assumes they are talking really enthusiastically about James Corden. —**MD**

Jenkins: Jenkins is the official Los Angeles–based driver of the pod. The stealth GFOP first picked me up in LA to drive me to the airport in late 2013. He looked sharp in in his black suit, had a gravelly cockney accent, and had the smooth, unflappable  persona of a former SAS man or contract killer. We started talking football and he ominously informed me, "I already know quite a lot about you, Mr. Davies," and our relationship grew from there. Originally from Balham South London, Jenkins moved to the US in the 1980s to work in the "import-export business." He has driven me several times since in Los Angeles, and Rog has speculated that he doesn't actually exist or is a figment of my imagination, like an imaginary friend.

Actually, Jenkins is a lovely man who looks a bit like Warren Barton's dad. —MD

Jersey, The:

THE TEN GREATEST WORLD CUP SHIRTS OF ALL TIME

World Cup uniforms originally played the simple role of separating one team from another. They are now among the most lucrative billboards in sports. The shirts, once cut from flannel in the 1930s, are now made of polyester, but they might as well be spun from gold. Adidas reported $2.7 billion in sales courtesy of Germany's success in the 2014 World Cup. Soccer's equivalent of turning water into wine.

The intense competition between the big three apparel companies—Adidas, Puma, and Nike—has fostered a frantic culture of creativity and reinvention in which soccer shirts have become a canvas and designs have the life expectancy of a fruit fly.

These chameleonic conditions make the challenge of judging which shirts are truly epic as subjective as deeming what makes great art. Legendary performance helps (see Brazil 1970) but is by no means critical. Indeed, the majority of the teams below fizzled in the early rounds (Zaire 1974). Some of the shirts are definitive old-school classics. Others are bold, avant-garde reinventions that redefine the genre. What matters most is the first impression. The distinctive swagger they grant a team running out onto the field for its World Cup debut, back when everything still seems possible, and the story lines of success and failure are yet to unfold. To steal a quote from Roman bard Horace (65–8 BC), the great shirts are "poetry without words": images which burn onto your retina, remaining there long after the team itself has been eliminated.

10. Peru 1978

The stark slash slicing through the shirt was a simple yet strikingly effective piece of design. The team were appalling, but if soccer were scored like figure skating, and points were factored in for style, Peru would, without a doubt, have instantly been hailed as World Champions. Instead they failed to emerge from the second group stage.

9. Zaire 1974

Once Zaire became the first Sub-Saharan team ever to qualify for the tournament, President Mobuto seized the opportunity to use the World Cup as a global public relations coup. He rebranded the national team the Leopards (they had been known as the Lions) to reflect his trademark hat and demanded victory. While their record (3 losses, 14 goals conceded, 0 scored) could not match the inflated expectations of an entire continent, their shirt design could. A three-part masterpiece of complementary design elements: An eye-catching logo in which a leopard is poised to attack an unsuspecting soccer ball; deceptively simple font-work; and floppy, casual yellow collars. Adidas designers on top of their game. Unfortunately, Zaire failed to emerge from the group stage.

8. Brazil 1970

Brazil's squad, loaded with the explosive firepower of Pelé, Tostão, Gerson, Rivelino, and Jairzinho, was one of the finest ever assembled. Their stylish, flamboyant soccer was the sport as if choreographed by Cirque du Soleil. This was the first World Cup

to be broadcast in color, lending the television footage an evocative quality which captured the warmth of Brazil's classic golden shirts in all of their finery. Brazil won the 1970 World Cup after defeating Italy 4–1.

7. Mexico 1978

Despite fielding the young striker phenomenon Hugo Sánchez, the Mexicans were dumped in the opening round, losing decisively to Tunisia, West Germany, and Poland. What lingered about their appearance was the sassy selection of Bay Area jeans and casual wear specialists Levi's, who delivered on their promise that "Quality Never Goes Out of Style" by inventing these snuggly verdant V-neck creations.

6. Holland 1974

Johan Cruyff's magnificent Dutch side played "Total Football," a radically free-thinking style of soccer that used perpetual movement and passing to confuse opponents. Trumped 2–1 by West Germany in the final, their brilliant orange shirt was the only thing that became a winner, enhancing the long hair and chilled-out vibe of the team. Cruyff was so indispensable he had his own customized uniform. Because the Jedi-like maestro was sponsored by Puma and the jerseys were made by Adidas, he received a tailor-made shirt with two stripes, instead of the trademarked three.

5. Denmark 1986

"They are red, they are white, they are Danish Dynamite!" So sang the fans of this deliciously attacking squad resplendent with mullet-wearing players. When it was unveiled, their jersey, a delicate half shirt made by Dan-

ish outfitters Hummel, was as coveted as the attacking verve of creative forces, Michael Laudrup and Preben Elkjaer. It ultimately became a stylish harbinger of their tournament fate, its unbalanced symmetry hinting that soccer is a game of two halves, of both attack and defense. Denmark crushed all comers in the first round, emerging as many critics' choice to win it all, but a 5–1 mauling at the hands of Spain served as a reality check. An offense with no defense will only get you as far as the second round, and Denmark were eliminated in the round of 16 after losing to Spain 5–1.

4. Croatia 2006

Long before Norway charmed the pants off the world with their fashion-forward curling attire, Croatia rocked the look in the 1990s with this controversial but audacious shirt, a singular style perfected here in 2006. As ever, function refused to follow form and Croatia failed to emerge from the group stage.

3. East Germany 1974

If the Cold War was decided *Project Runway*–style by Tim Gunn, we would all be living under Communism. At a World Cup played amidst global ideological turmoil, it was only fitting that East Germany would be drawn against West in the group stages. East Germany won the match, against all odds, 1–0. They also won the style war. Stout utilitarian fontmanship coats the breast, drawing the eye to the idealism of the logo. Together they project an air of menace sufficient to unnerve their more materialistic brothers from the West.

East Germany failed to emerge from the second group stage.

2. Argentina 1986 away kit

The white and sky blue stripes of Argentina's home jersey are a design classic. But in 1986, when Diego Maradona skipped through virtually the entire English team to prod home one of the greatest goals the tournament has ever witnessed, he was wearing this V-neck all-blue away shirt, which resembled the sports-casual look of medical scrubs. As he lacerated the English defense, the jersey appeared to coolly gloat, "I can just roll out of bed in my pajamas and still crush you." Argentina won the 1986 World Cup after beating Germany 3–2 in the final.

1. USA 1994 home and away

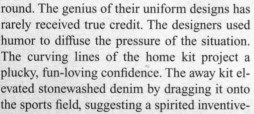

The USA hosted the tournament desperate to avoid the humiliation of becoming the first home team unable to safely navigate the opening round. The genius of their uniform designs has rarely received true credit. The designers used humor to diffuse the pressure of the situation. The curving lines of the home kit project a plucky, fun-loving confidence. The away kit elevated stonewashed denim by dragging it onto the sports field, suggesting a spirited inventiveness that many feared the team lacked. How good did these designs look? Even Alexi Lalas's ginger beard looked cool when he pulled them on. Despite their home field and sartorial advantages, the United States were elimi-

nated by Brazil in the round of 16 after losing 1–0.

Jewish Room: I was schooled at Liverpool College for Gentlemen, a centuries-old all-boys institution which was the last bastion of traditional English values in a city which, in the 1980s, was rotting away. Liverpool is to England what Baltimore is to the US. A once thriving port which had lost its raison d'être in the late 1960s and was subsequently crippled by a toxic mix of unemployment, poverty, and

Rog is second from the right. His table manners have only degenerated since then.

crime. The college was the one place in which time had stood still. Within its walls, the Churchillian spirit lived on: England still had an Empire, the monarch was beloved, and all boys were to be seen and not heard. A challenge to any of these tenets would earn an immediate yet savage thrashing of the bare buttocks courtesy of a teacher armed with a bamboo cane, cricket bat, or whatever was at hand that could act as an aide-mémoire. Constant canings notwithstanding, Liverpool College prided itself as being an oasis of civility against a backdrop of anarchy.

Being a Jew in a school in which chapel attendance, hymn singing, and generally "Serving the Lord" comprised 60 percent of the curriculum made for a turbulent time. Every school day began with the entire student body marching down to a prayer service at the school chapel. The entire school body minus heathens like me who had to report to a classroom popularly known as "Jewish Room." While our fellow Christ-believing classmates convened through hymn and prayer with their Lord, we infidels used our time slightly less productively, forced to sit in total silence, with perfect posture, at risk of the requisite caning from a master eager to punish us for an infraction of either rule.

Why the room was called "Jewish Room" in the first place was a theological mystery, ranking up there with the Turin Shroud. It contained a handful of Jews vastly outnumbered by twenty or so Muslim kids. A mini–Middle East where a majority simmered, incensed once more at the injustice of having the Jews somehow screw them out of naming rights. **–RB**

Jews, Best Team of All Time: In the infamous throwaway laugh line from the movie *Airplane!,* a flight attendant played by Julie Hagerty attempts to settle the nerves of an elderly, nervous passenger:

JULIE HAGERTY: Would you like something to read?
OLD LADY: Do you have anything light?
HAGERTY: How about this leaflet, *Famous Jewish Sports Legends*?

The movie scene may have been short but it has remained legendary. A sight gag that has reinforced the stereotype of Jewish athleticism and physicality in this country: Jews make great accountants, attorneys, and Mah-Jongg aficionados, but clinical strikers, marauding midfielders, or intimidating defenders, not so much. Hot-wired to win Nobel Prizes, we have always been seen as athletic interlopers.

To counter that cliché, I present history's greatest squad of the "Mosaic Persuasion." They might not be the best team in the world, but few can claim to have been so truly chosen.

GOALKEEPER

DAVID "DUDU" AOUATE (b. 1977) [P1]: Racing Santander, Deportivo La Coruña, Mallorca, Israel: Caused controversy in Israel in 2006 when he told a Spanish newspaper he would play on Yom Kippur if his club team forced him to. Right-wing politicians in Israel called for him to be removed from the national team for years.

DEFENDERS

BÉLA GUTTMANN (1899–1981): Hakoah Vienna, New York Giants, Hungary: Hungarian player turned coaching innovator who owned a New York speakeasy and returned to Europe after the Wall Street Crash, surviving the war, and finding fame as a tactical genius who coached Eusebio's Benfica to two European Cup victories. Benfica would not give Guttmann the raise he was looking for and he left in anger, supposedly after cursing the club. Despite making the final three times since, they have never won the Champions League again.

AVI COHEN (1956–2010): Maccabi Tel Aviv, Liverpool, Rangers, Israel: The first Israeli to play in English football when he left Maccabi Tel Aviv to join champions Liverpool for $285,000 in July 1979. Best remembered for the own goal he knocked home before redeeming himself by scoring the winner in a 4–1 home victory against Aston Villa that clinched the league title for Liverpool in May 1980.

JUAN PABLO SORIN (b. 1976): Juventus, River Plate, Villarreal, Argentina: Long-haired all-action hero known affectionately as "Juampi," the defender captained Argentina at the 2006 World Cup and was a one-man defensive wall despite being just five foot six.

JEFF AGOOS (b. 1968): SV Wehen, DC United, West Bromwich Albion (loan), USA: Prolific US international and own goal specialist who won over 130 caps over the course of thirteen years of action. After being the last man cut from the United States roster ahead of the 1994

BEST JEWISH TEAM OF ALL TIME

Gai Yigaal
Assulin

Striking Midfielder

Ronny
Rosenthal

Forward

Johan
Neeskens

Yossi
Benayoun

Eyal
Berkovic

Edgar
Davids

Midfielders

Jeff
Agoos

Avi
Cohen

Juan Pablo
Sorin

Bela
Guttman

Defenders

Dudu
Aouate

Goalkeeper

Jose
Pekerman

Manager

World Cup, he stuffed his training kit into a garbage can and set it aflame. Went on to represent the US at World Cups 1998 and 2002.

MIDFIELDERS

GAI ASSULIN (b. 1991): Barcelona flop, Manchester City flop, Mallorca, Israel: After starring with Barcelona B, and making his debut for Israel as a sixteen-year-old, the attacking midfielder wilted under the pressure of being hailed as "The next Messi." He later admitted, "I can never be him. He is the best player in the world; I'm a youngster trying to learn the secrets of football."

EDGAR DAVIDS (b. 1973): Ajax, AC Milan, Juventus, Holland: The Suriname-born Dutch international was known for his dreadlocks, sports goggles, and smothering defensive abilities in the heart of midfield. Louis van Gaal described his tackling abilities as those of a "pitbull."

JOHAN NEESKENS (b. 1951): Ajax, Holland: Midfield poet-warrior who dominated the game with the avant-garde Total Footballing Ajax team of the early 1970s. Sideburned of hair, he was known as "Johan Segon" (Johan the Second) in honor of his partnership with the iconic Johan Cruyff.

ATTACKING MIDFIELDERS

EYAL BERKOVIC (b. 1972): West Ham United, Celtic, Manchester City, Israel: Tiny creative visionary whose career was undermined by his apparent inability to mesh with coaches, players, and fans. Despite his peerless play in the final third, is best remembered for being viciously kicked in the head whilst lying prone on the turf by one of his own teammates in training.

YOSSI BENAYOUN (b. 1980): Maccabi Haifa, Racing Santander, West Ham United, Liverpool, Chelsea, Arsenal (loan), Israel: Israel's most capped player of all time with 96 caps, the diminutive Dimona-born midfielder became known as the "Negev Dagger" for his impudent passing ability.

FORWARD

RONNY ROSENTHAL (b. 1963): Maccabi Haifa, Club Brugge, Liverpool, Tottenham, Israel: The square-of-jaw, mulleted Israeli became a cult hero at Liverpool after netting a hat trick on his full debut. His pace earned him the nickname "Rocket," yet his inability to finish—he famously missed an open goal from three yards out—encouraged *The Guardian* to suggest that his nickname was shorthand for "a rogue rocket waiting to be aborted by mission control."

MANAGER

JOSÉ PÉKERMAN (b. 1949): Argentina, Colombia: Winner of consecutive South American Coach of the Year awards in 2012 and 2013, Pékerman was born in Villa Domínguez in Entre Ríos province, better known as Moisesville, the area where the Jewish gauchos, or cowboys, used to live.

SUBSTITUTES

STEVE BIRNBAUM (b. 1991), Defender: DC United, USA

JONATHAN SPECTOR (b. 1986), Defender/Midfielder: Manchester United, West Ham United, Birmingham City, USA

JONATHAN BERNSTEIN (b. 1984), Left Back: Chivas USA, UANL, Querétaro, USA

BENNY FEILHABER (b. 1985), Midfielder: Hamburger SV, Derby County, AGF Aarhus, New England Revolution, Sporting Kansas City, USA

YAEL AVERBUCH (b. 1986), Midfielder: New Jersey Lady Stallions, Sky Blue FC, Western NY Flash, FC Kansas City, USA

Johnny Foreigner: English football culture was dull, tactically inept, and violent until the Premier League rebranded itself in 1992. A five-year ban from European competition had made British football a backwater. The league was still primitive until a trickle of remarkable Italians, Frenchmen, and Germans braved the physical culture of English football and refashioned it into the most watched sports league in the world.

Many sneer at MLS for being an "elephants graveyard" or lucrative retirement village for football's ageing elite. Yet, in the early days of the Premier League, English football was derided for similar reasons. Players like Ruud Gullit and Gianluca Vialli arrived, way into their thirties, having won European trophies and dazzled in the powerhouse Serie A, to pick up one last paycheck on England's shores. An Italian journalist once told me that when Fabrizio Ravanelli, the White Feather, opted to join Middlesbrough after winning the Champions League with Juventus, the reaction in the Turin media was one of pity for him, as though the move was an embarrassment.

The English media were suspicious of the pioneering arrivals. When a thirty-year-old Jürgen Klinsmann arrived at Spurs in 1994, a *Guardian* writer welcomed him with a feature entitled "Why I Hate Jürgen Klinsmann," describing his cunning, flopping gamesmanship as everything the British game stands against. Within a couple of months, Jürgen had won everyone around with his ethereal talent, lashing home 29 goals, and forcing the English scribe to recant with a second feature, "Why I Love Jürgen Klinsmann."

The elder statesmen were just the beginning of the influx. The likes of Patrick Vieira, Dennis Bergkamp, Marc Overmars, Jaap Stam, Fabien Barthez, and Eric Cantona who followed transformed the face of the English game, making it the world's most cosmopolitan, yet the suspicion that surrounded their intent and motivation has never truly disappeared. Though technically and physically more gifted than their British peers, they are still "Johnny Foreigner"—the kind of man who will dive for penalties, mime the award of a yellow card to encourage the booking of opponents, and who does not like it "Up and at 'em."

John Terry Hat Trick: When a player scores a goal, an own goal, and receives a red card in the same game.

Joink: This is what I exclaim almost every time someone scores a goal in a highlight on *The Men in Blazers* show. Its etymology is hazy, even to me, and I invented it. But I believe I have been inspired by two of the great characters in modern television—*Pinky,* from *Pinky and the Brain,* and NeNe Leakes from *The Real Housewives of Atlanta.* "*Joink*" is their love child. First, Pinky. I understand the case for *Breaking Bad, The Wire,* or even *Battlestar Galactica,* but in my estimation, the greatest TV series ever made, in the pre-*Billions* era, is *Pinky and the Brain.* If you haven't seen it, the show features two genetically enhanced lab mice, who in every episode devise a plan to take over the world, and then fail, usually in spectacular fashion. Brain, the smaller of the two mice, is fiercely intelligent, dark, brooding, and slightly evil. Pinky, on the other hand, is a childlike, rambunctious, and good-natured idiot. Anyone notice any similarities to two bald English blokes? Anyway, one of my favorite things about Pinky is his verbal tics—he has several of them, like *"narf," "zort," "poit,"* and *"troz"* (the last of which he started saying after noticing it was "*zort* in the mirror"). *"Joink!"* is partially my own attempt to channel Pinky and offer an inane exclamation point to Rog's *Game of Thrones,* metaphor-filled analysis of the buildup. However, let us not underestimate the influence of NeNe Leakes from *The Real Housewives of Atlanta* on "Joink!" "Bloop!," her trademark expression to illustrate and underline the truth of what she is saying, had a profound effect on me when she started using the expression on *Watch What Happens Live.* Goals, after all, are football's only truth. **—MD**

Jonjo: To "Jonjo" is to do something wonderful one minute, and something self-destructive or slapstick the next. For example: Whilst representing Swansea, Jonjo Shelvey, playing against former club Liverpool, opened the scoring with a breathtaking strike after only two minutes, then gave away two goals courtesy of a pair of passes mishit straight to the feet of opposing strikers.

Judge Ivor Bennett Time: My father had two footballing rules he lived by. The first was "It only takes a second to score a goal." A relentlessly optimistic phrase he would habitually utter whenever Everton went behind in a game. As a child, I drew tremendous comfort from those words, only for my faith to be shattered in 1982 when Liverpool demolished Everton 5–0. As the clock ticked past the 90th minute, I remember turning round to my father and inquiring innocently, "We can still get back into this game, right, Dad? There are still at least five seconds left—we could score five goals in those seconds because it only takes a second to score a goal." After watching his footballing gods proven to have feet of clay, my father was in no mood to indulge me. "Don't be stupid," he spat sharply. "Only a fool would believe in that ridiculous cliché."

My father's second rule lives on. He firmly believes goals scored either in the 44th minute of the first half or the 46th of the second were debilitating for the conceding team. The first because their manager would have to tear up his halftime tactical talk and brief his team on the fly. The second because whatever instructions handed out in the locker room had immediately been rendered irrelevant.

If we are watching an Everton game and the team concede around the halftime break, his muttering groan of "that is the worst time to let in a goal" stings like salt in a wound. For what it is worth, his other great belief is that bedrooms should be kept cold. Very cold and damp, if possible. In Judge Ivor Bennett's mind, "a cold room is the first value that leads to success." —RB

K

Kissing the Badge: A common deceit perpetrated in the wake of a goal by footballers eager to delude fans they love their team as much as supporters do. To begin with, fans adored this symbol of fierce loyalty demonstrated by a player's lip touching polyester. Yet the gesture now happens so frequently, its meaning has been diluted. Indeed, the act is often the beginning of a disheartening yet well-worn spiral that sees badge kissing quickly followed by the signing of a long-term contract, only to lead to the ditching of the club you professed love for to leap to a bigger club within a matter of months.

Arsenal fans have experienced the numbing emotional degradation of this cycle more than most. In the 2000s alone, Cesc Fàbregas, Sol Campbell, Samir Nasri, and Thierry Henry all kissed the badge shortly before decamping for pastures new, making this smooch more akin to a kiss of death. Togolese striker Emmanuel topped them all, ditching the club for Manchester City, and two months later, charging the length of the field so he could celebrate a goal he scored against the Gunners in front of the North London faithful, who howled in powerless derision as he kissed the badge of his new team.

The unchallenged master of disingenuous badge kissing is Wayne Rooney. A player who came through at Everton from the age of nine, wore a "Once a blue, always a blue" T-shirt after a famous youth team victory, and swore he would never leave the club he had supported since childhood. After defecting to Manchester United, he led his new mob to a sterling 4–2 come-from-behind victory at Goodison Park. A feat he capped by celebrating in the faces of the Everton fans who once idolized him, before waddling off to kiss his badge in front of the traveling away supporters.

Three years later, he stunned the football world by announcing it was time to leave United for crosstown rivals Manchester City, as the club had lacked "ambition," only to sign a huge new contract within a matter of days. Badge kissing resumed shortly thereafter—as it did at Everton, he returned, like a salmon swimming upstream to die, in 2017.

English striker turned marble-mouthed commentator Ian Wright famously denounced these kinds of actions in his memorable quote "When you've been at a club five minutes and you kiss the badge, you are just mugging yourself off . . . you mug." He should know. After six years at Crystal Palace, Wright scored for new club Arsenal, and practically got to second base with his Gunner badge before the stunned Palace terraces.

Klingenberg, Meghan: An American hero known as "Yinzer Maldini." A third-degree tae kwon do black belt, nunchucks expert, and member of the 2015 Woman's World Cup–winning US team. Her play turned the team round, as the team struggled early on. In the 77th minute of the second group stage game against Sweden, the US were lackluster. A Swedish shot looped the ball toward the American net. Hope Solo was stranded. But there was Meghan, all five foot two of her, leaping up like Crouching Tiger Hidden Klingenberg to head

"Mummy"

the ball off the line. Afterward she came on our pod and modestly declared, "I was only doing my job," but that job to us is superhero.

Klopp, Jürgen: Less a manager, more a giant Teutonic Care Bear. A master motivator who knows he can incite the home fans into the kind of frenzy previously seen only in a peasants' rebellion by leaping around his technical area air guitar–style, or fulfill his player's tactical, physical, and mental potential by rewarding them with a post-match hug. Klopp's hugs, let me tell you, as someone who has been in one, are as close as a grown man can come to climbing back into the womb. When I lay in his arms, time stopped, my horizons of what is possible broadened exponentially, and I felt compelled to call him "Father." **—RB**

Knee Slide:
Step One: Score goal
Step Two: Charge toward corner flag
Step Three: Ask self, Is this AstroTurf—If Yes, Abort Now

Step Four: Ask self, Is it raining—If Yes, Attempt Sideways Twist And Slide Flourish

Kummerspeck: Rog's favorite German word. Literally "grief bacon," it is used to describe the fat you put on whilst grieving a loss. Few words better capture the emotions experienced the moment your team is eliminated from a World Cup. Your nation is out. Your dreams are dead. God does not exist. All that is left is for you to do some Anger Laundry.

Kung Fu Fighting: The phrase that has been the sign-off from our podcast from the very beginning. A tribute to Carl Douglas's 1974 smash hit, which we believe might just be the world's greatest one-hit wonder of all time.

It is hard to top perfection, which is why we believe Mr. Douglas never hit the big time again, yet what appalls us is the world has stopped talking about the texture and nuance of the importance of this song. We like to do what we can to promote its legacy.

L

Lalas, Alexi: Rog adores Alexi Lalas (*see* Greatest Footballers of All Time [according to Rog]). So much so that when EA Sports invited us to pick our greatest World Cup XI's of all time, momentarily blinded by loyalty and emotion, Rog selected Alexi as one of his center backs playing in a star-studded team including Johan Cryuff, Michel Platini, and Zinedine Zidane. Davo's team was stuffed with legends front to back. We submitted the lineups to EA and sat back as they simulated the game overnight and relayed to us the next day as a line-by-line match report. The game ended Team Davo 7, Team Rog 1. It began like this:

Minute 1: Kickoff

Minute 3: Ronaldo runs at Team Roger's defense. Alexi Lalas trips him on the edge of the area and receives a yellow card. Free kick Team Davo. Ronaldo steps up to smash the free kick past Lev Yashin's outstretched hand. Team Davo 1 Team Roger 0.

Minute 5: Diego Maradona exchanges a one-two with Pelé and is pushed to ground by Alexi Lalas, who receives a second yellow card and is sent off. Penalty Team Davo. Pelé converts. Team Davo 2 Team Roger 0 (Team Roger reduced to ten men).

Larkin, Philip (1922–85): Temperamental, misanthropic poet, jazz critic, and university librarian who reveled and mourned in his dual themes of self-loathing and the decline of postwar England in equal measure. His philosophy was best summed up in *This Be the Verse:* "Man hands on misery to man. It deepens like a coastal shelf. Get out as early as you can, and don't have any kids yourself." He did not like football, but most fans of mid-table clubs can relate to that ethos.

Ley, Bob: A doppelgänger for a young Kenny Loggins, no American has broadcast the World Cup longer than this man. Back when he started, Sepp Blatter was still a nice guy, Brad Friedel  was still a young guy, and even more hard to believe, England were still good. A tastemaking prophet for football in America, Ley was reported to have been present at the 1930 World Cup semifinal, in which the US were cruelly pipped 6–1 by a speedy Argentinian side on a rain-soaked field in Montevideo. Of the thousands of games he has covered, here are the five Bob believes were most memorable:

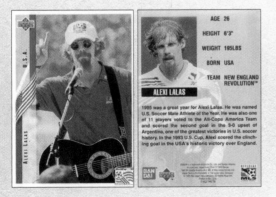

AGE 26

HEIGHT 6'3"

WEIGHT 195LBS

BORN USA

TEAM NEW ENGLAND REVOLUTION™

ALEXI LALAS

1995 was a great year for Alexi Lalas. He was named U.S. Soccer Male Athlete of the Year. He was also one of 11 players voted to the All-Copa America Team and scored the second goal in the 3-0 upset of Argentina, one of the greatest victories in U.S. soccer history. In the 1993 U.S. Cup, Alexi scored the clinching goal in the USA's historic victory over England.

1. USA 1 Algeria 0, June 23, 2010, Pretoria

"I was hosting the broadcast from our studios in Johannesburg. I was on air with Steve McManaman. We both knew the entire nation at home was praying for the US to progress. When Landon Donovan scored in the 90th + 1 minute, I have never experienced a moment like it. The audacity of the goal itself, the stage we were on, the drama and last-second nature of it all, and the way Ian Darke called it. Our World Cup ratings had been soaring. Americans had fallen for the tournament, in large part because of the way Bob Bradley's team had played. . . . As Landon's shot hit the back of the net, we created a lot of new lifelong American soccer fans in that second."

2. France 3 Brazil 0, July 12, 1998, Stade de France, St. Denis

"The game began with mystery. Would Ronaldo play? The first lineup sheet did not have him in the Brazil team. A second was then released with him in it. Irrespective, Brazil, the world's greatest ever soccer team, were never in the game. To be in the Stade de France and hear 'La Marseillaise' sung by 80,000 Frenchmen was enough to make me put aside every joke I have ever heard about the French. It was incredible. I knew then they would go up against the Brazilians and demolish them. And what a party at the final whistle. I spent the evening near the Champs-Élysées, watching Frenchmen sit on the hoods of cars speeding at fifty or sixty miles an hour, deliriously swigging bottles of champagne."

3. Mexico 0 USA 1, August 15, 2012, Azteca, Mexico City (friendly)

"The US had never won at the Azteca. The Mexicans were so confident they even paraded their Olympic team, who had just won a gold medal in London, at halftime. The fireworks they let off almost nailed us in the booth. Tim Howard stood on his head in goal, making a series of magical saves, then, in the 80th minute, Michael Orozco Fiscal bundled the ball

over the line at the far post. To this day, I have never understood why a defender was so far forward. At the final whistle, bottles, cans, and cups rained down on us. We needed to hold umbrellas during the postgame broadcast as the beer—I keep telling myself it was beer—thrown by fans soaked through our clothing."

4. Mexico 0 USA 0, World Cup qualifying, March 26, 2013, Azteca, Mexico City

"The final round of 2014 World Cup qualifying began terribly for the US, losing in the heat of Honduras. The next two games were home against Costa Rica and then down to Mexico. The prospect of having one point after three games felt very real. The "SnowClasico" allowed us to play with house money before we headed to the Azteca. We had no Tim Howard. Our defenders were young. Yet we hung on. You would never hang this game on the wall like a Rembrandt, but it taught America the beauty of a 0–0 draw."

5. Honduras 2 USA 3, World Cup qualifier, October 10, 2009, San Pedro Sula

USA 1 Costa Rica 0, World Cup qualifier, September 7, 1997, Portland

"Honduras had owned the US like a puppy dog, but in this game, on the road, the US had come back from two goals down twice to take the lead, which would qualify them for the 2010 World Cup. Then in the 86th minute, Jonathan Spector gave away a penalty. I was on the sideline, trying desperately to see the action over the shoulders of the Honduran soldiers with their submachine guns, ready to hold the crowd back. The Hondurans missed, and I marveled, watching this US side celebrate qualifying for South Africa, and how much they had matured along the way.

"The Costa Rica game was largely memorable for the debut of Thundersticks, aka the decline of civilization, until the 78th minute, when Tab Ramos drove the ball home and delivered the win that would take the United States to the 1998 World Cup. If you listen to the game broadcast, you can hear me slap my hand against the table with delight. You are first and foremost at the game to broadcast objectively . . . but the joy of international soccer is, you do root in your soul for your nation. That is what soccer is all about. No matter how much FIFA try to muck that up."

Liga, La: Akin to the Free Cities across the Narrow Sea. We know a strange land of riches exists. We know some control vast military forces, and that Barcelona and Real Madrid are as close as football can come to the Iron Bank of Braavos. Yet because the league is broadcast on a network which is barely accessible in the United States, its weekly narrative remains a distant, foreign whisper.

Liverpool: I grew up in the dark yet magical Liverpool of the 1980s. A time when Liverpool FC won so many trophies, the team seemed to be on a permanent victory parade through  the city's streets, showing off their latest piece of silverware. As a third-generation Everton fan in his formative years, witnessing Liverpool's stars perpetually cruise by aboard an open-top bus was a searing sight. The players lolling casually around the cup on the front of the upper deck, a pose that suggested winning had really been no sweat at all. Yet, as much as I abhorred Liverpool's success, I could not help but adore its contribution to our simmering, defiant, and to me, beautiful city. In the 1980s, Liverpool was economically troubled, yet the Reds and the Blues made it English football's capital. Football and music gave our town a global recognition that other urban areas— say Birmingham, Newcastle, and at the time, Manchester—did not possess.

I benefited from that halo firsthand. Once, as a high-schooler, I was on a sluggish train to Barcelona that was overrun by a band of Real Madrid hooligans. The gang worked their way down the train, breaking windows and menacing passengers in compartment after compartment. I happened to be traveling with two childhood mates from home, none of us blessed with fighting powers. As the sound of smashed glass and graffiti spray paint crept ever nearer, we flipped frantically through our tourist guide, desperate to discover how to scream "Not in the Face" in Spanish, to no avail. The Madridistas ripped open our compartment door, bandannas covering their faces.

"Where you from?" they bellowed. "Liverpool," we stammered back. The boys looked at each other, then shook our hands respectfully. Exiting the compartment, they proceeded to create mayhem in the carriage next door.

The city is both stigmatized by the violence which engulfed it in the 1980s and also feared for it. As a seafaring town looking out toward the Atlantic, Liverpool has always dreamed of itself less as English and more the capital of Ireland, or the fifty-first American state. The conductor Simon Rattle, a son of the city, once captured the essence of my hometown when he said: "New York is the only other place comparable. You don't like Liverpool: You either loathe it or you love it. And I don't know anyone who loathes it and comes from it. You don't have 'mittel-message' feelings about Liverpool. The minute I get off the train and hear the accent, I'm sold." **—RB**

Liverpool College Breaking Crew: Rog's short-lived breakdancing posse that existed in Liverpool's premier private school in the months between February and June 1987. The crew came together during the final year of high school, the exact time the powers-that-be had broken with centuries of tradition by allowing girls into our class "by way of experiment." This masterstroke meant that 10 pioneering girls were admitted into the midst of 100 sweaty, dirty boys. I am not sure if the explosion of hormones was audible, but the experiment was akin to chucking a handful of goldfish into a tank of piranhas. Before they arrived, 90 percent of us were still virgins. Within three weeks, amidst scenes worthy of Caligula, everyone, except the members of the school's a cappella group, was experienced in the ways of love. Early hip-hop in the guise of the Beastie Boys provided the perfect soundtrack for all that ensued. Their 1986 *Licensed to Ill* album informed our world view: "Babes, Bud, and beer." The more destructive our behavior the better.

By the time the actual Beastie Boys rolled into Liverpool with their live show, replete with giant motorized penis, all of us were ready to show them that the pupil had become the master. No sooner had the band taken the stage than they were battered with a barrage of beer cans. A friend of mine with a particularly good arm was able to catch their bald DJ, Hurricane, flush on the temple, knocking him off his drum riser. Ad-Rock ran offstage and reappeared with a baseball bat, attempting to line drive the incoming cans back from whence they came. A riot ensued. Even after the police fired tear gas into the rabid crowd, they stood firm, deliriously chanting, "We tamed the Beasties, we tamed the Beasties." I stood at the back of the venue, breathlessly paying witness to the carnage that surrounded me.

Ad-Rock was briefly arrested after the gig. The Beastie Boys left town, progressed and evolved, becoming one of the most socially aware bands of my generation, leading the fight for Tibet, and ultimately tackling the issue of domestic violence. In 2003 they released "In a World Gone Mad." Though the song is one of protest against the Iraq War, when I hear it I can only think of that night, standing at the back of the Liverpool Empire, as the tear gas filled the auditorium and chaos spiraled all around me. **–RB**

Longley, Luc: *Men in Blazers* is ostensibly about soccer, but we are unable to mask our true love of American sports. Baseball has always enthralled us, being as it is chess with chewing tobacco. We follow hockey because we do whatever Jeremy Roenick tells us. But since moving to America the NBA has always been sporting catnip. It is, after all, like watching a five-a-side soccer game featuring only players who have the handling mastery of elite goalkeepers. One of the joys of doing *Men in Blazers* is having the opportunity to talk with people you admire, like David Simon, Matt Weiner, and Laura Linney. So a highlight of our experience so far was having the excuse, during the 2015 NBA finals, to track down one of the heroes of my youth: former Chicago Bulls center Luc Longley.

The giant Australian center went out every night and ground out his game against some of the NBA's greatest big men. I was then a greenhorn, learning about the wonders of America on a daily basis, and so Longley was always an inspiration to me. He was a bloke who arrived all the way from Western Australia with nothing, and found cult fame and fortune by working his way onto the greatest team to ever play basketball and winning NBA titles. When I spoke to him, I could not wait to hear him distill the most important life lessons he took from his time with Michael Jordan. "Even in the most intense, competitive brain on the planet, there's always a place for humor," he responded. "Humor is the great equalizer," he added, before explaining how levity allowed him to raise the complicated team issues in a nonthreatening fashion, a crucial element in any winning team. As Longley himself reflected, "In life, it's the things that don't get said that do the most damage." **–RB**

Los Angeles: After emigrating to America in 1989, and a brief eighteen-month spell in Jamlando, Central Florida, I moved to Los Angeles in the spring of 1991. Like many who had made that cross-country drive before, I headed west with dreams of truly making it in show business and staying off the dole. I had the considerable advantage of being able to stay in my brother Will's, beautiful mid-century house in the hills just off Mulholland Drive. And other than his writing partner's nocturnal habit of cleaning his handgun collection after a few drinks, in the bedroom right next to mine, separated only by paper-thin walls, it was an amazing place to live.

In those early days, I cobbled together a living wage by teaching tennis on private courts in Beverly Hills, Brentwood, and Bel Air, reading scripts and writing coverage and freelance associate producing and writing on TV variety and game shows when they came up. I was immediately struck by three things in LA: how far away the beach was, how much more verdant it was than I ever imagined (the avocado and lemon trees, the bougainvillea!), and how much live football there was to watch.

To be fair, the football took some discovering, and it took place in a weird Spanish-speaking parallel universe at the magnificently dilapidated LA Coliseum and the enormous Rose Bowl on days when the gringos didn't need them for college football. But I saw some amazing matches in those stadiums. The 1991 Gold Cup was a classic. The USMNT beating Costa Rica, Mexico, and Honduras in successive matches. No more than a few dozen US fans were at any of the games, and watching the US team being booed by, and having all sorts of "matter" thrown on them by, Mexican fans in their own country is one of the most extraordinary things I have ever seen in sport.

Of course, the 1994 World Cup was a phenomenal bonus, and such an easy ticket. I saw all seven games played at the Rose Bowl, including the mind-numbing, heartbreaking final, culminating in Roberto Baggio's stunningly match-fixy, penalty shootout miss, way over the crossbar, to gift the title to Brazil. But my enduring memory of that tournament was watching Romanian maestro Gheorghe Hagi singlehandedly demolish an Argentinian team featuring Simeone and Batistuta in the last 16.

The 1996 Gold Cup returned to Los Angeles and this time featured Brazil. The final between Mexico and Brazil was a breathtaking game played in front of almost 90,000 fans at the Rose Bowl, but my favorite match was the US victory over Guatemala, also played in front of almost 90,000, at the Coliseum. Both went almost completely unreported by the media.

Then, on July 10, 1999, I sat in the stands with 90,000 others at the Rose Bowl again and watched the USWNT beat China on penalties for their historic World Cup win. At last the media took notice. But in that one amazing decade, in that one amazing city, in two historic stadiums, I had seen more international soccer in front of larger crowds than at any time in my life. I had fallen in love with football again. And Los Angeles was my wingman. —MD

Lowe, Rebecca: The Mother of Dragons, NBC's face of the Premier League. One of the most articulate, intelligent broadcasters on television, blessed with the ability to make the complex seem simple. Her path to success has not been easy. She grew up a Crystal Palace fan who used to walk to school with Peter Crouch. Yet she overcame those obstacles and has now contributed as much to the rise in popularity of the Premier League in America as anyone not named David Beckham.

Rebecca Lowe of the House Crystal Palace, First of her Name, the Unburnt, Breaker of Chains and Mother of Dragons

Here are her Five Golden Rules of Broadcasting:

1. Over-prepare: On live television, you can never be left without the knowledge. I never stop preparing. I am always reading and absorbing. I may only use 25 percent of what I research. But the unpredictable always hap-

Rog has not washed his bald patch since.

pens, be it a random goal scorer finding the net, a mystery board member turning up to watch the game, or a twenty-minute game delay. I am prepared for it all so I always have something to say and cannot be embarrassed.

2. Listen to what your panelists are saying. If you are not listening, why should the audience follow along at home? The natural tendency is to focus on composing your next question, but it is crucial you listen to your co-hosts. This sounds easy but the panelists are speaking for only thirty seconds and I have producers in my earpiece giving instructions throughout. This can come only from experience. Do the job for long enough and you develop the knack.

3. Know your panelists' habits, needs, and their rhythms. Some like to be set up for specific questions, others do not. Some give short, clipped responses, others like to fill their allotted time. Gain a sense of the perspective they like to shoot from. One might prefer to talk tactically, another reminisce from a player's experiences or rely on analogies. Appreciating these differences will allow you to develop the chemistry you need to succeed.

4. A stash of Black Bean Brownies. Robbie Earle claims they smelt like feet.

5. Don't stress about hitting breaks. Only you know the speed at which you talk. You will have a producer count down to commercials in your ear. With years of experience knowing your own pace, it becomes so automatic it is not conscious. It just happens by magic that at the exact second you can drop "Back in a mo . . ."

LTD: The acronym Ryan Seacrest and acquired taste English entertainer Paul McKenna text each other when they are experiencing "one of those rich moments" in which their lives just feel overwhelmingly complete. LTD stands for "Living the Dream." The revelation begets a very simple question: What kind of a person does that and why? Do both men really feel

This is the moment I realized I had left the price tag on the blazer.

good when they push send on that text, or do they exchange the message to keep up the charade, and no sooner have they sent it do they crumble onto their unmade bed, bury their head in a pillow, and sob sobs born of the sheer energy of keeping up the pretense?

LTN: What Rog occasionally texts Davo in moments of quiet repose. Acronym stands for "Living the Nightmare" (aka LTM, "Living the 'Mare").

Lucky Underpants: We both believe in the power of lucky underpants. Davo saves his for long-haul flights. Rog wears his on big-game days for Everton Football Club to give them the extra edge they need to prevail. The number one lesson learned from a lifetime of believing in lucky underpants is this: "They never really work, do they?"

Lumbersexual: A manufactured term conjured by style sections across the nation in reference to men who grow beards like Tim Howard's and look like they enjoy making love to wood chippings.

Lynch, Loretta: Eighty-third attorney general of the United States. America's great gift to the World of Football. The Argentine newspaper *La Nación* hailed Ms. Lynch as "the relentless attorney." In Paris, *Le Figaro* called her "the woman who rocked FIFA." We prefer to use the moniker bestowed upon the AG by the German media, where she was simply hailed as FIFA-Jägerin—the FIFA hunter.

To our shock and horror, Ms. Lynch is a *Men in Blazers* fan and she invited us to come to her office and talk football—from her first exposure to the game, developing mad skills in fourth grade at Lakewood Elementary School, Greensboro, North Carolina, and her message to Sepp Blatter and all those who wish to harm the game that they can do so no longer. Presenting her with the 2016 Golden Blazer was one of the most "Through the Looking-Glass" moments I have ever experienced. I just wish we had not left the price tag on the blazer. **—RB**

M

Making It in America: The tag line of *Men in Blazers* has always been "Soccer. America's Sport of the Future . . . as it has been since 1972." A slogan inspired by a pennant Rog bought off eBay that now hangs in our panic room, which proclaims "Soccer! America's Sport of the Eighties." Polls, though, show the sport is well and truly entrenched in the American firmament. The Luker-ESPN Sports Poll has determined soccer is America's second most popular sport for those aged twelve to twenty-four, outstripping college football, MLB, and even the NBA. The question then is—just when did the sport "make it"? We asked some of our friends to weigh in:

ROB STONE, broadcaster, FOX

It is so damn hard to select just one moment. World Cup '94 lit the fire. The Women's World Cup in 1999 was such a party, it left folks wanting more. The memories of Americans adjusting their time clocks to watch the US at World Cup 2002 in South Korea/Japan will long resonate, as will the moments when we shocked traditional world powers Portugal and Mexico, but if a gun was put to my head and one moment demanded, I would choose when the Real American, Landon Donovan, scored in the 91st minute against Algeria in 2010, moving us into the knockout stages. It resonated deeper and wider than any moment. The YouTube video of the bar in Omaha. OMAHA!! erupting after that goal,

still gives me goosebumps, and I watch it several times a year.

AMY ROSENFELD, producer, ESPN

Back in the day it was 1999 Women's World Cup final when I left the production truck for a last bathroom break before kickoff and took a peek inside the Rose Bowl to see 90,000 spectators inside the stadium for—shock! Horror!—a soccer game in America . . . and more than that, a women's soccer game. Then it went away again, as it did after the US run in 2002, but somewhere between Landon's goal in 2010 and Abby Wambach's 2011 strike against Brazil it all became real.

REBECCA LOWE, broadcaster, NBC

Two thousand fifteen when I went to watch a high school soccer game and there was a kid on the side in a Burnley shirt.

KYLE MARTINO, broadcaster, NBC

When they announced the creation of MLS I thought we had made it. I had already been in love with soccer for a long time, watching Italian Serie A and English football on the weekends, mostly in a different language. I was too young for the NASL so in my mind the sport had always been an import. As much as I dreamed of being a professional soccer player one day while watching Roberto Donadoni each weekend, it was the birth of our very own league that made that dream feel real. I sat in awe of that first game when Eric Wynalda cut the ball back and curled it in the corner. In my mind the sport had arrived.

ALEXI LALAS, broadcaster, FOX

I never knew that we had "made it." Fact is, we haven't made it yet, and I have no idea what it will look like when we do. But I kind of like it that way.

PAUL CARR, statistician, ESPN

When Landon Donovan scored his last-gasp winner against Algeria at the 2010 World Cup, I had no one to celebrate with. I was working for ESPN in a Johannesburg studio, surrounded by Englishmen who were more absorbed in England-Slovenia, which was taking place at the same time. When Donovan scored, I ran screaming around the studio with my arms stretched high, but I got blank looks from everyone around me.

Several hours later, I returned to the hotel. I started finding all the reactions from viewing parties, bars, and living rooms online. I had known people were watching back home, but the volume and intensity of the passion erupting coast to coast across the nation was overwhelming. I sat in my room and watched video after video after video, as tears trickled down my face. That's when I knew soccer had made it in America.

Managerial Fashion: In the 1970s, managers could pretty much be broken down into two categories: those who wore suits on the sideline, with the overall panache of undertakers, with a few wideboys who dared to dress like flash secondhand-car salesmen, and those who steadfastly committed to the tracksuit. We often wondered what the difference was between the two. Common wisdom had it that the suit suggested that the manager showered in his own private changing room, while the tracksuit meant the gaffer washed up with his players in their giant, communal bathtub.

Like so much in modern football, all that

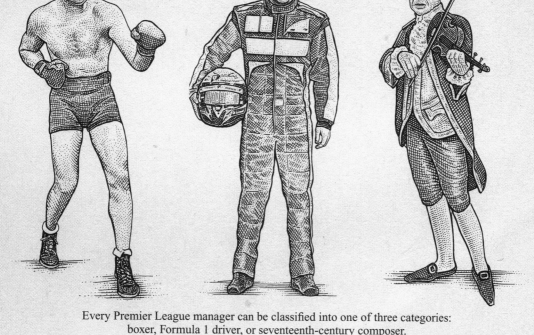

Every Premier League manager can be classified into one of three categories:
boxer, Formula 1 driver, or seventeenth-century composer.

has changed. A Premier League manager need not only be master motivator, tactician, sports scientist, and media handler. More important than his ability to field a team who can attack and defend is his signature style. Thus, it is impossible to think of Roberto Mancini without mentally conjuring his trademark scarf. Brendan Rodgers triggers thoughts of a man clad all in black like a poorly executed Johnny Cash waxwork. Arsène Wenger, a normcore sleeping-bag anorak; Tim Sherwood, his gilet; Tony Pulis and his devotion to Run-DMC–era shell-suits. José Mourinho and his flip-flop between Armani blazers (against mediocre teams) and training sweats as if he has just rolled out of bed (for big games, to show he could not care less about the opposition).

A GFOP, Jesse Dorsey once wrote with the observation that every Premier League manager fits into one of three categories:

A) an early-twentieth-century boxer
B) a recently retired Formula 1 driver
C) a seventeenth-century composer

Boxers: Big Sam Allardyce, Steve Bruce, Sean Dyche, Ronald Koeman, Craig Shakespeare, Slaven Bilic.

F1 Drivers: José Mourinho, Antonio Conte, Mark Hughes, Mauricio Pochettino, Tony Pulis, Marco Silva, Mauricio Pellegrino, Pep Guardiola, Brendan Rodgers (nose of a boxer, ego of an F1 driver).

Composers: Arsène Wenger, Manuel Pellegrini, Louis van Gaal, Jurgen Klopp, David Wagner.

We were once asked to think about what our signature motif would be were we to move into the upper echelons of football management. Davo believed he would dress as a schoolboy, replete with shorts and school cap. Rog favored a flower boutonniere, tweed blazer, mesh tank top, and sunglasses.

Man Bun: A favorite hairstyle amongst footballers and style trap that proves God has a sense of humor. Although thousands of men who have been influenced to grow their hair to Jared Leto lengths yank up their hair into a pony, scientists have discovered that the very act of pulling your hair tightly along the hairline can cause "traction alopecia," aka baldness.

Manchester City: An inspirational can-do story of triumph and self-improvement. For so long the Roger Clinton to United's Bill. The little brother transformed itself from longtime self-sabotaging laughingstock to "Noisy Neighbor" to World Power. All it took was an unprecedented investment from the Abu Dhabi royal family, who were looking for a platform to promote their region on the global stage and realized there is no communication system more powerful than Premier League football. Sheikh Mansour bin Zayed bin Sultan bin Zayed bin Khalifa Al Nahyan acquired the team in 2008 and pumped over a billion dollars into it, transforming the once hapless City into potent, rippled title winners by 2012—an extreme makeover even Charles Atlas would have found startling.

In any other realm, such a radical identity shift could be problematic—especially for supporters whose identity had been wrapped up in the club's tradition of being lovable losers. Yet football fandom is an emotional realm rather than a rational one where cognitive dissonance reigns supreme. Super-fan Noel Gallagher came onto our show and talked about the decades he followed the oft-slumping club around England and the delight he experienced in failure after failure. When asked if it was hard for him to savor the sudden, petro-dollar-fueled turnaround in the club's fortunes, he did not have to wait a second before replying, "Because we went so long and we went down so deep and low, it's like we'd all earned it."

Manchester United: The gold standard amongst English football teams: a juggernaut that rode unparalleled success on the field to financial nirvana off it. The club were beneficiaries of good timing. Until the 1980s, English football was run by an innocuous assortment of local businessmen who demonstrated a distinct lack of national ambition. Their financial model amounted to little more than "putting bums on seats" for home games. The creation of the English Premier League in 1992 changed everything, triggering a gluttonous gold rush. Some of the most sophisticated global sports business minds poured into English football to exploit the new frontiers of domestic, international, and digital rights, and the exploding universe of commercial opportunities.

No club seized the moment more than Manchester United. Their legendary coach Sir Alex Ferguson delivered title after title, empowering their commercial department to forge global partnerships across the world. No other team has such a dizzying array of money-spinning relationships. Cue photos of their sullen players standing in front of shiny machinery made by the club's official diesel engine partner, "Yanmar of Osaka," or cans of chips made by official savory snack partner, "Mr. Potato."

Under the ownership of the Florida-based Glazer family, Manchester United has achieved a status no other English club can dream of. First, they were reclassified as an "emerging growth company" registered in the Cayman Islands. Then, the Old Trafford club became the ticker symbol MANU, traded on New York's Big Board. For their board, that is ultimately the only table that matters. And because of that, I never root for Manchester United. Even if they were playing against an all-Evil starting eleven featuring Hitler in goal, Vlad the Impaler and Ivan the Terrible at center back, and Pol Pot at striker, I would root for Evil. —RB

Maradona, Diego: Few have used a World Cup as a platform to enthrall the planet. Fewer still have used the tournament to self-destruct and sully their own name. No man has done both to such radical extremes as Diego Armando Maradona, the Argentine icon who, in a career of excess, utilized the World Cup as the stage for both his greatest triumph and shattering humiliation.

In 1986, the strutting Number 10 delivered the single most virtuoso performance a World Cup has ever witnessed, inspiring an otherwise unexceptional Argentine team to victory. Just eight years later, El Diego tested positive for ephedrine doping (or fell victim to his thirst for an innocent energy drink called Ripped Fuel, depending on whether you believe FIFA or the player himself) flaming out mid-tournament, a theatrical exit bettered only marginally by Tony Montana at the end of *Scarface*.

Maradona's career was always built on brilliance, blurred boundaries, and spectacular overindulgence. Squat, impudent, and omnipotent, the player was part urchin, part prince. As he was just five foot five, his low center of gravity made him one of the greatest dribblers in the game. A French broadcaster described the player's inimitable control by suggesting his "foot was more like the paw of a cat." Almost impossible to knock off the ball, Maradona knew his opponents would attempt to boot him off the field, yet he would always quickly dust himself off and demand the ball again, drawing strength from the knowledge he was draining defenders of their energy.

Maradona's 1986 campaign is oft celebrated, and for good reason. The firestarter propelled his team to winning the Cup by all means necessary. In a roiling quarter final against the English, played at the Azteca in the shadows of the Falklands conflict, Maradona scored twice to seal a 2–1 victory. The first goal, when he used his left fist to reach over a six-foot-one goalkeeper and punch the ball into the net, became known as the "Hand of God" in Argentina. In England, it was referred to as the "Hand of the Devil."

Four minutes later, while the English were still reeling, he scored a goal that even a deity

1986. The true end of the Empire.

would struggle to replicate. A spectacular 60-meter display of the *Gambetta,* the Argentine art of dribbling, past six England players, the last two of whom desperately tried to take out the man rather than the ball. After witnessing the feat, the startled Argentine commentator proclaimed, "Good God! Long live football! Cosmic Kite! What planet do you come from?"

In 1994, the little warhorse prepared to drag his tattered body into battle one more time, aged thirty-three. His fourth World Cup would begin against Greece at Foxboro Stadium. A light aircraft buzzed above the field, pulling a banner that proclaimed "Maradona—Prima Donna" ahead of the game, and the star lived up to his billing. In the 60th minute of the 4–0 victory, Diego received the ball in the box, jinked to his left, and rifled the ball into the top corner, then celebrated the achievement in hopped-up

style, grabbing a sideline television camera and pressing his maniacal mug against it. Tight-lipped after the game, Maradona would only declare, "I'm letting my actions speak for themselves."

Four days later, the player was selected for random drug testing after a 2–1 win against Nigeria. FIFA quickly announced the Argentine had tested positive for five variants of ephedrine, an ingredient of over-the-counter cold medicines. "Maradona must have taken a cocktail of drugs because the five identified substances are not found in one medicine," said Dr. Michel d'Hooghe, a member of FIFA's executive committee. *The Guardian* would later note the way Maradona had celebrated his goal against Greece was as conclusive as any drug test, "Broadcast around the world, his contorted features made him look like a lunatic, flying on a cocktail of adrenalin and every recreational drug known to man."

***Men in Blazers,* Naming of:** When Rog and I simultaneously went on Sirius XM radio and Grantland in 2012, we needed a name and without any hesitation I immediately suggested *Men in Blazers:*

1. We are both men. Not particularly manly men but men all the same.
2. We love suits and ties and overdressing of all sorts. Rog enjoys hats. I enjoy handkerchiefs and tie clips. We both appreciate blazers. Though Rog is way more into tweed than me. Or any man.
3. When we first came to the US, everyone who was allowed on television to talk about sport was wearing a blazer with a logo on it, usually of the league they were broadcasting or the network they were broadcasting on.

So without any conversation that I remember, we knew exactly what to do. We hired a designer to design a blazer patch and a Latin scholar to translate "Men in Blazers" into that dead, poetic language. Slight hitch, though the Romans were very good at building straight roads, slaughtering Visigoths, and sorting things into groups of 10 and 100, they had horrible fashion sense and had completely failed to invent the blazer, or a word for "blazer" before their language died. So we opted for "Viri Recte Vestiti" instead. "Men Correctly Dressed." And despite my penchant for wearing my blazer and tie with shorts or knee-length joggers, and always with Adi Stan Smiths, we are "Recte Vestiti" at most times. **—MD**

***Men in Blazers* National Team:** In 2013, San Marino played England in World Cup qualifying. La Serenissima (The Serene Ones) then ranked 207th in FIFA's national rankings, were thrashed 8–0. Yet it was not their football that caught our eye. It was their footballers. Whilst the English team included such glam-

The jock tag on the bottom right of the jersey

orous global stars as Wayne Rooney, Joe Hart, and Frank Lampard, the enclaved microstate fielded a squad of players who had to finish their day jobs before pulling on their national team's jerseys. Goalkeeper Aldo Simoncini was a practicing accountant. The defense included two bank clerks and a bar owner. The midfield was bossed by Matteo Coppini, an olive oil manufacturer, and one of two professional squad members, Andy Selva, led the attack. The thirty-six-year-old plied his trade for Fidene in Italy's fifth tier.

Few international teams could make the case they work harder. Yet most of San Marino's work takes place off the field. However, their endeavor and truly amateur status was heartwarming, and we began to wonder what America's best amateur national team would look like. The *Men in Blazers* National Team was born to make that notion real. Within a week, over 4,000 listeners submitted their case to make the squad. Résumés from Butcher/Goalkeepers, Fireman/Midfielders, and Zookeeper/Strikers flooded in. Warren Barton bravely agreed to act as coach. A fax was fired off to San Marino's Football Association. Crickets ensued. The fax was resent. A subsequent version was dispatched to Gibraltar. We are yet to hear back. Thanks

World's first tweed football jersey

MEN IN BLAZERS

Viri Recte Vestiti

September 10, 2014

To Whom It May Concern:

We, at Men In Blazers, are honored representatives of the passionate football culture thriving across the United States. During the recent International Break, our nation became fascinated by the courageous exploits of your national team, the Mighty Gib.

Simply put, you have quickly become our favorite national team on the Iberian Peninsula.

In a modern footballing world that has become overwhelmed by money, brand-building, and ill-judged neck tattoos, your team's story is inspiring.

To craft a competitive international football team with an electrician as a winger, a fireman in goal, a cop holding down the midfield and a striker who is a shipping agent, is football as we love it. Honest. Transparent. Romantic.

UEFA may have you ranked at 54th in the continent, but confidentially, between us, what do they know about football?

Inspired by your example, we have invited our listeners to submit their names for consideration in an American National Team built in a similar spirit: The Men In Blazers' National Team. A squad consisting of the most talented football playing bar keeps, postal workers, bankers, and barely employed, yet talented footballing Americans we can find.

We floated the idea on last night's show and have already received over 1,000 applications. **We would like to challenge your British Overseas Territory to a single game of football, ideally at Estádio Algarve.** It would be stunning to have a game that would reinforce the spirit of aspiration and honesty and all that is good at football, as well as expose your team's story to every sports loving American.

We have skills. We have passion. And most importantly, we have air miles.

We eagerly await your response and can fly to Gibraltar International Airport at a moment's notice to discuss further at the Bayside Sports Complex. Nothing is more important to us than this.

Courage,

Roger Bennett   Michael Davies

www.meninblazers.com

@meninblazers

to Adidas, we have since developed a National Team kit—the world's first tweed football jersey—so we are ready.

Meola, Tony: One of America's least appreciated footballing heroes. A be-mulleted pioneer. A man who invested his passion and energy to build American soccer at a transitional time when it still lived in the shadows.

At a live show we did before the 2014 World Cup, he talked about the bewildering afterglow of USA 1994:

"It was a time of strange choices. We had fame but nowhere to play. I was offered a Hollywood role in a pirate movie and a chance to join the cast of *Tony n' Tina's Wedding* off-Broadway." The goalkeeper even had a stint as a kicker with the Jets. "I went to try out thinking it would just be me and coach Pete Carroll," he said, "but when I came out of the locker room there were hundreds of TV cameras there. To kick field goals in front of all those cameras was more nerve-wracking than anything I experienced in the World Cup."

When we asked Meola to describe the legacy of his career, he said something poignant that merits preserving in its entirety. "I met a guy from the 1950 team, Walter Bahr, when I was a kid on the U-19 World Cup squad, and he said, 'The only thing I want you to do is keep the ball rolling.' That was his expression, keep the ball rolling. All we did at the 1994 World Cup was push it along. There's a group of guys just after us that pushed it along, and now it's Michael Bradley, and Tim Howard, and Clint Dempsey and you know all the names, right? I just hope twenty years from now they're sitting up here with you guys pushing the ball along, and that for me is the legacy that I hope we left for all of you."

Mercersburg Academy: Life-changing boarding school in the crap part of Pennsylvania that I attended for the 1984–85 school year on an English Speaking Union Scholarship. I had never been to America before, and when I landed at Dulles Airport I was dumbstruck by the cops with guns, the green freeway signs, the

The school that gave us James Stewart, Benicio Del Toro, and Rebecca Lowe

massive Buick that I was picked up in and driven eighty-seven miles northwest to the Maryland-Pennsylvania border and my first visit to a real McDonald's and contact with real Americans. I ordered a Big Mac with large fries, a Coke, and a vanilla milkshake. And because they couldn't understand a word I was saying, I ended up with six chicken McNuggets, a black coffee, and an apple pie. I had spent six years longing to attend Mercersburg, ever since my some-what nerdy brother, William, had returned from the 'burg in the Summer of '79 with shoulders, beach blond hair, and a strong American ac-cent. He was no longer William. He was now Bill. And I liked Bill so much more.

The very first person I met at Mercersburg was a skinny, almost deranged Puerto Rican student who ran out of the dorm screaming Rolling Stones lyrics at me at the top of his hyperactive lungs. His name was Benicio Del Toro. The real one.

Almost 4,000 miles away from home, the only thing I missed about England was the football scores. I had actually never felt more at home. After spending my first weekend drinking RC Cola, demolishing pepperoni pizza from Romeo's, listening to go-go music and bingeing on the wonder that was American television—college football, *Miami Vice, Sat-urday Night Live*—I resolved to spend the rest of my life in America.

But my greatest discovery in that John Hughes movie of a year at American board-ing school was myself. Young Davo. Who I really was, in a country where the assumption was you were going to do great things, and the only question, how and where exactly you were going to do them. My God, I fell in love with America hard that first year. And I have never wavered. —**MD**

Messi, Lionel: To have watched the modern Barcelona team is to savor Marvel Comic su-perheroes writ large. Or, more accurately, writ small. In their prime, the Champions League–dominating Catalans possessed one of the

It is an honor to have been alive
to watch this man play.

shortest squads in football but compensated for their lack of stature with a confidence border-ing on the superhuman. First, their miniature stalwarts, Lionel Messi, Andrés Iniesta, and Xavi Hernández, were bold enough to lacer-ate opponents through the congested gut of midfield, cocksure their lightning-quick passes and movement meant adversaries could chase only shadows. Once Neymar and Luis Suárez signed up to lead the line alongside Messi for three golden years between 2014 and 2017, the threesome could have legitimately claimed to be the most awe-inspiring trio since the Bee Gees, conjuring a potent, whirling, yet precise brand of soccer previously experienced only on PlayStation consoles.

The team's success depended on the power of the collective. Yet, despite looking like he just wandered out of a local Supercuts, Lionel Messi has been its undoubted star. Known as *Pulga Atómica,* the Atomic Flea, the Argentine came to Barcelona at thirteen years of age because the Catalans were willing to cover the cost of a growth hormone treatment he needed at the time. Their investment has paid for itself many times over, as Messi has demonstrated a peerless ability to conjure up moments of magic in the biggest games, savaging opponents by accelerating from the seemingly safe deep waters of midfield, then navigating into a sliver of space between center back and left back with such velocity, it seems, in the poet Eduardo Galeano's words, "as if he was wearing the ball as a sock."

Once Messi enters the penalty area, opposing defenders' sense of confusion becomes palpable. The desperate attempts they make to chase down their quarry will be to no avail. They will pull up lame to avoid clipping the Argentine's heels, looking on in panic and praying their goalkeeper will come through.

Though his angle may be tight, Messi is ever aware the goalkeeper is obliged to cover his near post. He will leave his feet, defy gravity, and use the momentum of his upper torso to lure the keeper toward his left post while rolling the ball softly into the opposite corner. After scoring a goal just like this against archrival Real Madrid in the 2011 Champions League semifinal, he was asked by a breathless press pack how it is humanly possible to coordinate the variable calculations of trajectory, angle, and execution so rapidly. Messi downplayed the achievement. "It was all instinct," he revealed. "Only when I watched it later on television did I know what happened."

Middle Earth XI: Footballers come in all shapes and sizes. While the game is often physically dominated by the big men, we live to celebrate the tiny scurriers, all of whom look like hobbits or Ewok internationals.

Goalkeeper: David de Gea
Defenders: Tony Hibbert, Ryan Shawcross, Joleon Lescott, Leighton Baines
Midfielders: Jay Spearing, David Silva, Gareth Bale, Juan Mata
Forwards: Craig Bellamy, Fernando Torres
Super Sub: Tomas Rosicky

Milton Keynes: Town about forty-five miles northwest of London, where my dad unexpect-

Aerial view of alien landscape that is Milton Keynes. Hello, other Davos!

edly revealed to us that he had owned a house for several years when it casually came up in conversation in the 1990s. No one in my family has ever been to, or been invited to, said home.

The modernist-designed city, which began construction in 1967, is home to MK Dons Football club, after Wimbledon FC's controversial relocation there in 2003. In their sixteen-year history, the team's most notable achievement is the cultivation of a young Dele Alli, who was sold to Tottenham Hotspur in February 2015 for a fee in the region of £5 million. —MD

MLS Cup 1998: Of all the MLS Cups I have attended (one), this remains by far the most significant. It was remarkable for the fact that the two teams were coached by Bruce Arena and Bob Bradley, that Bradley's Chicago Fire won the Cup 2–0 that year AS AN EXPANSION TEAM, and for the majestic sight of the Bolivian playmaker Marco Etcheverry's jet black mullet, glistening like a localized oil slick in the late October Southern Californian sunshine. This was the first MLS Cup final at the Rose Bowl, and weirdly, though more than 50,000 people were in attendance, it was an intimate affair. I sat amongst DC United midfielder Richie Williams's extended family, and it felt almost collegiate, supportive, more celebratory than competitive. But it was Chicago's Polish small, Piotr Nowak, who was a class above every player in the game, and the way he worked superbly off their dominant tall, the ball-carrying Czech center back, Lubos Kubik, that really caught my attention. My theory of a world in which talls and smalls can and must work in perfect harmony on a football field was born. And also Jeff Agoos was there. —MD

Moleskin Pants: The ultimate winter pant cut from a fabric which, along with its cousin corduroy, are known as "fustian," for the way they are woven with thick cotton to create a dense fabric. To create moleskin, the fabric is brushed, allowing a furry nap to emerge. In corduroy, ridges are cut into the fabric to create exotic ruts. Origins are unknown, but often traced back to steelworkers in nineteenth-century Sheffield who admired the fabric's protective qualities—the tight weave fending off spark and flame.

Mortality: One of the only things in life that is as certain as Real Madrid or Barcelona reaching the Champions League final. Indeed, many social psychologists believe it is an awareness of our own mortality that drives us to be sports fans in the first place. "Terror Management Theory" suggests humans are drawn to symbolic systems that seem to provide narrative, meaning, and value with which we can both fend off fear, and connect to something seemingly permanent that will outlive us all. Like Norwich City.

Mourinho, José: Machiavelli in cleats. A master managerial motivator, whose preferred modus is to circle the wagons with his team and ride an "us against the world" mentality to glory. The intensity he employs in doing so tends to be furious, combustible, and ultimately self-destructive. A scorched-earth strategy that burns down everything around him. The Portuguese may bring silverware wherever he goes, yet devastation soon follows, as the manager tends to exit amidst scenes of discord and feuding after three seasons at any club.

Every time I have interviewed José, I have been blown away by his ferocious desire to twist a knife. The first time I filmed with him was July 2013 upon his return to Chelsea Football Club. Mourinho had just been spat out by Real Madrid after failing to come to grips with the politics of its ego-filled locker room, led, as rumor had it, by Cristiano Ronaldo.

My line of questioning was purely Chelsea-focused, but Mourinho drove the conversation to where he wanted it, segueing to a seemingly random conversation about the 2002 Brazil World Cup team. As our time together was extremely limited, my inner monologue was frantic, trying to understand why we had taken this detour and what I had to do to get us back on track. I needn't have worried. Mourinho leaned into his story, talking with wild eyes bulging about the goal-scoring abilities of Brazilian phenomenon Ronaldo, then he paused for a beat, smirked at the camera, and sneered, "the real one, the Brazilian one." The second our interview aired, this was the clip which blew up social media and became headlines all over the world, and one to which Portuguese Ronaldo even felt compelled to respond. Classic Mourinho. A man for whom football is a game of snubs, grudges, and scores to settle. One in which there is no limit to the amount of salt that must be rubbed into opponents' wounds.

I would wage a bet that if Mourinho was asked the classic philosophical leadership conundrum, whether it is better to be loved or feared, he would sneeringly pick a third way—to be hated. Yet to me, his career cycles of boom and bust stand as a reminder of a piece-of-life wisdom British comedian Matt Lucas gave us when he came on our show: "You will meet everyone twice in life," he said. "Once when you are on the way up and once when you are on the way down . . . so treat them accordingly."
—RB

Movies: Premier League football is shot from so many angles, and rife with so much narrative, fictional versions have rarely been able to compete with the drama of the real thing. Guy Ritchie came on our show and complained about the paucity. We are praying he will helm a remake of *Victory*. Here are our four best:

The Two Escobars (2010)
A documentary audaciously told by brothers Jeff and Michael Zimbalist, narrating the intertwined stories of the rise and fall of Colombian soccer, Pablo Escobar's gruesome reign as cartel kingpin, and the tragic career of doomed Colombian international defender Andrés Escobar, who was gunned down after scoring an own goal against the United States at the 1994 World Cup.

Victory (1981)
John Huston's epic Sylvester Stallone vehicle set in a German POW camp and loosely based on the urban myth of a Second World War "Death Match," between the best imprisoned professional footballers from Ukraine and the Nazi Air Defense Artillery football team. Worth watching just to see Michael Caine and Bobby Moore interchange passes with half of the late 1970s Ipswich Town team to set up Pelé for an overhead kick golazo. Stallone stars as cocky yet novice goalkeeper "Hatch." Stallone reportedly demanded his character score the winning goal. It had to be explained to the American that even with his great thespian range, as a goalkeeper, that would not be happening.

Gregory's Girl (1981)
Bill Forsyth's poetic telling of the relationship between a nerdy goalkeeper and the beautiful female striker who joins his high school team. A perfect combination of football and the rhythms and heartbeats of adolescent angst, this is the film Wes Anderson would have made if he had grown up in Glasgow, no doubt wearing a corduroy kilt.

Zidane: A 21st Century Portrait (2006)
Seventeen cameras follow the French legend around the field for the entirety of a game, focusing only on his emotions and reactions through the course of play. The hypnotic experience that results doubles as one of the greatest pro-bald infomercials of all time.

Mud: There used to be so much more mud in football. Mainly because there was so much more mud in Britain. Everywhere. We have shared stories on the pod about going to rugby or football training after school, getting covered in mud, and then because we both refused, as almost all boys did, to jump into THE COMMUNAL BATH (basically a lukewarm septic tank FULL OF SAME MUD), we would wait for the mud to dry, caked onto our little, barely

Just after the final whistle of a not particularly muddy encounter between Sheffield Wednesday and Burnley in the first division in 1969

Nottingham Forest's Viv Anderson charges past Terry Cooper (problems in sector 3.1) of Davo's beloved Bristol City at about 4 mph on a completely acceptable first division surface in 1980.

Frank Lampard Sr. defending a corner at the near post, or perhaps stuck to the post, during an FA Cup quarter final in 1975. West Ham won the cup that May. But Frank Senior didn't get all the mud off his legs until late October.

hairy legs, and then put our school uniforms on over said muddy legs and take the bus home. All boys of our age and era did it, and it is astonishing that more did not die of staph infections. Elite first division or FA Cup football, when we occasionally got to see it, was even muddier. —**MD**

Mullets: A bi-level haircut named from *molet* (fourteenth-century Middle English), *mulet* (Anglo-French), *mullus* (Latin), and *myllos* (Greek), the hairstyle has secreted its traces across history, appearing first on the Sphinx in Giza, being imported to North America on the head of Revolutionary War general Horatio Gates, and then perfected by *Facts of Life*–era George Clooney. The cut has many power bases, including the American South and in minor hockey leagues all over the Canadian prairie, yet few cultures have been such a global melting pot for the mullet as World Football. Its popularity can perhaps be explained by its ability to communicate so many different things. The "South American Mullet" (4.1), owned by Kun Agüero when he broke through with Atlético, said "Baller." Mesut Özil's blond "Mullet

4.1   4.2   4.3   4.4   4.5

of Youth" (4.2) said "I think differently." Newcastle and Spurs icon Chris Waddle's "Northern Mullet" (4.3) said "It's 1990 and I am English." The 1980s Bulgarian defender Trifon Ivanov's "Eastern European Enforcer Mullet" (4.4) said "I give you Levi's, you be wife?," and US 1994 goalkeeping hero Tony Meola's "Jersey Chic" (4.5) do screamed "I am just lookin' for a haircut that looks cool with stonewashed denim."

Munich: I have cheered for the Germans just twice in my life. Once, when my seventh-grade history class learned how Austria and Prussia joined Britain and Russia to put Napoleon back in his box after his return from exile in 1815. And a second time when Manchester United faced Bayern Munich in the 1999 Champions League final.

I watched that game in Dupont Circle, Washington, DC, at my local bar, which was stuffed to overflowing with English Premier League fans. When Bayern's dead-ball specialist Mario Basler spanked a free kick past Peter Schmeichel in the Manchester United goal after just six minutes, I sprang off my bar stool, punched the air, and emitted a belly laugh that was James Earl Jones–deep in tenor.

To my horror, the celebration was a solo affair, met by crickets. The bar man, a gregarious United fan, broke the silence by publicly dressing me down. "Roger, you're Jewish! How could you?" he exclaimed, adding with a hint of jingoism, "Besides, they're German. Does war mean nothing to you?"

The bar was too packed and the game too gripping for me to debate the point. Suffice it to say, when United summoned two stunning goals in injury time to pull off a miracle victory, I was as crushed as if I had been Bavarian, born and bred. **—RB**

Muppet Show, The: *The Muppet Show* was a US/UK collaboration right up there with NBC Sports and the Premier League, Fleetwood

Our role models

Davo's spirit animal

Rog's spirit animal

Mac, and Kanye West and Estelle. Turned down by every US network, the show was picked up by British commercial television impresario Lew Grade in 1976 and produced just down the street from Watford at Elstree. Of course, Rog and I have been greatly influenced by Statler and Waldorf, who now seem like early prototypes of the two of us. Rog's favorite Muppet is the piano-playing, poetry-reading, deep-souled, lovelorn Rowlf the Dog. Davo is moved to tears in every way by Beaker's rendition of "Oh Danny Boy" backed up by Animal and the Swedish Chef. **—MD**

Mustaches: When you think of the definitive mustaches in history—you think Stalin, Hitler, or Tom Selleck circa *Magnum P.I.* Yet Robbie Earle's November 2015 Facial Scrub deserves

to be up there. It is the 'stache which singlehandedly killed Movember.

N

Naismith, Steven: A player whose unique ability is born of the fact that he was born so blond, and with skin so white, he is borderline translucent. This special power makes him virtually impossible to defend. You cannot stop what you cannot see.

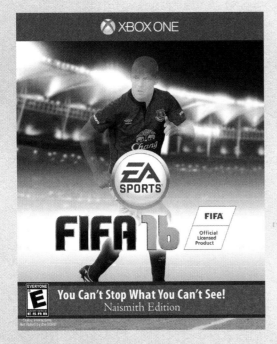

Naming Babies: My wife is American, with a penchant for English names like Jasper, Sebastian, and Charles that she has stored up from years watching romantic narratives unfold on PBS *Masterpiece Theater.* To me, those names are slightly less romantic, evoking memories of the Neanderthal rugby players who populated English public schools in the 1980s. So,

naming a child becomes essentially a business negotiation. After having four kids, my wife has unilaterally declared our baby-producing days to be over, so I can now reveal my five-step naming strategy:

Step One: Know where you want to end up

Have two or three names that are your true dream list. Make sure you are at peace with all of them. Keep this list to yourself.

Step Two: Open wildly

The opening salvo must be intrinsically believable, yet random in its ambit. For my first child, that list was "Garrincha" (after the great Brazilian footballer of the 1960s who overcame severe spinal and leg defects to become the greatest dribbler of all time, before drinking himself to an early death), "Hector" (after the Greek warrior who was killed in battle and had his body dragged in the dust by chariots), and "Primo" (after the great Holocaust writer/philosopher Primo Levi). None of these names should be acceptable to your partner.

Step Three: Wait one week, then present an even less acceptable slate of names

The second list must suggest a state of mind that is spiraling out of control and must be reined in. My list for my second kid was: "Wayne" (after Rooney), "Tirico" (after Mike), and Nixon (as in, the sweatiest president of all time). Invoking your favorite anchor of *Meet the Press,* a wilding name (Mance Rayder), or minor Baldwin brother (Daniel) will work just as well.

Step Four: Be prepared to live with the stress that sets in for up to seven days

It is an awful experience. But your child will thank you for it later.

Step Five: Unveil the true dream list. Be reasonable. Let your partner pick from a shortened ballot of four or five. In best cases, over time, they will come to think the selected name was their idea. Cede on the middle name as if it is a low-round draft pick thrown in as a makeweight in a blockbuster NFL trade. —RB

Newspapers: Being a Premier League fan means being exposed to the peculiar tenors of the English media and the adage "You can't tell a book by its cover, but you can tell English people by the newspaper they read." America! Here is a guide to your British news sources:

The Daily Telegraph

Pompous, older conservative, middle/upper class World War One poetry aficionados who mourn the loss of the Empire by placing cricket before family. When given the choice between great sex or finishing the crossword, unless the act involves Elizabeth Hurley, they would choose the crossword. Favorite musical duo: Gilbert & Sullivan. Most recently truly happy: D-Day (also and inevitably, Davo's favorite).

The Guardian (or *The Observer* on Sundays)

Middle-class liberal spelt-lovers with intellectual pretensions. Self-righteously preoccupied with the issues of education and ending all wars. Often facially haired with a predilection to roll their own cigarettes. Favorite lunch: Seitan Bake ("Long live the Other Wheat Meat!"). No other newspaper in the world is more often found protruding out of reader's duffel coat pocket.

The Times

Someone who has a hand in running the country, politically or in the corporate sector. Like to think of themselves as tolerant. Num-

ber of minority friends: zero. Most probably a member of an elite gentlemen's club. Most definitely a member of a sadomasochist dominatrix club (Davo's second favorite).

The Independent

A rare breed, as circulation is minuscule. Overly educated, often depressed, centrist underachievers who like long words with their breakfast and are really, really worried about the environment. Alternatively, someone who got to the newsstand late and discovered to their dismay all the other papers had sold out.

Daily Mail

Middle-aged, middle-class housewives who live in fear of rising house prices and are easily scandalized by the poor, immigrants, and "Gypsies." Pet hates: marijuana, welfare cheats, minorities, and all homosexuals, especially Elton John. Pet loves: the police force, Mrs. Thatcher, talented pet stories, public floggings, and George Clooney. Like to imbibe their news via short articles shorn of long words. Not bigoted, but firmly believe there is nothing wrong with the country that someone who could make the trains run on time could not put right.

Daily Express

Intolerant, easily outraged, and yet to recover from the trauma of Lady Diana's death. Employ a steady diet of gin and brash reality television to sedate themselves in the face of the terrorist threats to Britain's shores. Find conspiracy theories everywhere. Easiest way to improve England in a single stroke? Ban foreigners.

Daily Mirror

A reader whose great gift in life is wolf-whistling at random women. Low IQ masks an impressive ability to pass off entire articles as their own opinions down at the pub later the same day. A really great night out typically starts at the greyhound track, segues into a bout of binge drinking, and spirals into committing random acts of violence.

The Star

An audience eager to ingest a gossip-soaked tabloid that cuts to the jugular whether the subject at hand is politics, soccer, or well-endowed topless babes. Beloved by lager louts who believe there is nothing wrong with the country that a prime minister with a big pair of breasts could not put right. Also popular among young media-types who savor the paper's witty headlines as a guilty pleasure to accompany a traditional broadsheet like a cheap whisky chaser to a quality ale.

Nicknames, Best Footballer:

Brian "Toilet" McClair, Manchester United, 1987–1998. So called because he was so crap.

"Ginja Ninja" Paul Scholes, Manchester United, 1993–2013. The quintessential redheaded warrior.

Michael "Haunted" Mancienne, Wolverhampton, 2008–11. Say it quickly a few times.

Dennis "The Non–Flying Dutchman" Bergkamp, Arsenal, 1995–2006. A fear of flying prevented him from traveling to Champions League away games by plane.

Stuart "Jigsaw" Barlow, Oldham Athletic, 1995–98. Because he was known to "go to pieces" in the box.

"One Size" Fitz Hall, QPR, 2008–12. Say it quickly.

Jonathan "Village" Woodgate, Leeds United, 1998–2003. On account of his reputation as the Village Idiot.

Marc "Das Kampfschwein" ("War Pig") Wilmots, Standard Liège, 1991–96. A reference to the intense physicality he brought to any team he played on.

But Charles Barkley's nickname, "The Round Mound of Rebound," remains the best in sports.

1994: The year soccer changed in America. Just as Captain Kirk considered space his final frontier, the United States had been football's. Nineteen ninety-four changed that, because by hosting the World Cup, the US's qualification was automatic. That was a mixed blessing, as a woefully inexperienced squad faced four long years in which it was deprived of the one thing that could battle-harden the players: competitive matches that mattered. It didn't help that only a handful of American soccer players had found professional opportunities in Europe, and MLS was yet to exist.

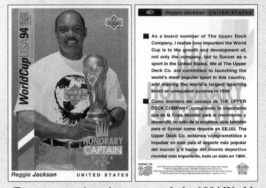

To encourage Americans to watch the 1994 World Cup, Reggie Jackson was enlisted to raise the profile of the tournament.

Desperate to avoid the humiliation of becoming the first home team unable to emerge from the tournament's opening round, US Soccer undertook a bold experiment, establishing a national residential training center for its team in Southern California. With no guarantee of a place in the final 22, and no definite path to a professional future after the tournament, the players moved in and took a leap into the dark.

By the time the World Cup kicked off, most of the US players had racked up vast international experience—up to 79 caps—without ever having played a professional game of club football. Few Americans understood that soccer could actually be a career. Alexi Lalas told us the story of how he was flying coach a week before the World Cup kicked off and an old woman who was his seatmate asked him what he did. "I am a soccer player," he replied proudly. The befuddled Midwesterner frowned with confusion as she pressed on with a follow-up question. "Yes dear, but what do you do *professionally*?" A week later, Lalas and his teammates ran onto the field to play Switzerland at the Pontiac Silverdome before a sold-out crowd of 73,425 and football in the United States has never been the same again.

Non-Celebrations: Uruguayan striker Diego Forlán once admitted that the experience of scoring a goal feels like the most intense orgasm. When players return to their former clubs, score a goal, and then refuse to celebrate, what damage does it do to their body's innards to suppress that emotion?

Not in the Face: A footballing term of fear ahead of a game in which a beatdown is a distinct possibility. Born of a phrase commonly used across Liverpool on Saturday nights throughout the 1980s shortly after 11 p.m., or pub-closing time. When thousands of intoxicated teens stumbled into local chip shops simultaneously, hundreds of fistfights fueled by alcohol and testosterone would ensue. The fights, like lives in the Medieval ages, were most often "nasty, brutish, and short." The loser would crumple into a bloodied ball on the tiled floor of the chip shop, and inevitably utter the words as a stoic plea, whilst the victor unleashed a string of stinging kicks to their person. "Not in the face," they would beg amidst

muffled groans whilst they were set upon. As an Everton fan, football often leaves me like one of those victims, moaning and curled up in the fetal position in front of my own television. —**RB**

O

The Observer's Book of Association Football: In the 1970s I constantly struggled for football news. I had very little access to the family newspaper (taken by my father in his slim, Samsonite Classic black leather briefcase in the morning and returned home late at night) and there was almost no live football, or any football coverage on television, except for the FA Cup final, major European club finals, and, every four years, the World Cup. Yes, there was *Match of the Day* on the BBC on Saturday night, but it

was way past my bedtime. And *The Big Match* on Sunday lunchtime on ITV, but my father didn't much like ITV, or the noise of football in general. My thirst for football knowledge was sated in three ways:

1. My obsession with, and semi-street-legal trading of, Top Trumps Football Cards on the Brooklands primary school playground (the trade for my hero, Geoff Merrick's, card, still ranks as a life highlight).

2. The weekly delivery, and devouring, of my bible, *Tiger and Scorcher.*

3. My almost nightly study of *The Observer's Book of Association Football.*

The Observer's Books were a series of small, pocket-sized books, published by Frederick Warne & Co. in the United Kingdom from 1937 to 2003. They were huge in the 1970s and they covered a variety of topics, including hobbies, art, history, and wildlife. I owned dozens of these books, or rather my father bought me dozens of these books, including *The Larger British Moths, Unmanned Space Flight, Tropical Fish, Small Craft, Firearms, British Birds' Eggs,* and *Tanks and Other Armoured Vehicles.* But the only one or two I ever really read were the volumes on *Cricket* and *Association Football.*

The 192 tiny pages were filled with chapters on all the major European club competitions,

BRITISHCOMICS.COM

the history of the game, and England's complete record in full internationals (back then it wasn't so depressing). My favorite section was the ten-page epic nonfiction novella on "World Stars of 1972–73." I was obsessed with this entry on Giacinto Facchetti, a man I had never seen play, but who was etched into my barely formed brain like some kind of mythic creature:

Facchetti, Giacinto. Left-back of Internazionale and Italy, but in reality a half-defender-cum-half-forward. Manages to combine these demanding roles through his tremendous physique and no mean skill. Born at Treviglio in Northern Italy and joined Inter-Milan in 1960 as a teenager. Developed by Helenio Herrera into a revolutionary full-back who swept forward and scored goals—often at critical moments in vital matches. Standing 6 ft 3 in., he is virtually unbeatable in the air and his long raking stride carries him over the ground in near Olympics time—10.5 seconds for 100 metres. Aged 29, he set an all-time Italian record in 1971 when winning his 60th cap. Further testimony to

his prowess is the fact that he has scored more than 50 League goals in a country where centre-forwards do well to get ten per season!

We did not have players like that in England. Bristol City's Geoff Merrick took about twice that long to run 100 meters and he was the best player I'd ever seen. The bulk of the book was devoted to a "Guide to the 92 Football League Clubs in England and Wales," including an exotic "Colour Guide" to all of their uniforms, their histories, their biggest wins, their heaviest defeats, THEIR PITCH DIMENSIONS, AND THEIR PHONE NUMBERS!!!!

If you're trying to reach Eddie Howe at the football club formerly known as Bournemouth and Boscombe Athletic, pitch dimensions x times x, you might try to get an operator on the phone and ask for Bournemouth 35381. —MD

Over-the-Head Clap for the Away Fans: One of the ritual tropes of modern football in which footballers on the road trot up to their penned-in supporters after the final whistle and give them a lackadaisical clap of thanks for making the journey, whatever the score line may be. Few token gestures carry such weighty significance, as the act reinforces the myth that the players care about the club in the same way fans do and share the same collective feelings about the result. In 2013, Arsenal's Per Mertesacker almost had a fistfight on the field with teammate Mesut Özil, when his fellow German, disgusted by his own performance after a 6–3 shellacking at Manchester City, ignored his orders to clap the long-suffering Arsenal faithful, prompting one English journalist to write: "Özil is a newcomer to the Premier League, a league that has a history of clapping fans more than any other place he's been before." Clapping hard is more important than playing hard.

Owen, Wilfred: The greatest war poet of all time in the mind of my second grade English teacher Mr. Stott, who insisted on teaching us nothing but First World War poetry for the entirety of the school year. Our classes would consist of him pointing to a pupil, making them come to the front of class and read aloud from  the classic First World War poetry anthology book, *Men Who March Away*. In our six-year-old voices, we would tremulously recite poems of mass slaughter, the experience of being mustard-gassed, or the trauma of shell shock. Stott would sit with his feet on the desk and hands behind his head, as tears rolled down his cheeks, weeping openly before us.

Wilfred Owen's poetry dominated that year. An English soldier bard who fought and died in the First World War trenches of France as an infantryman, writing a trove of poems that were published posthumously, including "Anthem for Doomed Youth," "Futility," "Mental Cases," and "Disabled." I can still recite one of the poems by memory: "Dulce et Decorum Est," a poem about watching a fellow soldier suffocate during a gas attack. The lines

In all my dreams, before my helpless sight,
He plunges at me, guttering, choking,
*   drowning*

gave me nightmares, and occasional bedwetting episodes until my early teens. Mr. Stott did not care, and in 1980s England, none of the parents complained. On occasion Stott would become so overwhelmed by the thoughts the poetry conjured in his imagination, he would sadly roll himself a cigarette, blowing his nose theatrically before lifting it to his lips, and mumbling a Wilfred Owen quote which, in his mind, was the reason why we were studying this devastating body of work at such a tender age: " 'All a poet can do today is warn,' lads," he would intone. "All the poem can do is warn. That is why the true poet must be truthful." —RB

P

Pants: A wonderful British expression meaning "crap." At the 2002 and 2006 World Cups I introduced a "pants" rating scale for grading teams and players. Great performances were awarded with "no pants at all." Crap performances with "Big Billowing Aladdin Pants." In between were briefs, boxer briefs, boxer shorts, short shorts, pleated golf shorts, cargo shorts, capri pants, jeans with holes in them, and Levi's Dockers. Incidentally, I have no idea where the expression "pants" comes from. In England, we call pants "trousers" and pants are actually underwear. Men's underwear tend to be called "underpants," perhaps the creepiest word in the English language. Women's underwear tend to be "knickers" or "panties" when they're sexy, or "pants" when they're just "pants." But pants can also be boys' or men's underwear. The word has this certain unisex, drab and yellow-stained connotation which doesn't take much of a leap to see how it could end up becoming a synonym for "quite crap." However, I have no idea of the etymology. This would be a good question for an English William Safire. **—MD**

Parrish, Steve: One of the great joys of 2015 was reacquainting myself with my old friend from Colfe's School in South East London,

Steve and I just eleven serious juvenile offenders away from each other in a school picture in 1981

The Panic Room 2.0

We moved into this one in January 2017. So much more luxurious than the original Panic Room from whence we first inflicted our crap show upon America in September 2014.

1. GFOP knitted scarf of Rog's nickname for Everton when they're playing well and he doesn't want to jinx them. Rarely needed. Never worn.
2. Entire original Panic Room was designed around existing light switch, which was so perfectly crap that we didn't want to hide or move it. Even crapper is that we've painstakingly and pointlessly re-created this light switch in Panic Room 2.0.
3. How Rebecca Lowe throws to break in her slippers. Still waiting for an American broadcaster to imitate this.
4. Our Lord and Savior Mike Tirico
5. A fake conspiracy of fake ravens

6. Original crap cat (other crap cat is an impostor)
7. These used to be in our fish tank.
8. Rog's heartwarming mantra (*see* page 29)
9. Ruud Gullit (not the real one)
10. This mug is a daily reminder of the $250,000 we lost on BlazerCon.
11. I was basically robbed at gunpoint right after buying this relic. World Cup on Coacabana Beach in 2014.
12. Original *George Michael Sports Machine* neon sign. It makes a lot of noise when we plug it in. It is the primary asset of Men in Blazers LLC.
13. Somehow this man did not score the winning goal from sixty-five yards in a World Cup final.

14. Disinterested staff of non-soccer-based Embassy Row TV shows.
15. Powerful studio lights to fully exploit our resplendent baldness
16. This is what some people in television call "engineering." All I know is that it breaks down a lot.
17. Tiny clock that tells me when I have to get on and off the air. I've never had the heart to tell our producer Jen that it's too small for me to read and I basically make my decisions on how anxious she sounds in my ear.
18. Another disinterested staff member of another Embassy Row TV show.
19. The technical term for this thing is "camera."
20. Another "camera"
21. Monitor on which we watch clips, ourselves, and always point and laugh at the squirrel in our show open.
22. Rog enjoys and excels at stick work.
23. Jack of Hearts for our GFOP Liam. It's there every show.
24. Green pens. Always green pens. Rog always steals my green pens. Note to self: must buy green pen company.
25. This is not water.
26. Sign I sometimes remember to hold up at the end of our crap show
27. Rog's chair. It also fears crossacks.
28. Davo's chair. They're the same height, but Rog looks taller on television, which is weird because I'm about a foot taller. I'm all legs. Rog has an absurdly long body.

THE GREATEST PENALTY KICKS OF ALL TIME

1. Anthony Knockaert—missed penalty which would've sent Leicester to championship playoff in 2013.
2. Sergio Ramos—missed penalty in semifinals against Bayern in 2012 Champions League.
3. Dennis Bergkamp—missed penalty in 1999 that would've sent Arsenal to back-to-back FA Cup finals.
4. John Terry—missed penalty in the 2008 Champions League final.
5. Asamoah Gyan—missed penalty for Ghana in waning moments of 2010 World Cup quarter final against Uruguay. Uruguay would go on to win in a penalty shootout.
6. Roberto Baggio—missed penalty in the '94 World Cup final.
7. Liu Yang, 1999 Woman's World Cup final—missed the only penalty of the shootout, which the USA would win.
8. John Aldridge—missed penalty in 1988 FA Cup final.
9. Billy Austin, 1926—missed a penalty for Man City in the final game of the season, which caused City to get relegated.
10. Oscar Cardozo—missed penalty in 2010 World Cup quarter final vs. Spain; Paraguay would lose 1–0.
11. Juan Riquelme—missed penalty against Arsenal in 2006 Champions League semis. Arsenal advanced 1–0 on aggregate.
12. Arjen Robben—missed penalty in 2012 Champions League final in ET.
13. Landon Donovan—missed penalty in 2009 MLS Cup final shootout.
14. Michel Platini—missed penalty for France vs. Brazil in 1986 World Cup quarter final.

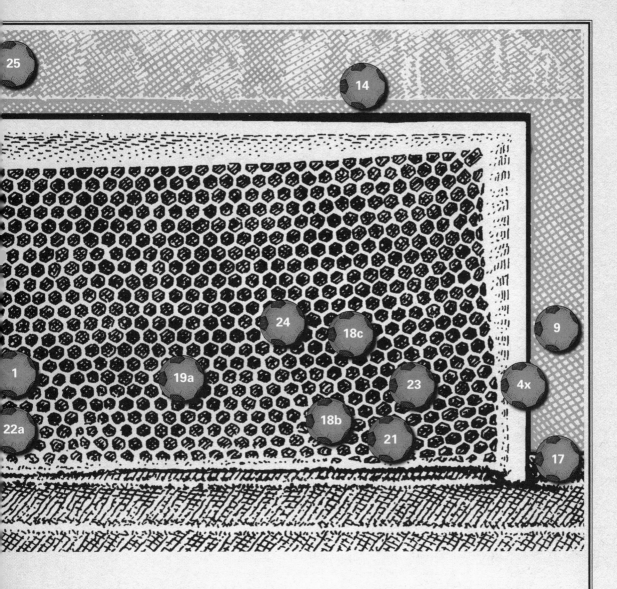

15. Beckham in 2004 Euros for England missed vs. Portugal in shootout; England lost the shootout 6–5.
16. Peter Devine for Lancaster City in 1991. Missed the penalty—didn't even reach the six-yard box and he injured himself.
17. Diana Ross in the 1994 World Cup pre-match festivities—one of the most miserable misses in athletic history.
18. (a.) Jamie Carragher, (b.) Frank Lampard, and (c.) Steven Gerrard all missed penalties in a shootout against Portugal in the 2006 World Cup.
19. (a.) Paul Ince and (b.) David Batty missed in the shootout for England against Argentina.
20. Darius Vassell—missed penalty for England in 2004 Euros against Portugal.

21. Gareth Southgate—missed penalty in Euro 1996 shootout for England vs. Germany.
22. (a.) Ashley Young and (b.) Ashley Cole missed in a shootout for England vs. Italy, 2012 Euros.
23. Didier Six—missed penalty for France vs. West Germany in 1982.
24. 2014, Carli Lloyd missed penalty for the USA against Germany in the World Cup semis.
25. 2003 Euro qualification vs. Turkey—Beckham missed a penalty terribly.
26. Robert Pirès vs. City tried to fake the kick but touched the ball.
27. 2009 Peace Cup, Del Piero had a brutal miss for Juventus.
28. 2012, Neymar with a shocking miss for Brazil vs. Colombia; thankfully it was a friendly.

Crystal Palace chairman Steve Parrish. Steve, though he looks about ten years younger than me, was in the grade above me at school and, though we weren't close, we hung out with the same general group of friends and genuinely liked each other. Yes, one of my best friends, Andy Rothery, had once tried to chase him through Chislehurst caves trying to kill him, but frankly, back then it was that kind of school, and Steve, by his own admission, may well have done something he shouldn't have with Andy's girlfriend. But on the whole, everyone liked Steve. He was simple. He liked cars, girls, and going down to the pub. In that respect, he was a lot like a lot of our other friends.

But Steve was different. He had a burning ambition to do something with his life. And he loved computers. In the early 1980s, he spent thousands of hours in "the computer room" behind the maths classroom on the second floor. Inside was a Sinclair 1k, a Commodore 64k, and maybe a couple of other early computers, totaling no more than 100k in memory. The son of a leading trade unionist in the printing trade, Steve eventually went into advertising on the print side, and what he learned in that room helped him revolutionize the business where he was hired, and turbocharged his career. Steve made a fortune in advertising, invested in dozens of other businesses, and eventually purchased a major stake in the football club he had supported since he was a boy. The second we set eyes on each other again in the crap part of SoHo, the memories came flooding back. In hindsight we wish we had been closer in our school days and never lost touch. But perhaps that would have been the friendship equivalent of scoring too early. —MD

Pelé: Jesus. Charo. Drake. True legends are always able to go by just one name. Edson Arantes do Nascimento—aka Pelé—is one such great. In the 1970s, even the most soccer-phobic American knew his name, thanks to his stint as the face of the NASL and the New York Cosmos. Yet the United States witnessed a Pelé cameo only in his twilight, long after the striker had broken through as a scrawny seventeen-year-old at the 1958 World Cup. There he introduced himself to the world in the final against host Sweden, flicking the ball over a dumbfounded defender's head, charging around him, and nonchalantly volleying the ball into the corner of the net.

His career became a long-running highlight reel, the face of a Brazilian team which won the World Cup three times over the course of twelve years. Fortunate timing, as the peak of his career coincided with the advent of live broadcasting, and his telegenic face, and natural ebullience, turned him into the game's first true star. He quickly became less a footballer— more a global billboard to hock MasterCard, Pepsi, or Atari.

For me, his career highlight came in the John Huston movie *Victory* alongside Sly Stallone. Pelé pretty much played himself, predictably scoring an otherworldly goal in the clutch game. Yet the years have not been kind to the Brazilian. A series of poor financial decisions forced the legend to try to keep himself in the news by making ever more ill-judged pronouncements backing corrupt Brazilian administrations, fueling a long-running war of attrition with Maradona, and then slumming it on an eerie set of Subway commercials.

Pelé at his best now only exists on YouTube. Watch the 1970 World Cup final against Italy. See the ball floated over toward the back post. Pelé is tightly marked by his defender, yet he will not be denied, leaping like a salmon from a stream to head the ball past a stunned goalkeeper. He knows he has scored the second the ball leaves his head, reeling away to celebrate. Snug of shorts, golden of shirt, he leaps into his teammates' arms, the embodiment of the joyous soccer fantasy that was the Selção Brasileira in its prime. —RB

Pie:
1. A baked dish of fruit, or meat and vegetables, typically with a top and base of pastry.

Footballers like pies.

Super Chefs like pies.

Frank likes pies.

Moe Szyslak likes pies.

2. A delicacy with prophetic powers baked in, we use on the *Men in Blazers* show to scientifically predict the outcome of football games.

Part of the holy trinity with Soccer: Football, Guinness, and Pies. The key is football; without it, we are all daytime drinkers and a pie is just horse meat.

The subject of one of our favorite football chants of all time. Inspired by 1980s footballing icon Mickey Quinn, a striker so fat he was nicknamed "Sumo," of whom opposing fans would chant:

Who ate all the pies?
Who ate all the pies?
You fat bastard,
You fat bastard,
You ate all the pies!

Pirlo, Andrea: An Italian footballing poet with more suaveness in the nail of his little finger than we will have over the course of our entire lives combined. Pirlo's face, hair, and late-career beard gave him the vibe of a rumpled bed post–tender lovemaking. Forged with his unique blend of vision, spatial awareness, and courtliness, they made him appear part elite athlete, part romantic poet. A trait reinforced by his willingness to cry softly on the field after rare losses, which made him transcendent. We once watched the Italian sob on the field after losing to Spain in the Euro 2012 final. It was sadder to experience than Tracy Chapman's debut album.

This is what it sounds like
when doves cry.

After Pirlo's glory-soaked Serie A career, his move to MLS and New York was the best thing to happen to the city since Piers Morgan left it. The American league welcomed a man whose postgame quotes were like Elizabethan love sonnets. While Pirlo's New York sojourn was mostly memorable off the field, who could not adore a man who says about his free kicks, "Each shot bears my name and they're all my children." But his greatest comments may be about his own humanity. On his looks, he once wrote, "If I glimpse the mirror when I get up, or before going to bed at night, I see a man of average ugliness. With stubble, an unruly mane of hair, a squint nose, slightly protruding ears, and bags under my eyes. But I also see a man who's completely happy with the figure staring back at him."

Poetry: I love poetry of all kinds. My three favorite poets are First World War poet Wilfred Owen, English classical curmudgeon Philip Larkin, and Wayne Rooney. I have not read

Wayne Rooney's poetry. I just adore the idea of those poetic abilities which were revealed in the BBC documentary *The Man Behind the Goals.* First, Rooney himself revealed he enjoyed writing love poetry to his wife, Coleen. She then told a story of how she recently went on vacation: "I went to bed with the kids and when I got up the next morning there was a poem on the side, which was nice."

What could such a poem look like. That written by a man who revealed in the same film that he proposed to his wife at a gas station. A player who speaks with such a thick Liverpool accent, foreign teammates such as Bastian Schweinsteiger and once manager Louis van Gaal told the press they "simply cannot understand what he says."

Maybe Rooney is like "President Reagan Mastermind" on *Saturday Night Live.* Phil Hartman played the former president as a moron in front of the press corps, yet once they exited the room, he snapped into life behind closed doors, suddenly demonstrating the mental faculty of a geopolitical genius. Maybe Wayne just pretends to be a bit simple in public, whilst in private the true Rooney pumps out poetic masterpieces with the fury of an English Allen Ginsberg. The true tragedy is, like a rabbi who shoots a hole-in-one whilst playing golf on the Sabbath, he can tell no one. **—RB**

"Polish Approach" to World Cups and Euros:
A theory posited by a Polish waiter in London who once told us: "We Poles always have a defined rhythm to the three group stage games we play at every major tournament in which we are inevitably eliminated. They even have ritualistic names:

Match day one: "The opening game in which everything is possible."
Match day two: "The must-win game in which our team's survival is on the line."
Match day three: "A dead rubber Game of Honor in which the result is irrelevant because the team is already eliminated."

Positive: My nickname at the University of Edinburgh, given to me as a freshman by the dry, laconic, precocious, seasoned wit of my friend James Symington. Usually used in conjunction with my first and last names—Mike "Positive" Davies—it certainly was not a compliment, but rather a criticism of my sunny disposition and outlook. It may also have been somewhat prescient, as it led many of my well-heeled English classmates to believe I was actually American. —MD

Pray for Guzan: A theologically challenging act, in reference to American shot stopper Brad Guzan, which became popular during the 2015–16 Premier League season, but after the player experienced back-to-back relegations with Aston Villa and then Middlesbrough, condemned all those who pursued it to consider atheism.

Pretty in Pink: Attending an all-boys school meant I first encountered actual real-life girls only when forced out onto the Liverpool bar mitzvah circuit. My success rate was somewhat handicapped by the fact that when it came to engaging the ladies, my approach was very much like the man who later became my role model, Duckie, Jon Cryer's dweebish New Waver in *Pretty in Pink*. My plan was based on a belief that if you focused on emanating style, the ladies will come to you. The great pro of this approach was that it put the prerogative squarely on the ladies to make the first move. Con being—they never did. When I think about the hours I dedicated to mastering Duckie's lines from the movie ("Once the Duckman . . . always the Duckman"), I pale. Did I really once believe these dud zingers would take me to the places I longed to go? Watching *Pretty in Pink* today, I realize what a nauseating turd Duckie is. If I ever met present-day Jon Cryer, I would punch him square on the nose for the central role he played in condemning me to the barren years I spent watching more naturally adjusted thirteen-year-olds grinding away on a dry-ice-filled dance floor to the horny sounds of Air Supply's "Making Love Out of Nothing at All." —RB

Pushkin, Alexander: In October 2014, a frustrated Arsène Wenger squared up to his eternal tormentor, José Mourinho, between the coaching areas on the sideline at Stamford Bridge. The two men pushed each other. No punches were thrown. Yet, José Mourinho managed to execute a remarkable tie flip, negating his own reach disadvantage by cutting inside and flicking his opponent's tie neckwear up in a stinging arc toward the Frenchman's nose. Watching Arsène Wenger attempt to fight, we were reminded of the great Russian author Pushkin, who died after dueling a man who had insulted the honor of his wife. His opponent, Georges d'Anthès, managed to fatally wound the noble yet doomed writer. On his deathbed, Pushkin attempted to die with honor, dispatching a message to his opponent assuring him that he forgave him for the entire incident. D'Anthès was reported to laugh upon receiving this missive, declaring with a snigger, "Well, tell him I forgive him too."

Q

Quotes, Our Favorite: As a child, I was always fascinated by the stories of early-twentieth-century exploration with which we were continuously regaled at school. Tall tales of ill-equipped teams of men who raced to be the first to climb impenetrable mountains, or traverse unforgiving, ice-cloaked passages. In those days, when Britain still had an Empire, their achievements were national victories.

The story which always stood out was that of Captain Lawrence Oates. One of five men who perished whilst attempting to return to base after being beaten to the South Pole by Norwegian Roald Amundsen in 1912.

Oates struggled with wet feet throughout the seventy-nine-day journey across packed ice. As they closed in on the Pole, they had the horror of encountering the abandoned remnants of the Norwegians' tent. Inside, a note from Amundsen informing them he had beaten them to it. Defeated and distraught, the small party attempted to return home, yet progress was agonizingly slow. Blizzards battered the party, and Oates, suffering from both gangrene and frostbite, had his big toe turn black and his body become yellow. His inability to walk bogged down the entire party, who, despite Oates's protestations, refused to leave him behind.

One the 17th of March, on his thirty-second birthday, Oates awoke and muttered his last words to the rest of his team, "I am just going outside and may be some time." He then proceeded to wander off into a −40°F blizzard and was never seen again.

Every year, throughout my schooling, our English teacher Mr. Stott would recount this story on the anniversary of Oates's death, inevitably breaking down with a wobble of his bottom lip whilst attempting to blurt out the explorer's last words of self-sacrifice. "I am just going outside and may be some time" remains my favorite quote in the world. For Mr. Stott it was a quote of virtue. The summation of all that it means to be an English Gentleman. To me, the story, and Stott's annual pantomiming reenactment, seemed faintly ridiculous and the quote became a life lesson I have never forgotten. A reminder to avoid life-threatening exertions. Why risk everything, when you can stay at home and watch football on your couch?
—RB

These lines, from the prologue to the play *The Time of Your Life* by William Saroyan, have got me through some dark times. And have helped me rationalize John Terry:

"In the time of your life, live—so that in that good time there shall be no ugliness or death for yourself or for any life your life touches. Seek goodness everywhere, and when it is found, bring it out of its hiding-place and let it be free and unashamed. Place in matter and in flesh the least of values, for these are the things that hold death and must pass away. Discover in all things that which shines and is beyond corruption. Encourage virtue in whatever heart it may have been driven into secrecy and sorrow by the shame and terror of the world. Ignore the obvious, for it is unworthy of the clear eye and the kindly heart. Be the inferior of no man, nor of any man be the superior. Remember that every man is a variation of yourself. No man's guilt is not yours, nor is any man's innocence a thing apart. Despise evil and ungodliness, but not men of ungodliness or evil. These, understand. Have no shame in being kindly and gentle, but if the time comes in the time of your life to kill, kill and have no regret." —MD

R

Rapinoe, Megan: The greatest spark plug American soccer has ever produced, known for her intelligence, fluidity, courage, and her signature blond bob. Justin Bieber loved it so much, he stole the style, only to sully it by wearing it in his prison mugshots. Megan's approach to football could double as a recommended approach to life. She jumped on the pod and explained, "Instead of waiting for things to come to me or instead of waiting for the game to come to me, I always just want to go get it."

Red and Blue: I generally believe that football is essentially a struggle between the forces of blue and the forces of red and that most people are drawn either to red teams or blue teams. Yes, there are huge exceptions, Brazil, Norwich, Newcastle, Leeds, and the preponderance of colors unknown to the human eye worn by teams in MLS especially when playing away. There are also teams like Barcelona and Crystal Palace (rarely mentioned in the same sentence) that play in both red and blue. But I regard that as simply unholy. Every team I support (except for a brief flirtation with Bristol City in my youth and Hibernian while at university) plays in blue, like Chelsea, Italy, and the Orlando Magic (never used in the same sentence) or in white with some blue— England and the USMNT and USWNT. I can't stand it when England play in red and actually find it hard to care as much about them when they do so. When I watch the World Cup final in 1966 it is almost always in black-and-white.

—MD

Referees: Premier League referees are paid a $84,560 per annum retainer and $1,700 per match. Over a season, that amounts to around $130,000 per man, of which each takes home about $90,000 after tax.

Would that be enough money for you to voluntarily expose yourself to the ridicule of players, and the global media on a weekly basis? A sociologist who analyzed the mind-set of professional refs determined the majority are "anal-retentive control freaks with no personality who are prone to childish sulking fits if they don't get their own way and who become worse the more attention they get." So, Dear Reader, have no pity for Premier League regulars like the late, great Mark Clattenburg. Know that the last thing they do before they leave the dressing room to take to the field and officiate is look in the mirror, soak up the noise of the crowd, and think "Everyone is here to see me."

Regrets: I have one rule I have always tried to maintain. To live a life free of regret. To this day, I have one regret that haunts me. A product of my first-ever visit to the United States when I arrived, as a fifteen-year-old, to spend the summer with my pen pal and his family in the northern suburbs of Chicago. Uncoincidentally, this journey occurred shortly after my beloved Chicago Bears had shuffled their way to victory in Super Bowl XX. To my horror, the entire team decamped to London shortly after my arrival to face the Dallas Cowboys at Wembley in the first ever NFL game to be played in England. The pain of missing the game was searing. The only way of salving it was to

Rog, bottom, with camera, waiting at O'Hare for Super Bowl Champion
Chicago Bears to return from London, Summer 1986

persuade my hosts to drive me to O'Hare International Airport so I could welcome them back when they returned to the United States. At 4 a.m. in the morning.

The waiting took forever. We were the only people other than the janitorial staff in the vast, empty arrivals terminal, so we killed the boredom by faking delirious crowd scenes for the local news crew who were covering the victorious return.

At long last, the Bears groggily deplaned. Coach Mike Ditka was the first to emerge from customs, chomping on a cigar, which he waved in my face as I approached, bellowing "These men are your heroes, leave them alone." That kind of logic was lost on a giddy fifteen-year-old desperately suppressing an erection the second I spied a series of fatigued, lumbering giants filing out behind him. Armed with a state-of-the-art technically complex 35-millimeter camera, which had been the choicest of gifts I had received for my bar mitz-

vah, I swooped amongst them, desperate to find my favorites and force them to pose for photographs. Offensive tackle Jimbo Covert was the first I recognized. I asked the six-foot-four Pennsylvanian if he would mind taking a photograph with me. "Fuck off" was his reply, so I quickly moved to plan B, snapping off my flash in his face.

Matt Suhey, the great blocking back, was more accommodating, posing for a photograph like a dandy in his head-to-toe Adidas garb. Then I spied Walter Payton ambling toward the baggage carousel and my nipples started to tingle. The man who would ultimately run 16,726 yards, who was on his way to a Hall of Fame career, and, more meaningfully to me, whose poster hung above my bedroom alongside Debbie Gibson and Danny DeVito, was standing right before me.

I summoned the courage to tap Payton on the shoulder as he waited for his luggage. The running back spun round and smiled, holding

Walter Payton tries to avoid teen Rog.

out his hand and introducing himself in his soft high-pitched voice. "Hi, I'm Walter." My tongue was suddenly so thick in my mouth, I could not summon words, but seeing my camera and being a pro, Walter knew the drill, living up to his nickname, Sweetness, as he summoned an elderly airport janitor to take a quick snap and draped his arm around my shoulders in a standard pose.

The janitor spent an age lining up the shot, but then lowered the camera before it had so much as flashed, a look of concern across his face. "It won't let me take anything," he muttered whilst staring at the camera in confusion. Realizing the shutter lock was on, I charged toward him with a sudden overwhelming panic, frantically pushing a series of buttons I prayed would allow my camera to come back to life.

Walter and I posed again. The janitor raised both the camera (and my hopes) before lowering it once again without a shutter sound. Walter had understandably had enough. "I'm sorry, I gotta go," he softly squeaked, ambling off with his trunk toward a waiting limo. The janitor handed me back my camera and shuffled off in silence, leaving me alone, with only the squeak of the baggage carousel for company. Since that moment, I have had family pets die, girlfriends I loved leave me, taking my heart along with them, and lost out in the final round of interviews for jobs I coveted, yet nothing has come close to the gnawing sense of pain I experienced watching Walter Payton, the man who embodied everything I wished I was at

that time, brush in and out of my life, without leaving any tangible evidence.

Relegation: Football's equivalent of the Moon Door through which teams may plummet (Sheffield Wednesday, Barnsley, Bradford City), never to be seen again. The suffering of American-based fans is practical: The team they have forged a deep emotional attachment to may never have a game broadcast on television again. Dodgy-pirated streams are the greatest test of the depth of all supporters' devotion. Yet for the players and the coaches the humiliation and pain of relegation is all too real. A pathos-filled Felix Magath once talked about the sorrow he felt after taking Fulham down. "This is worse than losing in two World Cup finals," the bespectacled German admitted. "Being the second-best team in the world is not as bad as being at the bottom of the Premier League."

Rhyming Slang, Cockney: The traditional patter emerging from London's East End in which "Pimple and blotch" means Scotch, a name check to the ultimate impact too much could have on a bloke's skin (as in Sir Alex likes a good Pimple and Blotch), "Mork and Mindy" (windy) describes the traditional weather at Stoke, and "Two Bob," short for "Two Bob Bit" means Shit (as in "You are Two Bob, Andros Townsend").

Ringwald, Molly: John Hughes's muse first appeared in my consciousness as a Ginger Vision courtesy of an enormous *Rolling Stone* profile in which she appeared, in my teen eyes, to be the most exotic, sophisticated, sensitive human being on God's green earth. The article talked about her upbringing outside Sacramento (which could not have sounded more alluring to my Liverpool-raised imagination), her father, who was a blind jazz musician (ditto), and her relationship with boyfriend Ad-Rock (aka the coolest human being on the planet). I was smitten, even before I read her talk about some movie called *Pretty in Pink,* in

Iona: "Did you feel it in your knees?" Andie Walsh: "I felt it everywhere."

which she alluded to the exact feelings of longing and loneliness which I was suffering from at that very moment.

There is a Yiddish word, *"besheret,"* which roughly translates through to "the single soul mate you are fated in life to meet and marry," and I was pretty sure at that moment that in Molly Ringwald I had just found mine. That belief deepened after I watched *Pretty in Pink* eleven times at the cinema, savored *The Pickup Artist,* and even survived my exposure to Molly's career wobble in the teen pregnancy drama *For Keeps.* Yet our relationship hit the rocks once Molly elected to drop off the Hollywood career radar and I interpreted the fact she decamped to Paris at virtually the same time I moved to America in the early 1990s as our final nail in the coffin.

When we had the chance to invite Molly to guest on the *Men in Blazers* show, I wanted to tell her how she had changed my life more than anyone else in the world, but I could not find the words. She came in, signed my bald head, and watched me reenact the lipstick trick from *Breakfast Club.* The best I could do was to ask her if she now believed her *Breakfast Club* line "When you grow up . . . your heart dies" was a life truth. She looked at me for a second, covered in red lipstick, and with her autograph scrawled with black marker across my bald head, and broke out in laughter. "No," she said, giggling. "Absolutely not." —RB

Rodgers, Brendan, aka "The Brodge": Liverpool manager, 2012–15. Either a modern-day retelling of the Greek Icarus fable or proof that even gods are mortal. By the time he was fired by Liverpool he was seen as a widely derided fraud. A dispenser of self-aggrandizing, delusional quotes such as, "My biggest mentor is myself because I've had to study and that's been my biggest influence" or "I've always said that you can live without water for many days, but you can't live for a second without hope." Yet in 2013–14, with Luis Suárez and Daniel Sturridge eviscerating all comers, his Liver-

pool were top of the table with just two games to go. Steven Gerrard's infamous slip against Chelsea triggered a savage implosion which denied Liverpool their first title in twenty-four years. A victory which would have seen Brendan Rodgers eternally hailed as a legend. Such are the margins between success and failure, heroes and villains in sports. Rodgers was left to shuffle off to Celtic, no doubt channeling the sentiments of Marlon Brando's Terry Malloy, "You don't understand. I coulda had class. *I coulda been a contender*. I coulda been somebody, instead of a bum, which is what I am."

Rod Lavers: The subtle ridge work and contoured style make this objectively the greatest sneaker of all time, edging the Stan Smith, and the all-white classic Puma G. Vilas.

Roger: Means "famous spear" from the Germanic elements *hrod,* "fame," and *ger,* "spear."

Rog's Ten Greatest Rogers of All Time*
1. Roger Taylor, Duran Duran drummer (1960–)
2. Roger Federer, Tennis star (1981–)
3. Roger Milla, Cameroonian footballer (1952–)
4. Roger Moore, Best Bond EVER (1927–2017)
5. Roger Maris, Baseball slugger (1934–1985)
6. Roger Ebert, Film critic (1942–2013)
7. Roger Staubach, NFL quarterback (1942–)
8. Roger Daltrey, The Who lead singer (1944–)
9. Roger Hargreaves, Mr. Men creator (1935–1988)
10. Roger Bannister, First sub-4-minute miler (1929–)

* *Clemens and Goodell disqualified just because.*

Rolling Stone: I know magazines are not what they used to be, but when I was fifteen and obsessed with America—a country to which I had never been, but come to adore via exposure to *Miami Vice, Hart to Hart,* and the Super Bowl Shuffle—I learned to feed my obsession by subscribing to *Rolling Stone* and having it shipped over from the United States of America.

In the 1980s, objects shipped by mail could take months to arrive, and even though the *Rolling Stone*s that dropped through my mailbox were already passed their sell-by date, I devoured them as if they were manna from heaven. I would tear at the pages as if our mailman had handed me a sliver of America itself as the magazine introduced me to movies *(Top Gun, Pretty in Pink, Back to the Future)* that would not be released in England for months, television shows (*The Equalizer*! *Perfect Strangers*! *The Wonder Years*!) that I would have to wait, in some cases for years, to see, and bands (Violent Femmes! The Hooters! The Long Ryders!) who would never crack the British market.

I could not care less. The images, photographs, and narrative appeared to be of a vivid world lived in Technicolor. After reading—or really, imbibing—*Rolling Stone,* to me England felt grimly cloaked in black-and-white in comparison. London-born comedian Matt Lucas best described the sensation I experienced when he came on our show and quipped, "On American television you had cool-looking characters, on British television everyone looked like a potato." As a clincher, the magazine always had a scratch-and-sniff insertion for Calvin Klein Obsession in the center, which overwhelmed my senses. It always smelled how I imagined Molly Ringwald would smell, a magical scent that lured me toward the United States like a sailor drawn onto the rocks by the songs of the Sirens. **—RB**

Ronaldo, Cristiano: The task of translating Ronaldo into the American sports pantheon demands fusing the competitive nature of Kobe Bryant with the self-importance of Terrell Owens, adding a dash of Zoolander, and topping it off with the arrogance and vanity of Alex Rodriguez. Like A-Rod, CR7 affects an aura that suggests he could easily let an afternoon get away from him while tracing the contours of his own reflection in the mirror.

This is a man who is 100 percent pure vaudeville villain, evidently living his life by an unspoken mantra "Why walk when you can strut?" A smile crosses his lips only to express derision toward the inferior inhabitants who populate his world: opponents, referees, and teammates who do not bend to his will. Goal celebrations are less spontaneous outbursts of joy, more validatory testaments to his own magnificence.

During Euro 2012 in Ukraine, one of the more interesting aspects of Ukrainian television's live broadcasts of the tournament was that whenever their commentator mentioned Cristiano Ronaldo, he would tag three puckered air kisses onto the end of his name. The gimmick perfectly captured the central tension of the Portuguese star's career: the battle for superiority between his undeniable skill and peerless ego.

Yet, strip away the rhinestones, precision-plucked eyebrows, and glistening waxed legs, and the Portuguese star is the complete athlete. Few players can torment their opponents in more ways. Like a five-tool baseball stud, Ronaldo in his prime was strong, swift, and superlatively coordinated, able to break legs with a move, score with power from distance, clinical calculation up close, or aerial audacity via his head.

That ability ensures that Ronaldo triggers extreme emotions. He is a player adored by his team's fan base yet loathed by just about everyone else. The man who once said "If God can't please everyone, I won't either" has offered a simple analysis of his detractors' motivations: "I think that because I am rich, handsome, and a great player, people are envious of me. I don't have any other explanation."

Baldness is Truth, Wayne Rooney. Baldness. Is. Truth.

Rooney, Wayne: When Wayne Rooney shattered English legend Bobby Charlton's forty-five-year-old international scoring record by netting his 50th goal on in September 2015, the English newspapers marked the feat by agonizing whether the Manchester United striker was a truly great player. Most agreed his achievement was remarkable as a sign of longevity and consistency, yet the achievement was undermined by the fact that so few goals came in top tournaments, and that in his era the English national team had been in decline. Yet above all, the moment was tarnished by the sense of unfulfilled promise that has haunted Rooney's career at the international level.

The stocky teen became England's then youngest international at 17 years and 111 days when he came on as a halftime substitute during a 3–1 friendly loss to Australia, and earned a call-up to the David Beckham–captained team into Euro 2004. The call-up came despite becoming ensnared in an unsavory nightclub incident in which he was alleged to have spat in a female clubber's face. *The Observer* prophetically called him "a snarling ball of aggression, too wild for some tastes, but a force impossible to ignore."

Watching Rooney at Euro 2004 was akin to witnessing a boy turn into a globally revered adult in fast-motion. He arrived in Portugal as an untested Evertonian prodigy. He left as a coveted world-class starlet. His two-goal man-of-the-match performance in a 3–0 victory against Switzerland could not have been predicted from the opening exchanges. A mali-cious studs-first slide into the goalkeeper saw the teenager yellow-carded within 18 minutes. The youngster's second and final warning came just three minutes later after he locked horns with the opposing striker in the center circle. But within seconds, Rooney channeled his manic energy with a purpose, becoming the youngest player to score at the Euros. Michael Owen crossed crisply from the left and young Wayne rose between two defenders to nod the ball past a flat-footed Jörg Stiel in goal. He then trotted calmly toward the corner flag, executing a celebratory cartwheel along the way (no small feat for such a thickset gent).

His legend would grow with every subsequent game. A second brace followed in a 4–2 come-from-behind victory against Croatia. Coach Sven-Göran Eriksson proclaimed, "I don't remember anyone making such an impact on a tournament since Pelé in the 1958 World Cup."

Whatever dreams they harbored were soon shattered during the quarter final against Portugal. Midway through the first half, Rooney chased down a routine long ball, only to pull up lame after the slightest of clips from a Portuguese defender caused him to lose his boot. He limped off with a broken foot, and England's chances departed with him. They fought out a 2–2 tie, only to be predictably eliminated on penalties. He was never the same player again.

Looking back over Rooney's international career, we located one of our favorite ever Rooney interviews. Ahead of his Euro tournament debut in 2004, an eighteen-year-old

Wayne Rooney participated in a question-and-answer with *FHM* magazine which included this riff:

Q: Will we see you experimenting with any daft haircuts?

Rooney: No, no, I don't think you'll see that. I think I'll just keep it the same.

Q: Not a mullet? What if the seventies footballer perm comes back into fashion?

Rooney: I don't think so, I think I'll just stay with me hair now.

Rule Changes: Football is the world's most popular game because of its simplicity. We humbly submit the following tweaks which we believe would make the sport perfect:

- A team should be awarded only half a goal if the goalkeeper saves a penalty, only for the penalty taker to smack home the rebound.
- A team should receive a goal and a half if the ball goes directly into the side or roof of the netting.
- Penalty Shoot-outs, which are too arbitrary a way to settle a game of football, should be replaced by full-team Dance-offs.
- Goalkeepers should have to take all their team's corners and then have to sprint back to cover their goal.
- Teams managed by a gent who has had a hair transplant start the season with an automatic 10 point deduction.
- All goalkeepers must be under five-foot-two-inches tall.
- Team with player sporting most creative neck tattoo automatically wins coin toss.
- Goals scored by an English player count double.
- Goals scored by an American player count triple.

Sad Nap: A term coined by MLB pitcher Brandon McCarthy, who talked about the emotions he experiences upon waking early to watch his beloved Liverpool, only to experience defeat. He defined it as "What you take after your team plays with misery in an early-morning Premier League game." Arsenal fans have assured us, there have been games their team has won, yet played so unconvincingly, they had sad napped even in victory. The first sad nap of the season is the least refreshing sad nap of all.

Schadenfreude: From the German "harm joy." The act of savoring somebody else's misfortune. Formerly, one of life's few true pleasures, though for Rog that simple thrill was destroyed by Dutch researchers who uncovered that schadenfreude is experienced only by those with low self-esteem in relation to those they envy. A truth hinted at by Martin Amis's belief "The English feel schadenfreude even about themselves."

Scoring Too Early: There are of course exceptions to this rule. You can never score too early at home (unless you're Aston Villa), and you can never score too early if you get a goalkeeper or last defender sent off in the process. Goals scored from blatantly offside positions or involving obvious handballs also do not apply. Substitutes can rarely score too early. You can never score too early if the player who has scored too early has never scored before or in memory for your club (the Obi Mikel exception). Also, you can never score too early in the snow. Finally, you can never score too early in any final, or knockout stage of the World Cup

in the Southern Hemisphere or Asia (unless, of course, you're England). The scoring-too-early rule generally expires at the 30-minute mark, but weaker teams playing against stronger teams, especially away from home, are always advised to keep games scoreless as long as possible, thus frustrating the home crowd, who put pressure on their players, and then nick a goal right at the end with too little time for the devastated home team to equalize. Also note that it is possible to equalize too early and definitely to celebrate too early. These last two often go hand in hand. Especially with Everton. (*See* Is That Your Analysis?) **—MD**

Scoring Too Early, Roger's Experience of: The Uruguayan writer Eduardo Galeano once declared "the goal is soccer's orgasm." Yet when Everton once went ahead against Chelsea, I realized, the initial rush I experienced as a lifelong Evertonian soon evaporated. No sooner had I punched the air and landed back in my seat than my stomach tightened, throat constricted, and a cold sweat descended.

At the final whistle, my dominant emotion was relief, the joy I experienced fleeting in comparison to the numbing "Black Dog" of a mood that cloaked me after impotent draws against Cardiff and West Brom in previous weeks. With Everton's victory came two realizations:

1. Against top-four teams, I feel more comfortable watching when the club I support have fallen behind 1–0 and are forced to chase the game as opposed to when they go ahead 1–0 and have to hold on.

SCARVES

An illustrated guide to tying a football scarf

The classic

The Italian

The *Apocalypse Now* general

Round the wrist, 1970s throwback

The tourist (the half-and-half scarf)

2. The buzz of victory pales in comparison to the pain of failure and defeat.

These are not emotions confined to Everton fans. Howard Jacobson, the Booker Prize–winning novelist, once memorably said that if Tottenham score in the first 10 minutes at White Hart Lane, 15,000 fearful Spurs supporters can be heard to whisper: "Too early . . . it's much too early."

One of the joys of living in New York City is that a psychoanalyst is never too far away. Indeed, my neighbor Barry Stern is a professor of medical psychology at Columbia University. After I had explained my predicament, he quipped, "I think New York Mets fans would have a lot to say about this," before launching into a psychoanalytical explanation in which "masochists" (his word) "turn passive into active" when faced by a traumatic experience over which they have no control.

"It sounds like you take control of the experience of disappointment by preemptively becoming disappointed," he told me. "You savor the anticipated loss when the team is down, a stance from which you can comfortably root for a win, without risking too much. Viewed like that, the 1–0 lead is inherently less pleasurable. Rather than enjoying your team being ahead, you manage the anxiety associated with them inevitably mucking up, negating the positive mood created through their lead . . . by spoiling it yourself. No more anxiety, just depression, and the familiar feeling of managing the weak sense of hope they might just pull this one out. [There's] no such thing as a happy football fan," he added, "except neutrals enjoying a game they don't care about." —RB

Scotland: One of the most beautiful parts of the world. A remarkable nation, vastly underappreciated because it is best known by the world courtesy of Mel Gibson's antics in *Braveheart* or via the self-loathing of *Trainspotting*. "We are the lowest of the low, the scum of the earth. The most wretched servile, miserable, pathetic trash that was ever Crapped intae creation."

Many young Englishmen come to know Scotland through football. Most searingly for our generation, it was Scotland 2, England 1 at Wembley in 1977. A game that began with Scotland's manager Ally MacLeod declaring, "I don't dislike the English, I hate their guts!" and ended with thousands of tartan-hatted Scottish fans storming the field and tearing down the goalposts at Wembley in scenes of giddy, lager-fueled ecstasy. Scottish footballers were revered back then—Dennis Law, Graeme Souness, and Kenny Dalglish were all world-class. Though the talent pool diminished, Scottish managers long predominated with the likes of Sir Alex Ferguson, David Moyes, and Alex McLeish, proving that all English players remain terrified of anything that emerges from a Scotsman's mouth.

The current dearth of elite Scottish football players, coupled with our adoration of Andy Murray, whom English people consider British in victory and Scottish in defeat, has long made us debate our favorite Scottish athletes of all time. Here is our definitive list:

5. Jim Clark (Kilmany, Fife, 1936–1968), motorsport, winner of the Indy 500 in 1965 and driver par excellence who landed a remarkable grand slam by starting on the pole, landing the fastest lap, and leading every lap in said race.
4. Dougal Haston (Currie, Midlothian, 1940–1977), for mountaineering, a student of philosophy before dedicating his life to wine, women, and climbing. He died after choking on his scarf in an avalanche.
3. Dr. John Cattanach (Newtonmore, Inverness-shire, 1885–1915), for shinty—the only shinty player in the Scottish Sports Hall of fame. A lieutenant for the Royal Army Medical Corps who died during the First World War at Gallipoli.
2. Willie Carson (Stirling, Stirlingshire, b. 1942), for horse racing, used his five-foot frame to ride 3,828 winners, including 187 in one season.

1. Robert Barclay Allardice (Stonehaven, Kincardineshire, 1779–1854), the world's greatest competitive walker and the father of the sport of pedestrianism. His most famous feat was walking 1,000 miles in 1,000 hours.

Seersucker: One of the most romantic American fabrics has its origins in the British Empire. Seersucker was popularized by British colonialists in the Indian Raj. Adapted from the Hindi adaptation of the Persian phrase, shyroshakar, referring to the bump and smooth of the fabric's stripes, the word originally meant "milk and sugar."

My love of the fabric preceded my knowledge of its Anglo origins. Indeed, few fabrics feel more American to my outsider eyes, as in the United States seersucker has become entwined with blue-blooded life in settings both Southern and Yankee. Yet it arrived on these shores as a working-class fabric, cheap and popular amongst rail workers and females in the military. According to *The New York Times,* seersucker made a class jump in the 1920s when college kids co-opted the fabric, "in a spirit of reverse snobbery." Newspaperman Damon Runyon wrote that his early co-option of seersucker caused "much confusion among my friends. They cannot decide whether I am broke or just setting a new vogue."

The first time I encountered it was back in my single days when I had the pleasure of dating a girl from Louisiana. We went to the movies and while we were in the line for tickets, I noticed the gentleman in front of me was clad in seersucker head to toe. I had never seen such an exotic, eye-catching, dandy fabric and could not prevent myself from reaching out and gently stroking the puckered weave with my fingers. The fellow never noticed, but it truly disturbed my date. I never went out with her again, yet my love of the fabric, which is the legacy of our relationship, more than compensated for her loss. **—RB**

Self-loathing: An underrated human emotion. Few traits can be more motivational. Zen philosopher Cheri Huber once said, "If you had a person in your life treating you the way you treat yourself, you would have gotten rid of them a long time ago." Channel that hatred. It is a gift. As Karl Ove Knausgaard admitted, "Self-loathing is the engine; fame is the fuel."

Shammgod, God: One of Rog's top four NBA stars of all time, alongside Luc Longley, Gheorghe Muresan and Sam Cassell. But undoubtedly the finest-named athlete of all time, just trumping Rodeo bull rider Ryan Dirteater, Reading goalkeeper Steve Death, and former Luxembourg defender Frank Awanka.

Shass: A shot that misses so badly that it turns into a pass. Daniel Sturridge specialized in shassing during his time at Chelsea. Many of his shasses turning into shassists. If you happen to shassist you have two choices, join in the celebration and accept the adulation for the pinpoint unselfishness of your pass, never letting on that it was completely unintentional. Or celebrate like an idiot, pointing at your flapping feet and walking like a clown and making a stupid face to make it clear that you don't know what you're doing. Most Premier League players choose the former.

Shirley Restaurante Rio: Rog and I would not have survived the World Cup without this place.

It's like Rio's version of Hollywood's Musso and Frank's, or The Palm, or a really crap version of Cipriani. It was tucked behind our hotel, on a little street (R. Gustavo Sampaio) just a block from Copacabana beach in the Leme section of Rio and I chanced upon it on our second day in Rio when I was running away from some young scallywags, heavily armed, who were trying to steal my watch, phone, money, jeans, and blazer. It's all wood paneling and waiters in white coats and black ties and has been

there forever. It's what some Brazilians refer to as a "traditional" restaurant (meaning strong possibility of food poisoning) specializing in Spanish-style seafood, like octopus vinaigrette, sardines, and paella. Here is my favorite Yelp review of the place:

> All dishes we ordered were over-cooked to the point where you could no longer tell if the seafood, even the octopus, actually was seafood or potatoes.

In many cities you would avoid a place reviewed like this like the plague. In Rio, that's basically the equivalent of getting two Michelin Stars. And moreover, Rog and I didn't get food poisoning there once. So we basically started eating every meal there.

By the end of week one, the waiters started greeting us by name—like "Norm" in *Cheers*—every time we entered. Though "Davo" was always a bit easier for them than "Rog." We drank all their best Malbec and Rioja, ate all their freshest (weeks old rather than months old) sardines, and started posting on social media about our special discovery. Problem. By the end of the World Cup the place was packed. We could barely get a table. And the giants of the English press—Henry Winter, Oliver Kay, and Paul Hayward—STOLE OUR FAVORITE TABLE.

Over the last couple of years we have heard frequently from GFOPs who have eaten at Shirley's. It's always made us rather miss the place.

The problem is, it's in Rio. And on our last day in the original Panic Room, at the crap end of Copacabana beach, Rog made me promise we'd never have to go back there. And I doubt the delivery service is very reliable. Or fresh. —MD

Sixty-six: Davo's favorite number. The year of his birth. The year England won the World Cup. A highway on which to get one's kicks. Mario Lemieux's retired jersey number. For real math nerds, 66 is a sphenic number, a triangular number, a hexagonal number, and a semi-meandric number. For really, really big math nerds, being a multiple of a perfect number, 66 is itself a semi-perfect number and, moreover, since it is possible to find sequences of 66 consecutive integers such that each inner member shares a factor with either the first or the last member, 66 is an Erdős–Woods number. For our more theologically inclined GFOPs, 66 is the total number of chapters in the Bible book of Isaiah. And the number of verses in Chapter 3 of the book of Lamentations. Of course, 66 is also the total number of books in the Protestant edition of the Bible (Old Testament and New Testament) combined. And, as everybody knows, it is the atomic number for dysprosium. Who can forget that 66 is the number of hot dogs eaten by world record holder Joey Chestnut in 15 minutes at the Nathan's Hot Dog Eating Contest in 2007. And finally, 66 is also the age, at publication, of Roger's least favorite recording artist, Phil Collins.

Size the Day: Bora Milutinović's enigmatic command to the United States Men's National Team ahead of the 1994 World Cup as revealed by Alexi Lalas at our 2013 Holiday Show. Alexi described Bora as a mix between "Yoda and Yogi Berra" and recommended Sizing the Day as a philosophy for life.

Rog Rog, meet Bora Bora

S.N.O.G.: Underused stat of near misses (shots nearly on goal). Based on Davo's observation that the obsession with shots on goal ignores the often more telling accumulation of powerful shots that evade the goalkeeper and nearly go in. Proof of the importance of "shots nearly on goal" over most shots on goal is that a curling shot that almost goes in is almost always greeted by a massive "Ooooooooooo" from the crowd. Shots hit tamely straight at the goalkeeper are, by contrast, usually greeted by "What happened to you, Matić?! You used to be good."

Soccer Players, Davo's Five Favorite Ever (non-Chelsea edition):

1. BOBBY MOORE

Bobby Moore was England's youngest ever captain and the West Ham left half, or left-sided central defender cum midfielder, and was just twenty-five as he climbed those Wembley stairs and wiped his hand on a velvet tablecloth before shaking the hand of Queen Elizabeth and lifting the World Cup. For every Englishman of my generation, he remains a national hero, years after his premature death in 1993 at the age of just fifty-one.

Sir Alex Ferguson, Pelé, and Franz Beckenbauer have described him as the best defender they "have ever seen," they have "played against," and "in the history of the game."

If you want to understand just how great a player was Bobby Moore, search for England

"Immaculate footballer. Imperial defender. Immortal hero of 1966. First Englishman to raise the World Cup aloft. Favourite son of London's East End. Finest legend of West Ham United. National Treasure. Master of Wembley. Lord of the game. Captain extraordinary. Gentleman of all time." This is the inscription on the pedestal of the statue of Bobby Moore at Wembley Stadium.

vs. Brazil in the 1970 World Cup. It was a group stage match, but many have described it as good enough to have been the final. Most England fans remember this game for Gordon Banks's "Save of the Century" from Pelé's header—and more on that later. But for me, it was Moore's two perfectly timed one-on-one tackles on Tostão and Jairzinho, that were class personified. After the final whistle, the Brazil players surrounded Moore to pay their respects, and Pelé ended up with his shirt.

In 1976 Bobby Moore came to the US to play for the San Antonio Thunder in the NASL (he later played a season in Seattle for the Sounders also). He also has the great and distinct honor of having represented Team USA along with Pelé and Giorgio Chinaglia in a friendly game against England in Philadelphia to commemorate the Bicentennial.

2. GORDON BANKS

"It's something that people will always remember me for. They won't remember me for winning the World Cup, it'll be for that save. That's how a big a thing it is. People just want to talk about that save."

That's what Gordon Banks said thirty-two years later to Jairzinho, the Brazilian forward who had set up an unstoppable shot against him that fateful day in Guadalajara at the 1970 World Cup. You watch it on YouTube today, and it still defies logic. Not only that Banks got to the ball, from Pelé's powerful header, down to his right, pinpoint and low into the corner, from six yards out, from Jairzinho's laser accurate cross, it's that Banks also tipped the ball up and over the bar, to prevent Pelé from getting the rebound. Pelé was in disbelief that it wasn't a goal and this, apparently, was the ensuing exchange:

"I thought that was a goal." (Pelé)

"You and me both." (Banks)

"You're getting old, Banksy, you used to hold on to them." (Bobby Moore)

Banks was born in Sheffield, the son of a bookmaker (not strictly legal), and left school

A split second before the "Save of the Century," Pelé is screaming "Gol!"— one of the only recorded instances when the Brazilian great celebrated too early.

at fourteen to work as a bagger for a local coal merchant. After moving up the ranks in Yorkshire amateur league football, and a short spell in the British Army in Germany, Banks started his career at Chesterfield Town before being spotted by first division Leicester City. He became a new style of keeper, ordering and martialing the defense in front of him, the Joe Hart of his generation but sane. He won the 1964 League Cup, the 1966 World Cup, and the 1972 League Cup, after moving to Stoke City. In October 1972 he lost sight in one eye in a car crash and was never the same keeper again. In 1977 he joined the Fort Lauderdale Strikers of the NASL and became the league's Goalkeeper of the Year, conceding just 29 goals in 26 games, a league defensive best. He played one more partial season with Fort Lauderdale in 1978 before his retirement. However, it is Banks's international career that really makes him one of the greatest goalkeepers in the history of the game.

After the group stage classic in 1970 against Brazil in Guadalajara, England were expected to go far in the tournament. However, Banks came down with a terrible bout of the Eartha Kitts (that's rhyming slang) and missed the quarter final with West Germany. Up 2–0, to my eternal shame, Chelsea's goalkeeper and Banks's understudy, Peter "the Cat" Bonetti, let in three goals, starting with one absolute, Rob Green level howler, from a tame Franz Beckenbauer shot. During Banks's 73 international games he kept 35 clean sheets and lost just nine games.

3. CARLOS ALBERTO

Carlos Alberto Torres, known always simply as Carlos Alberto, scored the astounding fourth goal in the humiliation of Italy in the 1970 final in Mexico City, and it was the emphatic exclamation point on a total football move of such extraordinary individual skill and team telepathic beauty that Alberto has described the goal as a "carnival." I got to know the goal intimately when working on the documentary

The Thickening

series *I Scored a Goal in the World Cup Final* in 2010 and it is, for me, by a hundred miles, simply the greatest World Cup final goal ever scored.

The move started with the Brazilian center forward, Tostão, naturally picking up the ball at left back. The ball then passed through all but two of the team's outfield players on its way to the goal's stunning climax. Clodoaldo dribbled past four Italian challenges in his own half, before passing to Rivelino, who knocked it nonchalantly forward to Jairzinho on the left wing. On the left a few meters outside Italy's penalty area, Jairzinho passed to Pelé, who was standing to his right at the top of the key. Pelé then casually passes the ball to no one. Literally into space. And you're thinking, what the f is he doing? Then, seemingly from nowhere, the massive figure of Carlos Alberto speed lollops into the scene and smashes it into the far corner of the net. Golazo Joink.

After a phenomenal club career in Brazil, the ball-playing, goal-scoring, game-reading, gentlemanly central defender came to play in the US for the New York Cosmos and the California Surf. While working on an earlier documentary, *Once in a Lifetime,* that I executive produced about the Cosmos in 2006, I was blown away by how valuable the contribution of Carlos Alberto was to the star-laden New York Cosmos team that won the title in 1977 and 1978, and then again in 1982. Pelé and Chinaglia got all the glory, and justifiably, but it was Carlos Alberto who often seemed to hold the whole team together. A total footballer. And an amazing man.

4. PAUL SCHOLES

"In the past fifteen to twenty years, the best central midfielder that I have seen—the most complete—is Scholes." —Xavi

Ginger power

Admission: I loved watching Manchester United in the 1990s and early 2000s. They played thrilling attacking football. And they were hard as trucks. Schmeichel, Pallister, Irwin, Nicky Butt, Roy Keane, and Jaap Stam provided the leadership, muscle, and brawn. Cantona, then Sheringham, Yorke, Andy Cole, and Solskjaer were breathtaking and clinical. Beckham—though it is so fashionable to belittle his ability and reduce it to "a great right boot" (when you're a right-footed playmaker, set piece taker, and winger, "a great right boot" can come in somewhat handy)—was an electric and total footballer in his prime. And Ryan Giggs possessed a combination of work ethic, bravery, an unparalleled engine, scintillating speed, and exacting passing, crossing, and finishing that made him arguably the greatest Premier League player ever. They were managed by the greatest club manager in the history of the game, Sir Alex Ferguson. But for me, the player I tuned in to watch, and was always blown away by when I saw him live, was the stocky, pink-skinned, red-faced, ginger assassin, Paul Scholes.

I first became aware of his potential magnificence when watching his full international debut for England against Italy at the Tournoi de France World Cup warm-up tournament in June 1997. At just twenty-two, he completely bossed the game from midfield, setting up Ian Wright with an audacious long pass for the opening goal after 25 minutes. However, after Glenn Hoddle was fired by England, no England manager seemed to be able to get the best out of Scholes, let alone play him in his best position. But for Manchester United, it was a completely different story.

The Ginger Ninja scored 155 goals in 718 appearances for the club. But it was not his stats that set him apart. It was his footballing intelligence and the fact that his key contributions so often came at exactly the right time and changed the outcome of so many games. My words simply cannot do him justice. Here's what others have said about him.

Socrates: "He was good enough to play for Brazil. I love to watch Scholes, to see him pass, the boy with the red hair and the red shirt. He had quality and character."

Zinedine Zidane: "Scholes was my toughest opponent, the complete midfielder and undoubtedly the greatest midfielder of his generation."

Laurent Blanc: "I tell anyone who asks me—Scholes is the best English player."

Edgar Davids: "I'm not the best, Paul Scholes is. Every one of us is just trying to become as good as him."

Thierry Henry: "United always had many amazing players, but whenever we faced them we were always, always, always scared of what Paul Scholes could do. Ask anyone from that old Arsenal team, they will tell you the same. If you let him play, he can kill you. The way he plays: one touch, arriving late into the box, the way he strikes the ball, his vision, his passing. Incredible."

5. ROBERTO BAGGIO

I witnessed two unforgettable moments at the 1994 World Cup at the Rose Bowl in Pasadena that will haunt me forever. The first was looking straight across at Andrés Escobar from the third row opposite the edge of the Colombian penalty area, lying on his back, hands behind his head, after he had scored that fateful own goal against the United States which resulted in his murder.

Before the ponytail, there was the mullet. Hair hero.

The second was standing amongst the Italian fans where the penalty shootout took place at the end of the final between Italy and Brazil and screaming as the man who had become my hero during that world cup, Roberto Baggio, sent his penalty flying over the bar to gift the World Cup to Brazil.

Baggio had set the tournament on fire that summer, and with England having failed to qualify, I was cheering full-throatedly for my beloved Italians. In the knockout stages, Baggio, nicknamed "Il Divin Codino," the Divine Ponytail, for the hairstyle he wore for much of his career, dazzled with guile and goals. He could dribble, curl free kicks, pass, shoot, and score. And in true Italian fashion, his ability to protest decisions, his innocence, and his gesticulations were all on another level. He almost single-handedly willed that Italian team into the finals, and on that boiling hot day in Pasadena gave it his all. It took me days to recover from the heartbreak of watching Italy lose that penalty shootout. To this day I believe that a shootout is a completely inappropriate way to end any World Cup game, let alone a World Cup final. Because of what happened to one of my heroes, Roberto Baggio. And because England are crap at them also.

Sockless: Guy Ritchie once briefed us on the cardinal rules governing the decision by men to forgo socks in the summer: "It's a dangerous game. Thin ice. Treacherous waters under that ice. I gotta tell you," he said. "It's not a game I'd usually play with. You gotta be Italian or Mediterranean. You gotta have olive skin. But the big game, the big game is when you got little pink legs and you're prepared to go bold."

SoHo, The Crap Part of: The Crap Part of SoHo, the area that developers and real estate agents ambitiously like to describe as West SoHo, Northern TriBeCa, or Hudson Square is a neighborhood in lower Manhattan, approximately bounded by West Houston Street to the north, Canal Street to the south, Sixth Avenue (Avenue of the Americas) to the east, and the Hudson River to the west. To the north of the neighborhood is Greenwich Village, to the south is TriBeCa, and to the east is the not crap part of SoHo. The area was once known as the Printing District, and today remains a center of media-related activity, including in advertising, design, communications, and the arts. Since 2006 it has been home to the Embassy Row studios. Within the neighborhood is the landmarked Charlton-King-Vandam Historic District, which contains the largest concentration of Federalist and Greek Revival style row houses built during the first half of the nineteenth century. The most prominent feature within the neighborhood is the Manhattan entrance to the Holland Tunnel. The tallest structure in the neighborhood is the Trump SoHo hotel. We also have a Chipotle, a Just Salad, a Pret a Manger, a Hale and Hearty Soup, and at least two Starbucks. The Ear Inn on Spring Street is one of the oldest bars in New York City, built in 1817 by one of George Washington's aides.

George Washington, John Adams, Aaron Burr, and John Jacob Astor have all resided in the CPOS. Today, the Embassy Row studios occupy the same illustrious city block as a meth clinic.

Spain: A nation able to shuck a rich tradition of brilliant yet fragile chokers, by unfurling an intoxicating team who dominated all comers between 2008 and 2012 with their mesmerizing,

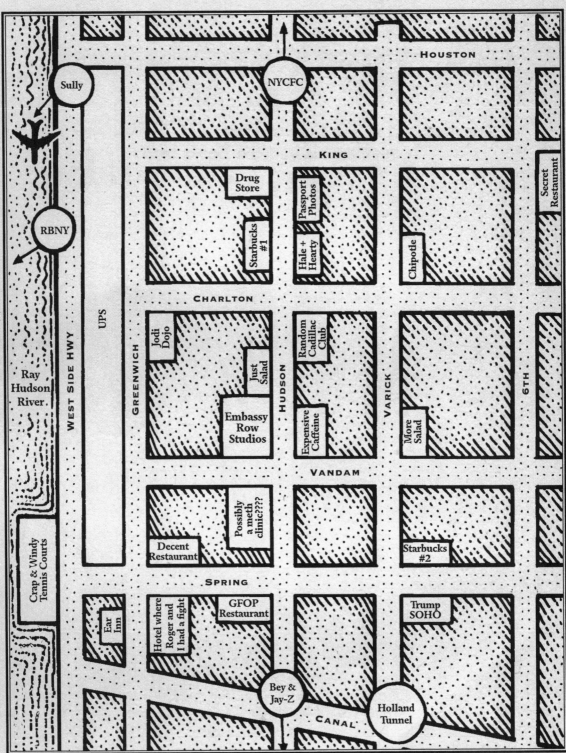

suffocating, possession-hungry squad which was tactically and psychologically peerless.

If Tyrion Lannister were a footballer. . .

When we were growing up in the 1980s, Spain were so erratic and delicate even England could take them. Before every major tournament they were always amongst the favorites, dispatching a talent-rich flair team, stuffed with as many Josés, Miguels, and Enriques as they could start. Their group stage would always begin well, but once opponents like Northern Ireland, essentially a pub team, worked out how to out-muscle them, the Spanish challenge would quickly meet its end, like the Arab swordsman in *Raiders of the Lost Ark* whose dashing scimitar foreplay was undone by Harrison Ford simply pulling out a pistol and shooting him.

The dual rise of Real Madrid and Barcelona into global super-clubs shattered that reality, empowering Spain to develop a strain of player under laboratory conditions, born with the psychological ability to defy pressure and be comfortable as front-running winners. The core of players like Iker Casillas, Xavi, and Andrés Iniesta played on national teams since they were fourteen, affording them an almost telepathic familiarity needed to play their inimitable "tiki-taka" football that emphasized movement and tiny passes to paper-cut defenders to death.

Imagine a midfield of scheming Tyrion Lannisters holding on to possession with their cunning combinations, moving forward at will, yet knowing their opponents could not score if they never touched the ball. Critics decried the football as boring, yet the only boring feature was that this team in their prime removed the suspense from the game. It was clear to all before kickoff that Spain would end the winners. The joy of watching those victorious tiny Smurfs confuse and befuddle Gargamel-esque opponents over and over again was a pleasure that was only truly appreciated once it was gone.

Speeches, Davo's Five Favorite of All Time: I love a good speech. Like Jamie Vardy's "Beers on the coach on the plane" classic in the dressing room at Swansea after breaking the Premier League consecutive game scoring record. But I also like great speeches. The ones that make you run away from the hall or television or prematch tunnel or halftime dressing room and make you do something, like rip off your shirt and yell. When Aeschines spoke, they said, "How well he speaks." But when Demosthenes spoke, they said, "Let's march against Philip." Speeches are a huge part of football, especially at halftime, but few managers have approached the oratorical power of the following:

1. We shall fight on the beaches, Winston Churchill, June 4, 1940, Westminster, London

Churchill's inspirational speech to Parliament just days after the humiliating yet miraculous evacuation of the vast majority of the British Expeditionary Force from German-surrounded Dunkirk, had to acknowledge an enormous loss, pay tribute to the men and women who had ensured a miraculous outcome, and prepare the nation for an almost inevitable invasion. It did all of the above. The unforgettable climax of the speech still gives me goose bumps, and if you listen to it, I defy you not to run from your house, ripping your clothes off, screaming "War Pig!"

"Even though large tracts of Europe and many old and famous states have fallen or may fall into the grip of the Gestapo and all the odious apparatus of Nazi rule, we shall not flag or fail. We shall go on to the end. We shall fight in France, we shall fight on the seas and oceans, we shall fight with growing confidence and growing strength in the air, we shall defend our island, whatever the cost may be. We shall fight on the beaches, we shall fight on the landing grounds, we shall fight in the fields and in the streets, we shall fight in the hills; we shall never surrender, and if, which I do not for a moment believe, this island or a large part of it were subjugated and starving, then our Empire beyond the seas, armed and guarded by the British Fleet, would carry on the struggle, until, in God's good time, the New World, with all its power and might, steps forth to the rescue and the liberation of the old."

As British historian Simon Schama has written, Churchill's words were "the lifeboat and the blood transfusion. They turned the tide." His speech made all who heard it believe that Britain could stand against the might of the Germans and hold out until the Americans entered the war. By the end of the month, the Battle of Britain had commenced, and shortly after that, the Blitz, the devastating German bombing of London and other major cities by the German Luftwaffe. But by the end of the summer, the Royal Air Force was more than holding their own in the aerial war. Churchill spoke to Parliament again on August 20. "The gratitude of every home in our island, in our Empire, and indeed throughout the world, except in the abodes of the guilty, goes out to the British airmen who, undaunted by odds, unwearied in their constant challenge and mortal danger, are turning the tide of the World War by their prowess and by their devotion. Never in the field of human conflict was so much owed by so many to so few." By the middle of September, the RAF were inflicting heavy losses on the Luftwaffe, and by the end of October the battle was truly won. It was a defensive victory.

And as a Chelsea fan I can particularly appreciate that. The offensive victory commenced four years and two days after this speech when the American and British military, together with forces from Canada, France, Poland, Australia, Czechoslovakia, Greece, Luxembourg, Holland, New Zealand, and Norway, began crossing the Channel back into France and started pinning the Germans all the way back into their own area. They might be brilliant at football. But the Germans didn't like it up them.

2. An ideal for which I am prepared to die, Nelson Mandela, April 20, 1964, Pretoria, South Africa

One of the many aspects of this eloquent, measured, and powerful speech that make it so remarkable is the fact that it was delivered in a Pretoria courtroom, from the dock, at the beginning of his trial for sabotage, high treason, and conspiracy to overthrow the government. Were he to be found guilty, Mandela faced the strong likelihood of being sentenced to death.

"This then is what the ANC is fighting. Their struggle is a truly national one. It is a struggle of the African people, inspired by their own suffering and their own experience. It is a struggle for the right to live. During my lifetime I have dedicated myself to this struggle of the African people. I have fought against white domination, and I have fought against black domination. I have cherished the ideal of a democratic and free society in which all persons live together in harmony and with equal opportunities. It is an ideal which I hope to live for and to achieve. But if needs be, it is an ideal for which I am prepared to die."

On June 12, 1964, at the conclusion of the trial, Mandela was found guilty on four charges of sabotage and was sentenced to life imprisonment.

3. Giving us freedom or giving us death, Emmeline Pankhurst, November 13, 1913, Hartford, Connecticut

Delivered to the Connecticut Women's Suffrage Association under the leadership of Katharine Houghton Hepburn (the mother of the movie actress). She was on a tour of the US, attempting to persuade American audiences in general, and suffragettes in particular, to adopt the same militant tactics as she had in Britain. She brilliantly ties her argument to the Yankee tradition of revolution and civil war, persuading her audience that not to allow women to use violence, when they had fought two wars, a revolution to free themselves, and a civil war to end slavery, was inconsistent. The entire audience would have been aware that just four months earlier, Emily Davison, one of Pankhurst's followers, had thrown herself in front of the king's horse at the English Derby and given her life to the cause.

"That is the way in which we women of England are doing. Human life for us is sacred, but we say if any life is to be sacrificed it shall be ours, we won't do it ourselves, but we will put the enemy in the position where they will have to choose between giving us freedom or giving us death."

4. This is not the Worcester, Mass., Boat Show, is it? I am sorry. I have made a terrible mistake, Will Ferrell, June 4, 2003, Harvard, Cambridge, Massachusetts

Dressed in full yacht club uniform, and entering dancing to "Celebrate good times, come on!" by Kool and the Gang, Will Ferrell delivered the comedy graduation speech to end all comedy graduation speeches.

"Let me paint a picture of what it's like out there. The last four or, for some of you, five years you've been living in a fantasyland, running around, talking about Hemingway, or Clancy, or, I don't know, I mean whatever you read here at Harvard. The novelization of *The Matrix*, I don't know. I don't know what you do here.

"But I do know this. You're about to enter into a world filled with hypocrisy and doublespeak, a world in which your limo to the airport is often a half hour late. In addition to not even being a limo at all; oftentimes it's a Lincoln Town Car. You're about to enter a world where you ask your new assistant, Jamie, to bring you a tall, nonfat latte. And he comes back with a short soy cappuccino."

5. We are going to keep the community center, Hugh Grant as George Wade, sometime in imaginary 2002, Legal Aid, somewhere in Brooklyn, New York

The boy gets girl back inducing speech from *Two Weeks Notice*, my favorite romcom ever. And I love a romcom. Makes me cry every time, even when I'm not on a plane. Hugh Grant reminds me so much of my brother. And Sandra Bullock is the Willian of female movie stars—unsure about her at first, but now always so good, even when everyone else around her is crap.

"I need your advice on one last thing, then I promise you will never hear from me again. You see, I've just delivered the first speech I've written entirely by myself since we met, and I think I may have blown it. I want to ask your thoughts. Okay? Then I will read it to you.

" 'I'd like to welcome everyone on this special day. Island Towers will bring glamour and prestige to the neighborhood and become part of Brooklyn's renaissance. And I'm very pleased and proud to be here. Unfortunately, there is one fly in the ointment. You see, I gave my word to someone that we wouldn't knock down this building behind me. And normally, and those of you who know me or were married

Spite-tracking: The newfound ability and willingness of wide attacking players (particularly Pedro and Hazard), to track back and defend under a new manager (Guus Hiddink, Antonio Conte), after showing absolutely no interest in doing the same under their former manager (Mourinho), for whom wide players tracking back was a central tenet of his tactical philosophy. Distant relative of spite-striking (Diego Costa). And spite-playmaking (Cesc Fàbregas).

Stay in Charge: Joe Blake has been my friend for almost twenty years. At the wrong side of fifty he is, in every way, the prototype for the most interesting man in the world, if the most interesting man in the world was younger, better-looking, and more in charge. The concept of "staying in charge" started to be propagated by Joe sometime around the advent of text messaging amongst American males. It is his regular sign-off. But it is written with purpose. It means never let anyone, and most of all yourself, feel like you're not in control of a situation. Particularly an uncomfortable situation. Or when you're not actually in charge. Those three simple words have powered me through breakups, firings, insane negotiations, awkward social encounters, and facing Rog across the table in my office on Tuesdays after Chelsea have lost and Everton have won. Stay in Charge doesn't mean being an a-hole or insensitive, it just means own your reality, believe in yourself, and act in a way that you can always be proud of. It is the single greatest piece of advice I have ever been given. And it has become the single piece of advice I most often, almost exclusively give. So, whatever you have to deal with after putting down this book—do it with purpose and self-belief. Stay in charge. **—MD**

to me can attest to this, my word wouldn't mean very much. So why does it this time? Well, partly because this building is an architectural gem and deserves to be landmarked and partly because people really do need a place to do senior's water ballet and CPR. Preferably not together. But mainly because this person, despite being unusually stubborn and unwilling to compromise and a very poor dresser, is . . . she's rather like the building she loves so much. A little rough around the edges but, when you look closely, absolutely beautiful. And the only one of her kind. And even though I've said cruel things and driven her away, she's become the voice in my head. And I can't seem to drown her out. And I don't want to drown her out. So, we are going to keep the community center. Because I gave my word to her and because we gave our word to the community.'

"And I didn't sleep with June. That's not in the speech, that's just me letting you know that important fact." **—MD**

Stoke: Old English *"stoc"* meaning "place" or settlement. The modern area—a collective noun for six old towns—has not changed much since then. Depending on how you experience it, Stoke is either a region lost in the past of

England's fading fine china industry or a futuristic glimpse of what postapocalyptic Britain could look like.

I had traveled there to film an interview with then Stoke City goalkeeper Asimir Begović and made the mistake of stopping off at what felt like the "downtown" equivalent in search of some fish and chips before heading to the airport. Picture a semideserted dilapidated shopping area in which not a chain store could be seen, only small, run-down stores with crude puns in the name like "Floors for Thought," a home furnisher's, and "Our Soles," a shoe outlet.

The only other human beings visible were kids roving in small gangs. I pegged them between the ages of eight and twelve, though it was hard to tell, because I am not good at decoding the age of molemen. As we had driven into the area, a number had stared at us without emotion whilst we searched for parking. No sooner had we jumped out and started to feed the meter than a small knot sauntered toward us. As I squinted at them in the late afternoon light, I saw to my astonishment they were all armed with bricks and hammers. One girl had a five-foot-long piece of lumber, casually propped against her shoulder. As a stab of panic kicked in, I made a rough calculation of the distance to the chip shop and realized we would never make it, and so made an executive decision to abort mission and dive right back into the car. Even as we sped off, the facial expressions of the Stoke brick-wielding urchins did not change. They remained eerily emotionless. It felt like middle England had been taken over by zombies à la *World War Z*. Once I had regained control of my sphincter, I muttered a silent prayer for Geoff Cameron and urged the Lord to deliver him from all evil. **—RB**

Stone, Rob: An American hero. The Kofi Annan between American soccer's Israel and Palestine (Warren Barton and Eric Wynalda) on the FOX Soccer couch. Rog believes a Rob Stone eau de cologne would grant all those who

wear it instant desirability and the appearance of great dental work.

Subbuteo: The obsession of every football-loving European under the age of thirteen in the 1970s. An era akin to the dark ages, in that video games had yet to be invented. All we needed to fire up our imagination back then was a team of tiny little  plastic men on weighted bases we would flick at a giant hollow football around a tabletop "pitch" laid out on the bedroom floor.

Teams could be purchased in hundreds of colors and combinations to match any football fan's real-life club. I played with Everton as my home kit, and the Israeli national team as my alternate away combination. Though the figures themselves were just an inch high, when I flicked them with my fingernail I experienced a singular dizzying delight, and was instantly transported from my own dank, damp surrounds to such fantastical sporting

My carrying case was my prize possession when I was nine. My teams were Israel and Everton. Note the oilie sticker bottom left, which made it all extra cool.

cauldrons as the Maracanã, Wembley, and La Bombonera in my imagination.

My Subbuteo passion peaked in 1983. I welcomed in New Year's Day by spending much of the afternoon in a state of Subbuteo-induced frenzy as I lined up my players for a team photo shoot. The diary I used to keep calls the plastic men "My best friends in the world." The off-centered photo I finally took of them does not do their square-jawed masculinity justice. It mattered not, for even as the shutter snapped on my camera, the technological revolution was sweeping the globe and was poised to turn my world upside down.

At the end of the year, my bar mitzvah rolled around. Its legacy was a ZX Spectrum personal computer with its tinny sound, garish colors, and a primitive soccer-action game, *Match Day*. The game graphics may have had all the subtlety of a kindergartener's crayon drawing. Its crowd could best be described as "senior citizen's belch." Yet the game was crack-cocaine addictive. A small pile of books and cassette tapes soon began to build on the formerly hal-

The team lineup for a preseason photo

lowed Subbuteo turf suddenly unused in the center of my bedroom.

When I became a father of sons, and those kids turned seven and five respectively, I unpacked the Subbuteo relics—the replica playing field and the two, heroic teams—from my wardrobe. The knot of excitement I experienced in my stomach as I fastidiously laid them out in my boys' New York bedroom was almost incapacitating until I looked up at my kids and

I kept voluminous notes on every game. Note: Pennants were exchanged before big games.

saw them recoiling as they stared back at their father and the twenty-two plastic figures he was maniacally flicking around the flimsy polyester cutting.

To me, the little plastic players were humans with free will. (*actual size*)

I quickly returned the players to their plastic carrying case, and folded the playing field back into neat squares. We have not talked about the matter again. One of the players now adorns my desk, fitting in between a signed Hank Greenberg baseball and an Alexi Lalas action figure. Whenever I glimpse the little plastic Subbuteo fellow, in his standard pose, with arms poised for action at his sides, I am reminded of this dream world propelled by the power of imagination, fantasy, and projection. No different really than the Premier League is to me today. **—RB**

Superstitions: Football is rife with them. Be it the Holy Water former Italian manager Giovanni Trapattoni used to sprinkle on the field pregame, supplied by his sister, the nun, or John Terry, who used to listen to the same Usher CD and sit in the same seat on the bus pregame. Players and coaches are not the only ones suffering from the magical burden of superstition.

If I am watching Everton Football Club, and they happen to be down a goal at halftime, I believe that the act of my moving seats—from the armchair to the left side of the couch—can empower Everton to force themselves back into the game. I do this even though I am over 3,000 miles away from the game and the players have no knowledge of my tactical furniture shift. To be honest, I do this even if the game I am watching is DVR'd and not live. If you are reading this, you may well be reminded of certain irrational behaviors you exhibit whilst watching the team you love: a certain item of clothing that must be worn, or a particular onion dip which it is compulsory to serve.

All of this only began to make sense to me when I read the work of twentieth-century American psychologist B. F. Skinner, who explored what he called "Superstitious Conditioning." Skinner studied pigeons and would reward them with food pellets if they followed his training and learned how to play "Take Me Out to the Ball Game" on a xylophone. Skinner noted how his subjects would perform behaviors he had not taught them—little skips, or dances—but that they thought were part of the conditioning and so incorporated into the ritual of xylophone playing. So even though we may be different—Everton fan or Chelsea supporter, Arsenal or Spurs—we are all just pigeons hungering after food pellets. **—RB**

T

Take That, Gloria!: A phrase that captures the extent to which football support is emotional rather than rational relayed to us by my Arsenal-loving friend Dan Harverd, who went to watch the Gunners battle Liverpool in the 1987 League Cup final at Wembley. When Arsenal took the lead in the 83rd minute, a stranger sitting behind Dan leapt into the air and repeatedly screamed "Take that, Gloria!" Dan has always been an inquisitive type of gent, so as the excitement surrounding the goal died down, he turned round and asked the stranger who this mysterious "Gloria" was. With no hesitation, the middle-aged Arsenal fan explained Gloria was the name of his ex-wife, a Liverpool-born lass whom he had come home from work one afternoon and found in bed with his best friend. The more we think about this story, the more we realize football fandom is actually quite rational after all. —RB

Talisker: The only Scotch I drink, distilled since 1830 on the remote Scottish island of Skye. I drink it for the memory as much as the taste—and the taste is heavenly. Yet I first supped Talisker, when a good mate of mine, Dan (*see* Take That, Gloria!), and I elected to mark the last day of university by hitchhiking to the most remote part of the country we both could think of. With the spirit of manic adventure gripping us, we found ourselves on a highway entrance ramp just outside of Leeds at five o'clock in the morning.

In our hands we carried a cardboard sign proclaiming "Isle of Skye" in black marker. We had giggled as we wrote it. The destination seemed as nonsensical as selecting "Mars" or "Qatar" as our goal. Yet within three or four minutes of revealing the sign and extending our thumbs to passing motorists, an open-backed truck screeched to a halt in front of us. "Get in, lads," the driver boomed. "I am going to the Isle of Skye." When the driver said "in" he technically meant, "into the back of his truck." A wagon that was packed full of dead sheep. And so we sat there confused at what had just occurred as we bounced around for ten hours on the back of a wagon's worth of animal corpses.

Rog, about to hitch to Skye and have his life changed forever

We drove through the day, and as the afternoon light faded we found ourselves on the small ferry connecting Skye (population 10,008) to the mainland. The scenic isle is famed for its rugged cliffs, medieval ruins, and scattered fishing villages. Dan and I saw none of that. We set up a small tent in a field near the Talisker distillery and did not leave it for a week, until the smell of the local Scotch oozing from our pores had finally overwhelmed the stench of rotting mutton. —RB

Tattoos: Footballing life, a combination of piles of cash and too much free time, can create both a culture of boredom and a yearning for self-expression. As a result, world football has become Ground Zero for terrible tattoos as elite athletes compete to make a statement by inking

The Worst Tattoos in Football

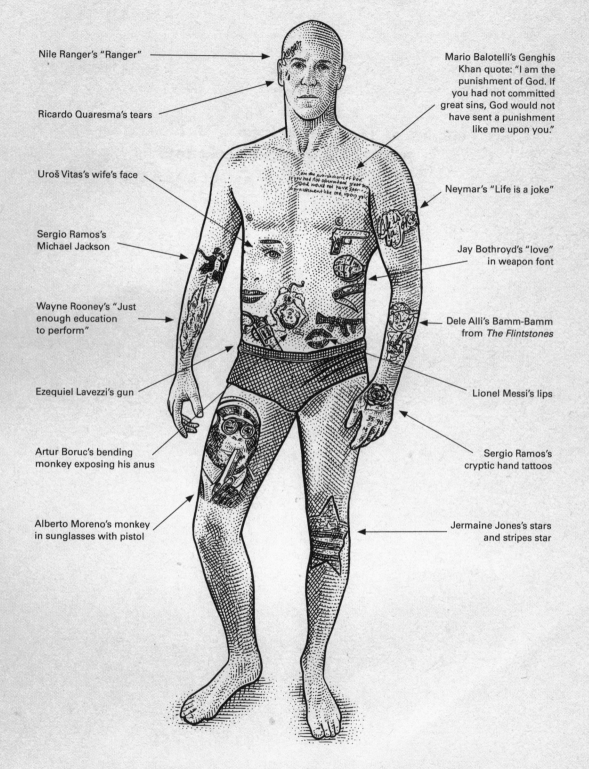

Nile Ranger's "Ranger"

Ricardo Quaresma's tears

Uroš Vitas's wife's face

Sergio Ramos's Michael Jackson

Wayne Rooney's "Just enough education to perform"

Ezequiel Lavezzi's gun

Artur Boruc's bending monkey exposing his anus

Alberto Moreno's monkey in sunglasses with pistol

Mario Balotelli's Genghis Khan quote: "I am the punishment of God. If you had not committed great sins, God would not have sent a punishment like me upon you."

Neymar's "Life is a joke"

Jay Bothroyd's "love" in weapon font

Dele Alli's Bamm-Bamm from *The Flintstones*

Lionel Messi's lips

Sergio Ramos's cryptic hand tattoos

Jermaine Jones's stars and stripes star

THE WORST TATTOOS IN FOOTBALL

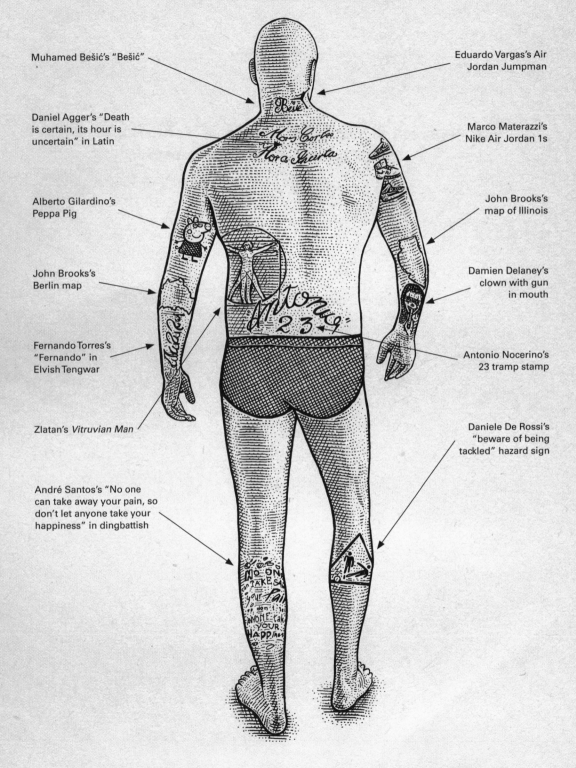

Muhamed Bešić's "Bešić"

Daniel Agger's "Death is certain, its hour is uncertain" in Latin

Alberto Gilardino's Peppa Pig

John Brooks's Berlin map

Fernando Torres's "Fernando" in Elvish Tengwar

Zlatan's *Vitruvian Man*

André Santos's "No one can take away your pain, so don't let anyone take your happiness" in dingbattish

Eduardo Vargas's Air Jordan Jumpman

Marco Materazzi's Nike Air Jordan 1s

John Brooks's map of Illinois

Damien Delaney's clown with gun in mouth

Antonio Nocerino's 23 tramp stamp

Daniele De Rossi's "beware of being tackled" hazard sign

the tools of their trade—their own limbs, demonstrating worse decision making than jailed Russian criminals or even Arsenal-era Nicklas Bendtner in front of goal. Dragons, full-sized angel wings, and Michael Jackson portraits abound. The worst though is Polish goalkeeper Artur Boruc, who has etched a monkey around his belly button. It is portrayed bending over, exposing its sphincter which is exactly where his belly button is. A sight gag. For life.

Tattoo: Which Would We Get?
DAVO: Form is temporary, class is permanent" or "England first, football second, Chelsea third"
ROGER: "Everton: America's team, not in the face, not in the face"

Team Talk: Some managers believe the English legend Sir Alf Ramsey to have uttered these borderline Churchillian words to urge his charges on to victory in extra time during the 1966 World Cup final: "'Ou've won it once. Now 'ou'll have to go out there and win it again"—others put no stock in them at all. Another ex–England manager, Sven-Göran Eriksson, revealed there is so much adrenaline flowing around the locker room during a game, a manager "might as well drink a cup of tea, as the players will not hear a word he says." Yet my favorite team talk of all was given by Sir Alex Ferguson. Former United captain Roy Keane told the story in his autobiography of how Sir Alex just walked in and said, "Lads, it's Tottenham." Three words he knew that would ensure victory.

Tennis Players: Growing up in England, it was never wise to use the word "Jewish" in public, and so the small community adopted the code word "Tennis Player" for common usage. Such a phrasing is common around the world. In Montreal, they employ the word "Eskimo" for the same purpose. A friend of mine from Cleveland used the word "Amish." Our London cousins preferred "Merchants of Tennis," which always seemed poetic yet cumbersome.

Until I understood what the term was and why it was used, my mother and grandmother seemed to be perpetually engrossed in conversations about tennis. Once I was clued in, the code word quickly became second nature. Fast-forward twenty-five years, and the proud moment my father and I took my oldest son, Samson, then six years of age, to his first Everton game at Goodison Park. The Blues were playing West Ham, who fielded American international Jonathan Spector, a Jewish defender from Illinois.

Once Everton took to the field, Goodison Park turned into a cauldron, and by the time the PA announcer rattled through the West Ham lineup of "Green, Faubert, Da Costa, Upson, Spector . . ." you had to scream just to be heard by your seatmates. However, the presence of a Premier League footballer of the "Mosaic Persuasion" was such a rare occurrence, I felt compelled to alert my father to his existence, which I did by bellowing, "Dad, the West Ham defender is a TENNIS PLAYER." To which my six-year-old son who was sitting sandwiched in between us proudly added, "Yes, and he is JEWISH too." My father paled instantly, diving on my grandson as if he could somehow stuff the offending word right back into this mouth. He looked around in panic as if a horde of three hundred Cossacks would come riding our way and cut us down like in the Old Country. Oddly enough, we happened to be sitting in a block of Russians, family members of Everton's Moscow-born midfielder Diniyar Bilyaletdinov. Luckily they spoke no English, and so the pogrom of my father's imagination never came. But I have always been fond of the code words Jews around the world have employed to mask their identities and have collected them faithfully over the years. Here are my ten favorites:

Accountant, Akron, Ohio
Black Belt, Birmingham, England
Canadian, Detroit, Michigan
Cossack, London, England
Irishman, Toronto, Canada

Jazz Singer, San Francisco, California
Jedi, Los Angeles, California
Kissinger, Washington, DC
Moaner, London, England
Versace, Miami, Florida —RB

"There Are Two Kinds of People in the World . . .": The fact that we say this all the time on *Men in Blazers* suggests that we should know by now that there are far more than two kinds of people in the world. Here is a definitive list of how the world is split:

There are two kinds of people in the world . . .

. . . Those who are Red, and those who are Blue.

. . . Those who wonder what Julia Roberts was thinking when she married Lyle Lovett and those who wonder what on earth Lyle Lovett was thinking when he married Julia Roberts.

. . . Those whose parents left their bedrooms intact as a shrine when they left home and those whose parents immediately converted their childhood bedroom into a "Mum's gym/Dad's home office" combo.

. . . Those who have a recurring dream they are flying (Rog's dad) and those who have a recurring dream they are falling from the sky and plummeting toward the ground (Rog's mum).

. . . Those who love summer and the opportunity it brings to show off their body in shorts and muscle tees and those who crave the snuggly embrace of a good chunky cardigan that winter offers.

. . . Those who hate their birthdays and attempt to avoid any public celebration and those who need to be feted by a week of Viking-esque pageantry.

. . . Those who watch *Men in Blazers* and those who have good taste in football podcasts and television.

Tie Knots with Kyle Martino: Kyle Martino is a man blessed with many skills. A US international who has seamlessly transitioned into broadcasting, he has become most famous for his ability to conjure the most perfectly swollen, bulbous tie knots ever seen on television. Kyle was good enough to reveal his black belt tie-knotting techniques. Go for it America.

Step One: Choose the right material. The secret to bloated tie knotting lies in the fundamentals. It is all about the girth of the material you arm yourself with. You need a tie that feels it is made from the kind of fabric that could be found hanging from your mother's drapes.

Step Two: Go Cantona. Collars up . . .

Step Three: You are looking to line up the skinny part halfway down the fat part for optimal results to come.

Step Four: We are crossing once. Start with standard knotting approach. Do not be afraid to keep things basic at the outset.

Step Five: Arlo White talks about the corridor of uncertainty behind the defense. What we are creating here is the "Triangle of Absurdity." This is the crucial move. This triangle is the foundation. It is as fundamental as the hair gel that keeps my hair up. It is like a fullback overlapping the winger and the center back overlapping him. A double overlapping run.

Step Six: Now you know that something is happening. That you have a big fish hooked on the line. You are in the Major Leagues. You are not going home from the bar alone. If you are an all-out girth-lover, the art lies in not pulling up the knot too hard. The dirty secret of television is you do not have to pull the tie down too far. You can just mask the tie end with your jacket and hide all the wires.

Step Seven: Look at yourself in the mirror and ask yourself, what kind of guy am I going to be today? I am going to be the guy with tie elephantiasis. You are committing. So be prepared. Know this is the tie equivalent of when Mike Tyson got that face tattoo.

The Tingling: That electric nipple feeling which strikes any football fan when they watch Romelu Lukaku barrel toward the opposition defense with the ball at his feet, or Eden Hazard mesmerize his opponents with a through ball that cuts out the backline. In truth, the feeling

can also be caused by hormonal changes, nerve damage, or medication applied to the nipple area. A GFOP, Brian Dickerson, wrote to us to provide an analysis of the overall malady:

Hello gents—

My wife and I watch your show religiously . . . well—more like I watch your show religiously and she sits next to me checking Facebook and glancing towards the TV and laughing. During a recent episode—she mentioned that she believes Rog is suffering from a condition called "paresthesia."

Not realizing what she was referring to at the time—I hazarded a guess. "Is paresthesia a cause of baldness?" She replied: "Not that . . . the nipple tingling."

You see, my wife is a lactation consultant . . . and nipples are her area of expertise. (She's seen more nipples than you and I ever will by a long mile. Even you Davo.)

She went on to explain paresthesia is a sensation of partial numbness or tingling of the nipples that can come as a result of a tight-fitting bra or shirt . . . and from the sound of it, Rog may have a pretty serious case.

Fortunately there is an easy-to-use product she recommends to her clients in cases like this. Rog should be in touch if he needs advice for the brand of Nipple Butter he needs to employ.

Best—

Brian (& Dawn) Dickerson

Tiny Bananas: Landing in Brazil the day the 2014 World Cup kicked off, we experienced two striking first impressions. The first was the extent to which Brazilians so admired Barry Manilow that they named a beach after one of his songs. The second was just how tiny their bananas were. As if they had been harvested off bonsai trees by a pack of Smurfs.

A spot of speedy research unearthed the fact that Tiny Bananas were first reported in sixth century BC Buddhist writing. Also known as "Lady Fingers," the fruit are a product of a lack

of water and intense heat, which force a banana to charge through its development process at helter-skelter speed. Their omnipresence across Rio made us imagine modern-day Brazilian tourists walking around New York City awestruck. Not at the Statue of Liberty or Times Square, but at the immense size and girth of our wholesome American fruit.

Tiricoism: A monotheistic spiritual movement founded during the 2014 World Cup based on a loose set of precepts which posited ESPN's on-air personality, Mike Tirico, is a deity largely based around his permanent state of near-ecstatic bliss. Rog and Davo were the first disciples of this Tirico death cult, which has yet to spread.

With the high priest of Tiricoism

Toilet: Rog's nickname as a youth. Stolen from Brian McClair, a Scottish striker who plied his trade at Manchester United in the early 1990s, but who was so crap he earned the endearing fan-generated nickname "Toilet."

Top Trumps: Simply put, the greatest card game ever invented. According to seven-year-old Rog and any child, in any British schoolyard in the long summer running up to the 1978 World Cup. The rules were simple. The players divide up the cards, and call a category—"Goals" or "Games Played." The owner of the highest-scoring card wins the rest. Just looking at the

WORLD CUP '78

TOP TRUMPS

FREE pack offer inside !

Argentina

Daniel Killer

World Cup Appearances	0
World Cup Goals	0
International Appearances	19
International Goals	2
Height	6' 2''

Brazil

Alberto Rivelino

World Cup Appearances	12
World Cup Goals	6
International Appearances	117
International Goals	38
Height	5' 10''

Scotland

Archie Gemmil

World Cup Appearances	1
World Cup Goals	0
International Appearances	23
International Goals	2
Height	5' 5''

West Germany

Berti Vogts

World Cup Appearances	12
World Cup Goals	0
International Appearances	86
International Goals	0
Height	5' 5''

France

Michel Platini

World Cup Appearances	0
World Cup Goals	0
International Appearances	13
International Goals	8
Height	5' 10''

Holland

Jan Peters

World Cup Appearances	0
World Cup Goals	0
International Appearances	12
International Goals	2
Height	5' 5¾''

Iran

Ali Parvin

World Cup Appearances	0
World Cup Goals	0
International Appearances	81
International Goals	19
Height	5' 7''

France

Dominique Rocheteau

World Cup Appearances	0
World Cup Goals	0
International Appearances	10
International Goals	2
Height	5' 9''

cover card tells you this game was produced in a more innocent time. A time in which a company could produce a World Cup product featuring images of the world's best football players, replete with their stats, and not have applied for a single license nor trademark. There is not a single mention of the word "FIFA." This game is a throwback to an age before corruption had even been invented. Michel Platini is involved—but only as his own playing card. Back then he was just a curly-haired young midfielder yet to take the world by storm.

The greats are all here. Rivelino, Dino Zoff, and Deyna. Back then, English football was immensely parochial. In the pre-Internet era, these trading cards were the first time we had heard of any of these players. We would flick through and see the bold perm of a player like Daniel Killer of Argentina or the rippled thighs of Paulo César and gasp at their beauty. We reproduce a glut of the cards here in the hope you see fit to take a pair of scissors to this book, and make your own set, and be transported to a more innocent time when football was clearly just a game, Sepp Blatter was an unknown, and the World Cup was yet to become a solar eclipse which would cast its shadow across the entire globe.

Tramp Stamp: The weekend *Men in Blazers* launched on NBC, our screens were graced by a stout ginger-haired Stoke City fan who reacted to his team scoring by uncorking a wobbling dance of celebration which revealed to a global viewing audience the Slipknot tramp stamp he had inked onto his lower back. The world recoiled in horror as this one gentleman undid decades of dedicated promotional work by the Stoke Tourist Board. We have oft wondered since then, whether his could be the worst tramp stamp of all time. Here were three deemed worse by GFOPs:

3. Grateful Dead logo
2. Barry Manilow's signature
1. That Southern guy from the reality show

Party Down South who has a tramp stamp that says "Tramp Stamp."

Transfer Deadline Day: The day the transfer window closes is one of our favorites of the season. The Premier League is always built on narrative, fantasy, and hope but for the last thirty-six hours of the window that sporting telenovela goes into overdrive. Every football fan believes in leprechauns, dodos, unicorns, and a top-four finish as the emotions of surprise, boredom, fear, love, and hate collide on a cliché-ridden day in which these terms run rife:

"come and get me plea"
"derisory offer"
"waiting for the fax to come through"
"dream come true to return to my boyhood club"

It's a day propelled by middle-aged English football journalists who shamelessly work themselves into a frenzy before a live worldwide audience, frantically working their phones to fill the dead air, even if nothing is happening.

A day of rumors and gossip in which the EPL becomes TMZ—and Twitter comes alight with rumors Messi has been seen at Norwich airport or that someone's brother's hairdresser's dad works security at Bournemouth and has just escorted Mario Balotelli into the Vitality Stadium.

A day in which the driver-side car window reigns, a mysterious camera angle allowing the interviewee to cloak their intentions rather than shed light on them.

When clusters of acne-ridden English youths linger outside of stadiums late at night, surrounding reporters as they break news. Like villagers ready to storm a castle. Proof there are some corners of England in which the medieval ages have never ended.

A day of domino effects—when one move will suddenly trigger a spasm of others—some of which will be season-altering, some sure to stink more than Drakkar Noir.

Random Brazilian superstars jet into Manchester never quite sure if they have just signed for United or City.

When an Instagram photograph of incoming players wearing their new club colors can send grown men and women into raptures.

Some teams will acquire the missing piece they need to put them over the top.

Others will sabotage themselves and poison the locker room culture with desperate last-minute panic buys. Still others will have their heart ripped out of them by teams higher up the food chain. Disaster hangs over every fan like a guillotine blade. At the same time, the delusion the cavalry is about to arrive never leaves you—especially if you are an Arsenal fan. And that is what makes it such a special day—twenty-four hours lived suspended between doom and hope, agony and delirium—the distilled essence of football fandom.

"Trap It with Your Thumb": My father is offended by many things. All noises made by all football crowds. Tomato ketchup, which is to be avoided at all costs ("ersatz and vile"), and especially by children. The use of the word "hopefully." Hugging. Closing a car door too firmly or not firmly enough. Cowering from the rain. Grunting by tennis players. Sound, in general, emanating from his grandchildren or their toys. However, THERE IS NOTHING MORE OFFENSIVE TO MY FATHER than the sound of silverware clanging against china as people (how he refers to us, his family) stand up from the table and clear our plates. Hence, his highly effective and strangely satisfying solution. Line up your silverware, knife and fork, or, God forbid, fork and spoon, next to each other on the plate, and trap it with your thumb against the plate before you even think of rising from the table. These five words were said to us so often as children that to this day I cannot come to the end of any meal without reciting them to myself. Or under my breath to waiters or busboys as they clear my meal. —MD

Tropical Clime: A weather condition prevalent in such fine nations as Suriname, Guadeloupe, and Montserrat that creates a quandary. What is the most appropriate blazer fabric to counter tropical humidity? We are asked that question all the time. Michael admires linen in principle, yet its creaseability makes it a hard fabric to rely on in reality. A Japanese chambray is his blazer of choice, as the way it creases only adds to its allure. Rog dreams of a summer tweed but adores seersucker, the fabric of American democracy. If he owned a football team, the home kits would be cut out of seersucker.

Truth in Football: "There is no truth in football." This was said to me by either Barry Hearn or Joey Barton. And as I have never met Joey Barton, it must have been Barry. Or maybe Warren Barton. Whoever said it, it has become one of my central tenets in the observation of Premier League and international football.

What is the truth of the situation that forced Mourinho out of Stamford Bridge so abruptly in December 2015? Was it the Eva Carneiro fiasco? Had he lost the players? Was it the players' fault? Or was it a combination of all of those? Were there additional reasons we still haven't heard about?

When is a handball deliberate handball and when is it not deliberate? When is allowing the ball to strike the hand so negligent that it reaches the level of deliberate intent? How many players would ever deliberately handle the ball in the area to concede a penalty?

What level would an MLS team fit into in the English league system? Are the present Arsenal team better than the Arsenal Invincibles, who went unbeaten in the league in the 2003–04 season? Who's better, Harry Kane or Jamie Vardy? Were either of them as good as Diego Costa? Was Diego Costa actually evil? Often Rog and I watch the same "truth," the same match, and see it completely differently. Stendahl, major GFOP, once wrote, "I cannot provide the reality of events, I can only convey their shadow." Rog and I often, clearly, see different shadows.

"The truth is rarely pure and never simple." So says one of Oscar Wilde's characters, not much of a GFOP, in *The Importance of Being Earnest*. The truth is, most "truth" is only true as far as it is verifiable, and much truth is only opinion. Which is my way of concluding that Diego Costa is just misunderstood. —MD

Tuxedo T-shirt: The only T-shirt it is permissible to wear past the age of forty.

Tweed: A fabric that appears to have romance woven into its fibers. Dirty Harry wore it. So did Miss Marple. The earthy fabric has noble roots. Woven on Scottish estates to keep the aristocracy warm whilst they hunted and fished in winter. The fabric's names resound as if they tumbled from a D. H. Lawrence novel: Gamekeeper, Thornproof, and Cheviot, the latter named for a breed of white-face sheep that populate the Scottish borders. Harris Tweed is the definitive brand. Protected by British law, and marked by the distinctive orb logo, the fabric has been handwoven by an islander on the Outer Hebrides.

The manufacturers of Johnnie Walker recently unveiled a new Harris smart fabric that permanently gave off the smell of whisky. Yet, every tweed garment I own already smells of Scotch in my mind, because to wear a tweed jacket is to don a magical cloak that stirs up the wearer's imagination. Which is why it makes perfect sense to me that George Mallory would attempt to climb Everest wearing the fabric. Yes, he died, and his body was entombed in a block of ice for seventy-five years, but as I am sure he would have agreed: Style hurts. —RB

U

Unbelievable!: Arlo White informed us that his producers have banned him from saying this word. Their logic: If something is unbelievable it could not, by definition, have happened. When Leicester City lifted the Premier League trophy after their fantastical 2015–16 campaign, perhaps at our prodding, Arlo, a lifelong Leicester fan, screamed, "Some might say this is unbelievable . . ."

Universal Language of Football: Every professional team is a veritable Tower of Babel. Composed of personnel ingathered from across the footballing diaspora. Goalkeeper Petr Čech once admitted he spoke to his Arsenal backline in three languages—French, German, and presumably Huttese. But not every footballer is blessed with Čech's polylingual ability. Footballers, after all, are not always known for their IQs. It is no surprise then that the world of football has developed its own sign language. A kind of Premier League Esperanto:

I am an awful person (The fictional red card)
I am angry (The managerial cold shoulder)
I am REALLY angry (Storming down the tunnel)
I am on the verge of self-combusting (Throwing your gloves down on the pitch)
I hate my current team and wish I had never left my old one (The non–celebration goal celebration when a player scores on a former club)
I am in control of all affairs (Manager attempting to effect calm by scribbling in notebook furiously when his team concede)

I probably did foul him, but please don't call it (Diving motion)
I just had a baby (Thumb-sucking goal celebration)
I am angry (The half butt)
I am aware human beings are powerless in the face of fate (Managers checking their watches in injury time)

US Soccer Badge: We adore US Soccer and have since we first saw the be-denied World Cup team swagger onto the field in 1994. Yet, if you take our passion for US Soccer, and think about its antonym—that is the extent to which we hate the US Soccer logo. It is less than a logo, more a placeholder. The soccer ball flying wildly was the most insecure sporting design decision ever made. A symbol of a craven need to provide the rest of the country with an aide-mémoire as to what sport is being played here.

Where to begin? Perhaps with the crap font which resembles Tablet Gothic Heavy Oblique or even Futura Bold Oblique. The three stars which top off the design connoting only the designer's desperate desire to fill in empty space

Old and crap   New, yet still crap

with "football-like stuff." And the actual trajectory of the ball—hurtling upward—suggests the badge is either celebrating a goal kick or a wildly hacked shot over the bar.

USMNT: The Quest for a Crest

In 2016, US Soccer retired that crest and replaced it with a new confection . . . a shield with thirteen stripes said to symbolize the original colonies. The consensus amongst fans as "underwhelming," deriding the design for its "Autobot" qualities, comparing it to a discarded design for a Marvel superhero's shield. We could do better. Mediocre clip art would be better. As a public service we have invited three of our favorite designers to take a crack at a logo worthy of being eliminated in the round of 16 come World Cup 2022.

Peter Mendelsund and Oliver Munday

Gregg Kulick

Kamp Grizzly

USWNT: The Movie

The USWNT's 2015 World Cup victory engaged the nation in a sense of ecstatic collective rapture, summoning the kind of emotions that heretofore had been catalyzed only by a made-for-television movie on the Hallmark Channel. Recognizing the size and nature of the opportunity, we interviewed squad members during their march to triumph and asked them whom we should cast in the Hallmark movie. Below are their choices.

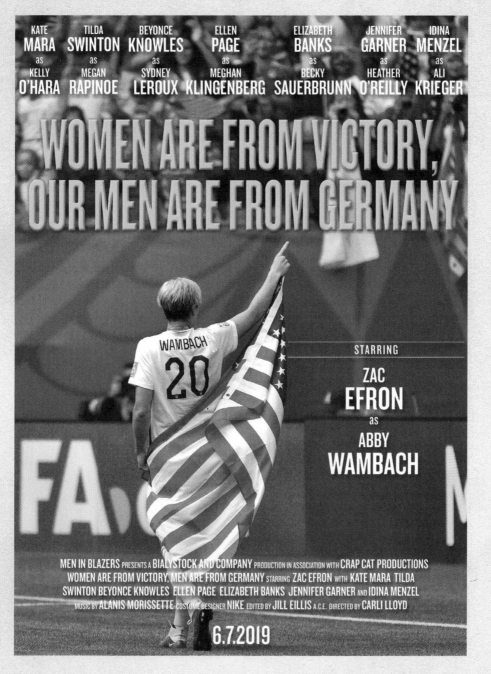

V

Van Buren, Ashley: Holder of the @AVB handle, New York–based writer/producer/director who was constantly mistaken for former Chelsea and Tottenham manager André Villas-Boas, and, therefore,  constantly subjected to misdirected but vile abuse on social media.

> **Follow Ashley Van Buren** @avb
> Reminder that I am NOT the UK football coach, so if you send me a death threat meant for him, I'm gonna tweet you a musical theater lyric.
> 9:55 AM - 15 Dec 2013
> 3,844 3,844 Retweets 1,008 1,008 likes

van Gaal, Louis: The Dutch manager arrived at Manchester United in 2014 with his Champions League winning pedigree and rolling gate, parading around with arms behind back, stomach pushed out like a spike-crested peacock, hair stiffly at attention, and lips pursed as if in vague disgust.

In July 2014, van Gaal announced it would take him three months to figure out his strategy and execute that vision. Yet, a year later, his United squad remained paralyzed, favoring possession over purpose, and sterile territorial dominance over the creation of goal-scoring chances. Watching the English tabloid media crack the Dutchman's stoic mask was as harrowing a spectacle as bearbaiting. Van Gaal was transformed from a man of arrogant self-confidence to a broken, confused old man, haunting the halls of Old Trafford like a depressed turkey. By the time the sixty-three-year-old Dutchman was finally fired in May 2016, it felt like a mercy killing. With the arrival of José Mourinho, Manchester United instantly became 79 percent more tactically astute, yet 87 percent less comic.

Villainy: Football is a spectacle as much as a sport. A human drama incorporating triumph and failure, glory and pain, heroes and villains. Every act of creative brilliance can be matched by a moment of unfathomable stupidity and violence. Both become forged in spectators' memories and cause the adrenaline to flow, creating players we love, and others we love to hate.

French philosopher Roland Barthes wrote about the critical role rule-breaking heels play in his essay "The World of Wrestling." "For a fan nothing is finer than the revengeful fury of a betrayed fighter who throws himself not on a successful opponent but on the smarting image of foul play." In soccer as in wrestling, it is not just the unpredictability of the violence that thrills the viewer, it is the emotional hook his act creates, keeping the audience glued to the game, desperate for the evildoer to be defeated. Not just to lose, but be made to pay.

In that light, let us take a second to pay homage to the game's assorted villains and thank them for their two-footed tackles, untamed egos, and hint of evil. Be it the casual racism of John Terry, the oral fixation of Luis Suárez, or our imagined dark side of Martin Škrtel, a man who looks like he partakes in ethnic cleansing as a hobby. These vaudeville villains are why we watch the game. As José Mourinho so sagely recognized when Diego Costa had clutched his face in playacting agony in order to persuade a bewildered referee to send off an Arsenal defender, "If you want to speak about Diego Costa with me, just say he played like he has to play and that's why you have full stadiums, you sell to televisions all around the world for millions and millions because the game has to be played like that."

Villas-Boas, André: Luís André de Pina Cabral e Villas-Boas, also known as AVB, replaced Carlo Ancelotti through the brutally fast-moving, Russian-propelled, early-twenty-first-century revolving door of Chelsea managers in 2011. Ancelotti had committed the crime of a second-place finish in the Premier League after winning a Premier League/FA Cup double the year before and AVB no doubt highlighted that in the PowerPoint he prepared to pitch the job. Just like the PowerPoint he prepared when applying for a job at Burnley one year earlier.

"He sent a very detailed and lengthy application for the job. His CV and PowerPoint presentation were amazing. Even by today's standards there was some complicated stuff in it, with some things that I didn't understand," said former Burnley chief executive Paul Fletcher when explaining why he didn't give the young Portuguese coach the job.

In his forlorn and desperate spells at Chelsea and then Tottenham there was always something rather sad about AVB. He was younger than his senior players. And seemed to grow more gingery with every loss. He knelt a lot, and held his chin and analyzed. But this always seemed designed for the cameras. So we would think he was really thoughtful and tactical. He was like the hot new marketing guy at the hot new company who everyone thinks is so cool until they realize they don't understand a word he's saying, or what he's trying to do, or even if

he knows what he's really saying or trying to do. He did always dress well. But the stealth Gingie never seemed so surprised as when his team actually won. Or equalized.

Von Trapps: Jürgen Klinsmann's 2014 US Men's National World Cup Team. A talented group of innocents empowered by the guiding hand of a strong, dedicated governess on the

The Von Trapps, back in the good old days

eve of Anschluss. As with anything good about *Men in Blazers,* the name was created by a GFOP, Chris Ferris, who won our 2013 competition to craft a better nickname for the US Soccer team than the current placeholders, "The Yanks" and "The Stars and Stripes." Despite a protracted battle with Wikipedia's guardians, the Von Trapps was never given official Wiki status. Klinsmann was fired in November 2016. The nickname died with him.

Possibly our proudest achievement

VINYL

To take my mind off football, I have tried to develop hobbies, like collecting vinyl. This pursuit quickly turned into collecting football vinyl. One day, I would like to have a Sirius channel where I just spin Johann Cruyff's polka or Rod Stewart's rollicking release with a doomed Scottish World Cup squad. —RB

W

Wanker, Full Kit (till what age acceptable?):
Wearing a full kit—jersey and shorts—to show your support of a team. Cute when you are a child, but a deviant war crime when you are a grown-up, as it suggests either that you are mentally blurring the distinction between fan and player, or worse, that you are delusional in that your childhood dreams of becoming part of a Premier League team remain intact. What then is the threshold past which the naïveté of youth becomes an egregious social faux pas? Puberty.

Wanker Sign: The Essence of Football fandom. Grown men delight in taunting opposing players and fans by cupping their hand as if grasping an imaginary cucumber and  then jerking said hand up and down frantically, deliriously oblivious to an age-old wisdom: Sticks and stones may break my bones but wanker signs will never hurt me.

    Wanker, Double-fisted: As above, but with both hands. It is medically impossible to do this without being caught on camera by the television broadcaster.

War Pig!: The nickname of once Belgium National Team coach Marc Wilmots, who was known, whilst a player, as "Das Kampfschwein." Apparently war pigs were common in ancient war. Though we could not imagine a less useful animal to armor up and take into battle—even "war giraffes" seem of more im-mediate practical use—it turns out they were largely used after being set aflame and pitched against attacking clusters of war elephants. The first ever *Men in Blazers* tie, hand-crafted in Scotland, by master tie designers General Knot, celebrated that discovery by being emblazoned with silk war pigs.

The Belgian World Cup manager
who inspired a tie

Watching: The single question we are most often asked by newer American soccer fans is a variation on "How do you 'watch' football?" Do you follow the ball, the players, or the space on the field? And how, in a game which is for-ever fluid, can you tell who is on the ball all the time? The truth is, it is very different watch-ing the sport in stadium, which empowers a fan with a clear view of the formations and the movement of play, and viewing it, as we most often do in the United States, via television, where the passage of play is compressed into the box of the screen.

To gain a sense of how a professional watches the game, we asked Arlo White, NBC's lead football commentator, to describe his philosophy:

"The names of the players are the one thing in your professional life you are expected to get right as a commentator. A lot of it is familiarity. You see their positional habits over and over. During warm-ups, you do stare at the players. The colors of their boots. Who is wearing gloves, short sleeves, long sleeves. These are the 'tells' but the commentary position is vital.

"I was once covering the US Men's Team against Scotland in Jacksonville in a cavernous NFL stadium. Because of the distance between the booth and the field, NFL broadcasters have a spotter to ensure they always know who is touching the ball. I did not. Worse, the US played in a striped shirt with gray numbers which were impossible to see from the broadcast position. It is humanly impossible to tell Steve Cherundolo and Landon Donovan apart. Landon got a hat trick in that game but I called it so tentatively because I was never sure if it was really him on the ball.

"Fog hurts. Rain can kill you as it changes the players' haircuts. At the Etihad we used to broadcast from a gantry bolted onto the roof of the stadium, which had worse sight lines than the worst seat in the stadium. The weather was terrible and the wind howled in, driving a pouring rain. Aston Villa were the opponents that day, and when they took off their tracksuits after warm-ups they revealed maroon quarters with gold numbers. I immediately knew I would not know which center half was on the ball for the entire game and just snapped into self-preservation mode, completely focused on who is on the ball and who has it next and not the wider game.

"As a commentator you want to be able to shout out the name of the player as he scores, but in a game like that, you simply describe what you see and wait for the TV replay, be-

cause the worst thing you can do is shout out the wrong name of a goal scorer. As in real estate, so in football. Watching it well is simply about location, location, location."

Way Less Bald in Person: Davo is way less bald in person. Many people say this when they first meet him after having only previously seen him on television. (*See* Balding Sectors). He is also much taller and athletic in person. He is also writing this entry.

Wayne Rooney's Twitter: A font of modern-day source material and inspiration for scholars of medieval literature for it is written in a language akin to Chaucer's *Canterbury Tales* or *Sir Gawain and the Green Knight*. Off the soccer field, in the comfort of his own home, Rooney seems to derive a particular pleasure in tweeting in Middle English. After being involved in a slapping incident against Cardiff, Rooney was booked, and the commentator, former Liverpool hardman Graeme Souness, suggested the United player had an "exploding head." A furious Rooney tweeted:

"Sourness [*sic*] the rules are u kick out u should be off. Souness medel gives left hook he's done his job. Haha brilliant."

A further tweet read: "Sourness was sarcastic for everyone biting," though it is unclear what this referred to.

Welsh: Adj. meaning "Crap" as in Welsh Xavi (Joe Allen), Welsh Barcelona (Swansea City).

Wendepunkt: After the US Men's National Team defeated Mexico 2–0 on September 10, 2013, a game that virtually guaranteed qualification for the 2014 FIFA World Cup, I told Rog, on the pod, that had I been in the post-match press conference, I would have asked US coach Jürgen Klinsmann a one-word question in German: *"Wendepunkt?"*

Wendepunkt literally means *turning point*. And I saw this game as a turning point for how the US Men's Team would be supported, could play football, and could be believed in. A turning point for how far I believed that Jürgen the German could take his team of Americans (and a few Germans and Norwegians) into the tournament in Brazil. But it was another German who inspired my use of the word.

My favorite German author in school was Thomas Mann. Mainly because he wrote the shortest stories, or novellas. My favorite one was *Tonio Kröger,* all about a sad-eyed, dark-haired, highly artistic, super-sensitive German boy—literature's Mesut Özil—who always seemed to suffer even during his happiest times. Perhaps the central concept of the novella is that it is a fictional narrative restricted to a single suspenseful event, situation, or conflict leading to an unexpected turning point—or *Wendepunkt.*

I see *Wendepunkt*s in football everywhere—hard tackles, sendings off, goals scored too early, uncalled penalties, key substitutions, managerial firings—mainly because I know that the Premier League and FIFA World Cup writers have read a lot of German literature. Most of it novellas. Because they're shorter and those guys have to read a lot for inspiration.

But also, because no football season or tournament sees a straight line from start to finish for the eventual winner. The narrative bobs and weaves, teams soar, then fade, and die. Every team meets its challenges and potential *Wendepunkt*s, good and bad, but only one team will react to every setback, own goal, and disappointing result against Bournemouth at home by making it a turning point. And *Wendepunkting* themselves all the way to the title.* —MD

*or fourth-place finish, in the case of Arsenal.

Wheels Within Wheels: A phrase to shut down any conversation about life, the machinations of which are far too mind-boggling for mere mortals to comprehend. Like the infinite nature of space, the reality our world is really a flat plate supported on the back of a giant tortoise, or Arsene Wenger's inability to buy a reliable, healthy defensive midfielder.

White, Arlo: Commentator, Leicester City fan, legend. Arlo once revealed to us that when he used to complain to his father about how far he had to travel at the weekends to cover Premier League games, his dad would shake his head and remind him of the earthly truth, "It's not coal mining, is it."

One of the joys of Arlo White is that he and I both love the Chicago Bears. Not only that, by complete coincidence so seismic it would shock even Gwyneth Paltrow in *Sliding Doors,* Arlo and I both experienced a live NFL game on the very same night in the very same place. August 16, 1986, at Soldier Field. The Super Bowl–defending Bears of Walter Payton and Jim McMahon welcomed the hapless Indianapolis Colts. I was there having spent three weeks with my Chicagoan pen pal on the North Shore. A thirteen-year-old Arlo, replete with ginger mullet, was visiting family. These are his photographs. When we made this discovery, Arlo marveled, "Just think how ordinary a preseason game against the Colts was to all but two members of the crowd that night." —RB

White Hart Lane: 1) The home stadium of Tottenham Hotspur between 1899 and 2017. 2) The legal name taken by Gary Lane, a bricklayer from Woking, to demonstrate his devotion to Tottenham. Even though the club are now moving to a new stadium.

Who Wants to Sex Mutombo?: Dikembe Mutombo and I were both born in 1966. Other than that, the Congolese-born retired NBA center and I have almost nothing in common. I fouled out of the only basketball game I ever played for the Colfe's School Under 12s against St. Olave's. Mostly out of politeness for always putting my arm up for a foul. And I think I remember going 0 for 4 from the line. We didn't even have real basketball uniforms. We wore white T-shirts and gym shorts and it was, frankly, embarrassing. I knew what real basketball teams looked like. My sister, Rebecca, had attended the Harlem Globetrotters basketball camp in 1974 in Luton. She was, for several years, the only kid in our neighborhood who could actually do a real lay-up. Anyway, all very different from the seven-foot-two, eight-time NBA All-Star Dikembe Mutombo, who is responsible, allegedly, for one of the greatest phrases in the history of sports, sex, and parties. My great and insane friend Bruce, who has been known to charter a helicopter to *Men in Blazers* events, who basically owns Connecticut and has the ugliest golf swing in American history, used to play INTRAMURAL basketball against Mutombo at Georgetown for the Flying Baldinis (yes, seriously) and "regularly beat them." But HE IS NOT THE PERSON who told me that during the height of his Hoya basketball fame, Dikembe Mutombo would sometimes go to college parties and scream upon arrival—"Who Wants to Sex Mutombo!" And guess what. He wouldn't have said it if it didn't work. —MD

World Cup: An event held once every four years as a way for FIFA's gilded and privileged executive committee members to extract manila envelopes stuffed with dollars from desperate cronies around the globe. We applaud FIFA for their creativity and sense of humor in terms of awarding the next two World Cups to Russia 2018, Qatar 2022, venues both barely more suitable than an ISIS-controlled caliphate or, on reflection, USA 1994.

WORLD CUP, ROG'S FAVORITE GAMES

Argentina 3 vs. Netherlands 1 1978

Back then, we knew nothing about the fact that the tournament had been staged by a brutal military junta who had waged a barbaric "Dirty War" against their own people. That the tournament had been co-opted as a global public relations coup and, to prepare for it, slums had been swept of their inhabitants, many of whom were imprisoned or even disappeared.

We were also naive to 35,000 tons of free grain Argentina had conveniently shipped to Peru to ensure they beat Peru by more than four goals, which they needed to edge out Peru on goal difference.

I was a wide-eyed seven-year-old who was used to English football. A game lived out in run-down stadiums that reeked of spilled beer, chip shops, body odor, and police horse turd. This was the first World Cup I had ever seen. Live football was a scarce commodity in the 1970s, and it is one of the earliest games of foreign football I had ever watched live. I watched wide-eyed at the exuberant scenes beamed back live from Argentina as if they were being transmitted from life found on Mars. Games which burst into life before the second teams took the field as thousands of toilet paper rolls, streamers, and newspapers shredded into confetti greeted the players as if the whole stadium was exploding in joy.

Couple this with the fact that Netherlands were so graceful in their orange jerseys, long hair, and silky confidence. They passed poetically, they scored insouciantly from distance, they fielded the van der Kerkhofs, a pair of identical twins. Compared to English football, which was so agricultural back then, it looked like the players were actually using their hands to throw the ball around. In the final, they faced the hosts, Argentina, who though they played robust, fluid football were very much the vaudeville villains of the tournament. For all of the skill, this was a team that excelled in gamesmanship, diving and writhing in agony one minute, then jumping up to play on miraculously the next. To our English eyes, players were meant to hobble on unless decapitated, so there was something evil in their performance. When they won in extra time, courtesy of two goals from the admittedly dashing Mario Kempes, the confetti rained down, yet the spectacle felt fundamentally wrong. Cruel, unforgiving theater to my innocent eyes. A game of football had not just been lost. There was something cosmically wrong with the world which would have to wait four long years to be fixed.

Brazil 2 vs. Italy 3 1982

In 1982, English football remained sufficiently compartmentalized from the rest of the world for us to know very little about other teams until the tournament kicked off. Yes, we knew Brazil were an unstoppable machine, but that was about it. In the early group stages we would watch with jaws dropping as we became intimate with their ebullient, surging style. The greatest soccer-playing MD of all time, Socrates, would fling the ball to the white Pelé, Zico, who was guaranteed to find the deep-lying runs of the suave Falcao.

I had never seen players take the field with such joy, eager to play football as a form of artistic self-expression. That trait would ultimately come back to haunt them, like a dog poised to choke itself on its own collar. The team needed only a draw to progress against the dour, defensive Italians. Yet this was a game in which the Europeans came alive. The suave striker Paolo Rossi had the match of his life, netting twice, only for Falcao to peg a magnificent equalizer. The perm-haired Brazilian celebrated by running with arms outstretched, the veins in his wrists bulging from the screen as if it was a 3-D movie, a celebration I spent the next twelve months perfecting whenever I shinned home a goal on the schoolyard. Rossi was not finished though. Though the Brazilians should have shut the game down, they kept pressing for a winner they did not need, allowing the Italians to poach a goal, eliminate the Brazilians, and consign them, along with the 1974 Dutch, to the title of Best Team Never to Win It All. I took a photo of Rossi to my barbers when it was time for my next haircut. In the mirror, I saw my mother mouth to the hairdresser what I now realize were instructions to just give me a short back and sides. When the haircut was finished, I told the hairdresser I did not look like Paolo Rossi. He told me it was because my face was different.

England 1 vs. Argentina 2 1986

Diego Maradona's 1986 destruction of my beloved heroes by means most foul, then was a brutal life lesson. A crash course in ethics. The game, played in the shadows of 1982's Falklands Conflict, saw *El Pibe de Oro* score two of the most celebrated World Cup goals of all time. One illegitimate, in which Maradona used his left fist to reach over the six-foot-one goalkeeper and punch the ball into the net and became known as the "Hand of God" once the Argentinian admitted it had been scored "a little with the head of Diego and a little with the hand of God." Four minutes later, while the English were still reeling, he scored a solo goal even God would have had problems replicating, singlehandedly lacerating the entire English team, while, in the words of the British commentator, "turning like a little eel."

So breathtaking was the goal that Steve Hodge, the English midfielder charged with covering Maradona, revealed that it was all he could do to suppress the urge to clap as the ball went over the line. After watching my heroes emasculated in failure, I felt far less charitable. At the final whistle, my brother and I charged outside, desperate for the kind of emotional release that can be gained only by playing football in the street.

Overwhelmed by grief, and desperate to vent, I blasted the first shot that came my way straight through the window of our home. Before the shattered glass had finished falling from the window, my father came outside to find me standing in the middle of the road with tears of anger still stinging. Rather than being annoyed, my father shared our pain. He simply hugged us both. "I understand, lads," he said. "I understand." —**RB**

X

X, Our Favorite Players Whose Names Begin With: Xakane, Nkosiyabo—South African defender born in Bloemfontein, South Africa, the City of Roses. Once of Black Leopard FC, he now plays for FC Cape Town, or as the locals call them, the African Beasts.

Xanthopoulos, Petros—Greek International defender known as Xýlinon teîkhosis, Greek for "wooden defensive wall."

Xavier, Abel—A willingness to dye his beard extraordinary colors was this Portuguese international's most memorable skill in a wandering career which took him from Everton, to Liverpool, all the way to LA Galaxy.

Xavier, Bruno—Winner of the Golden Ball at the 2013 Beach World Cup, currently playing for the FC Barcelona beach soccer team.

Xisco—A striker who moved from Deportivo La Coruña to Newcastle and was dubbed the worst forward in the club's history by the local newspaper after his $8 million spawned just a solitary goal.

Xumetra, Jordi—The Levante midfield journeyman has made one appearance for the Catalonian national team.

Y

Yiddish: No language does pure spite more creatively.

Ale tseyner zoln bay dir aroysfaln, nor eyner zol blaybn—af tseynveytok.	May all your teeth fall out except for one—so you can get a toothache.
Zol dayne fis vern farholtzene dayne bokyh ful mit vaser un dayn kop gemakht fun gloz azey ven ayer fis vern farbent, vet ayer boykh zidn un dayn kop vet plastn.	May your feet be made of wood, your stomach be filled with water, and your head be made of glass so when your feet catch fire your stomach will boil and your head will explode.
Zolst vern a blintz un a kats zol dikh opsen.	You should be turned into a blintz, and a cat should eat you.
Oyf doktoyrim zolstu dos avekgebn.	You should spend it all on doctors.
Gey in dred un bek beygl.	Go in the ground and bake bagels.
Tsen shifn mit gold zoltsu farmogn un dos gantse gelt zoltsu farkrenkn.	Ten ships of gold should be yours and the money should only make you sick.
Zultsu hubn a groys gesheft mit skhoyre: un vus di hust zul men ba dir nisht beytn, un vos men beyt zulst nisht hubn.	You should have a large store and whatever people ask for you shouldn't have and what you do have shouldn't be requested.
Du drayst zikh arum vi a furtz in rusl.	You wander around like a fart in pickle juice.

Young Ones, The: Cult BBC television series of which twenty-six episodes, each a golden nugget, were made between 1982 and 1985. Set in a student house shared by four comically social reprobates, the spectacularly surreal show featured more violence, squalor, and gross-out humor than the entire BBC output that preceded it. A generation of British kids learned to swear like sailors just by watching. I was eleven when it first aired, and like everyone my age I was instantly hooked, even though I only understood approximately 37 percent of what was going on at any one time. **—RB**

Z

Zaha, Wilfried, and Other English Players with Foreign-Sounding Names: When Rog and I were growing up, England players had perfectly ordinary English names like Colin Bell, Martin Dobson, and, my favorite ever, Brian Kettle. Yes, there was an occasional Bonetti, or Le Tissier, but on the whole, English players sounded like English players, looked like English players, and played like English players. Like crap. Recently, though England are as wonderfully crap as ever, at least our players are starting to sound as exotic as our continental competition—Adam Lallana and Dele Alli are now almost automatic starters for England. Kyle Walker is about the most American name I could imagine. Jesse Lingard, Michail Antonio, Jay Rodriguez, and the above-mentioned Wilfried Zaha have all been called up to the senior team in recent years. Players such as Junior Stanislas, Nathaniel Chalobah, and Watford's "Troidini" are waiting for their opportunities. Of course, this will have no effect on the quality of England's football whatsoever. But we'll sound better during the team announcements.

Side note: If Troy Deeney were Argentinian, or Brazilian and Italian, and went by the mononymous "Troidini" instead of the more thuggish, loutish, English Troy Deeney, I strongly believe that we would think of him as one of the most exotic and skillful players in the Premier League. The same does not apply to "Waynrooni." —**MD**

Zidane: When France lined up to play Italy in the 2006 World Cup final, I had no idea my life was about to change forever. The game is largely remembered for Zidane's actions. The bald French legend opened the scoring with a cheekily chipped Panenka penalty kick, then succumbed to a moment of madness, butting Marco Materazzi in a sudden, shocking act of violence.

In the final moments of the game, I watched numb with shock whilst making fumbling attempts to dress for a wedding. The aftershocks of Zidane's sending off meant I must have buttoned up the front of my shirt with muscle memory.

As the game was about to go to extra time, my wife said sharply, "Roger, we have to go." She rarely calls me by my full name. It is reserved for our rare arguments, and moments of extreme stress, and its utilization is akin to an emotional alarm bell. "Babe," I said. "It is the World Cup final . . . the wedding will have to wait." "Roger," she said, "the wedding is on a *boat*. If we don't rush now, it will have left the dock without us on board."

Retrospectively, I realize this moment must rank as the greatest testament of my love for my wife: Dumbstruck, I let her click off the television broadcast of the 2006 World Cup final and followed her with a seething obedience out of the apartment into the street. Being yanked away from the World Cup in a pre–smart phone era was emotionally devastating. Akin to a spaceman being cut off from his air supply mid–moon walk. I followed my wife in body, yet not in mind. By the time we had reached South Ferry and boarded the wedding boat, I was in a very, very dark place. My mood worsened when I heard the Italians ultimately won on penalties. Surrounded by Americans who were giddily celebrating the impending nuptials, not just unaware we had all missed one of the most psychologically fascinating finals the World Cup had ever seen—but brazenly unaware the entire tournament had even taken place—sent me into a spiral of doom. I attacked the bar with the fury Zidane had propelled his cranium into Materazzi's midriff and vented by skulking around the periphery of the celebration, scowling, and avoiding human contact.

It was at the bar that I encountered a man whose countenance was different to all the others. Indeed, his curt dismissiveness and body language, which seemed to indicate he had no interest in being on a wedding boat on the Hudson, had the effect of making me feel like I was looking in the mirror. As he ordered a glass of Malbec, I heard his English accent. Though it was the plummy tone of a Southerner, I still warmed to his general disregard.

"Are you furious not to be watching the World Cup final?" I ventured.

"Furious enough to have contemplated sinking this boat," he replied.

"I'm Rog," I said, holding out my hand.

"Michael Davies," he replied.

And this is how I met Davo. The man my wife calls "my other wife." The moral of the story is pretty obvious: If you are ever forced to leave a World Cup final to witness a wedding you could not give two craps about but which happens to be taking place on a boat, make every opportunity to drag yourself up that gangplank before the vessel departs. It might just change your life. —RB

Acknowledgments

We want to thank all those who made this book happen. First of all. Glory be to God, for handing it to Rog, fully written, on top of Mount Sinai amidst fire, smoke, blackness, darkness, and thunder whilst Davo frantically organized the smelting of a Golden Calf back at base camp.

We are honored to have found a home at Knopf and are indebted to the quiet genius of our editor, Andrew Miller. A gent who reminds us of the last great Romantic poet with his endless well of patience and creativity and who would look really good behind the keys of a harpsichord. Thanks also to Rita Madrigal and the patient, creative genius that is Zakiya Harris at Knopf. We are also indebted to our designer, the great Peter Mendelsund, who said at the outset, "Let's design the best-looking football book of all time." Alas, we did not come close, but it was a lovely, and momentarily thrilling, idea.

Thanks to our agents, Jay Mandel at WME, the last great bookman, and David Larabell at CAA, the most optimistic gent in the business. Thanks also to all at Embassy Row and Sony Pictures Entertainment. Massive thanks and love to John Johnson, our Tony Award–winning theater producer. We are indebted to you for your support, passion, and creativity.

We are indebted to all of our NBC Sports family: Mark Lazarus, Jon Miller, Pierre Moosa, Adam Littlefield, Michael Kane, Ron Wechsler, Michael Carey, Maria Hartunian, Julie Schwarz, and all the talented crew up in Stamford, Connecticut. Home of the most friendly, strategic broadcasters in sports. We love working with you and admire the leaps and bounds you have made with the coverage of our sport in the United States.

We raise a glass to the whole NBC Premier League team, the Two Robbies, the One Kyle, Rebecca Lowe, Khaleesi, who all have done so much to grow the game we love in the country we love. The remarkable thing about all of you is that you are just as great in real life as you are on the screen—a reminder that authenticity is a key to life success. Arlo White is also a talented demigod, and talking of theology, Mike Tirico is an inspirational mensch. Thank you for giving the world its fastest-growing religion, Tiricoism.

Thanks also to all our colleagues in the tiny world of football broadcasting. We are indebted to each one of you for pushing the ball up the field: President Rob Stone, Alexi Lalas, John Strong, Eric Wynalda, Warren Barton, Stu Holden, Brad Friedel, and the team at FOX. Max Bretos, Herculez Gomez, Ian Darke, Super Julie Foudy, Julie Stewart-Binks, and TT at ESPN. The legend and icon and wonder Ray Hudson, as well as Phil Schoen and Kay Murray at beIN. We still revere the pioneers of FOX Soccer News: Mitch Peacock, Carlos Machado, Jeremy St. Louis, Eoin O'Callaghan, and the true innovator Michelle Lissel.

Massive gratitude to Bill Simmons for all of the support he and his team gave us at Grantland. Working with Bill and David Jacoby was a total delight. We remain grateful to all at ESPN for their misguided belief in us. Especially John Skipper, who is a true friend of the sport. Paul Carr, you blow our minds. Our great friend Bob Ley is the man we both want to be. Suave, sophisticated, verdant of hair, and an out and proud lover of football back in the day when that was a foolhardy act of courage.

Thanks to those who have had the poor decision making to be repeat regular guests on our podcast: John Green, Billy Beane, Steve Parrish, Barry Hearn, Jordan Morris, Aaron Dessner, John Oliver, Seth Myers, Becky Sauerbrunn, Dax McCarty, Kyle Beckerman, Bradley Edwin Guzan, Megan Rapinoe, and the inspirational Heather O'Reilly.

We raise an Xbox paddle to everyone at EA Sports, especially David Pekush and Paul Marr, for making FIFA—the game, that is—quite seriously, the silent hand that has grown the sport of football in North America; to all at Guinness, especially Jim Sias, and Ernesto Bruce and Zola Short at Adidas.

Thanks to all who have toiled in the crap part of SoHo to build *Men in Blazers* over the years. To the patient, patient Jen Simons and human wonder Jen Proctor, two terrific producers. Lexi Tannenholtz is a remarkable human being who breathed life into so much that is truly suboptimal. Jonathan Williamson is the single most creative, passionate, detail-oriented, calming visionary we have ever worked with. May Ipswich Town please return the Premier League at least once before the Apocalypse. Thanks also to Alex Tepper, David Ziplow, Evan Matthews, Rachel Chodor, Nick Koss, and Justin Rodriguez.

Our love and thoughts go to Alan Zapata and his family. May he rest in peace. Alan was our audio engineer and technical deity who passed far, far too soon. There is not a day that goes by that we do not miss his work and personality.

To Julie Schuck and Peter, that weird Australian dude she married on that boat on World Cup Final Day 2006, which both of us attended begrudgingly. Your marriage has produced two beautiful kids and our terrible show. Proof that even on the worst nights out, great crap can happen.

To all of our Great Friends of the Pod. We are inspired by the ongoing roiling conversation we have with you on a daily basis and never take it for granted. You are brilliant, creative, and loving. Some of you even have hair. We raise a glass to our original GFOPS who listened to Pre-MiB "Off the Ball" back when we had a handful of listeners and could name them all: Black Bile, Jason Kennedy, Josh Kail, Don Steele, One Wolf, @Seaux_Yves, Matthew McAllister . . . all over the country. noitsrebecca. Sweet Bobby, @DanteFlorence, @BinkyMarsh, and @EnglishBob1. To more. To more. COURAGE. KUNG FU FIGHTING AMERICA.

Rog would like to thank

Thanks to my brilliant, patient, talented assistant, Brad Feldman, who has toiled with me on this book—and so many weird projects—with a level of detail I wholly lack. Thanks also to the human phenomenon Dana Ferine, under whose loyal watch all this madness started.

I will always be grateful to Joe Scarborough, Mika Brzezinski, Alex Korson, and all at *Morning Joe* who invited me onto their show back in 2010 when football had no rights to be on it.

Eric Wattenberg at CAA is a top gent. I love what you do and the style in which you do it. Thanks also to the mighty David Larabell, and Vanessa Silverton-Peel.

I am grateful to the mighty Howard Handler, John Hock, Dan Harverd, David Katznelson, Courtney Holt, Rachel Levin, and Michael Cohen (not the Trump crony, but the one who is the most optimistic Arsenal fan of all time) for their continued counsel and support.

From the football world, Kyle Beckerman, Heather O'Reilly, Clint Dempsey, Jürgen Klinsmann, and Roberto Martínez have all been remarkable human beings at different times in my career, as have Neil Buethe, Michael Kammarman, and all at US Soccer.

In terms of life and meaning, I am forever in the debt of all of the following: Primo Levi, A Flock of Seagulls, Heaven 17, Adam and the Ants, Aztec Camera, "I'm Afraid of Me"–

era Culture Club, New Order, KRS-One, the Stone Roses, Molly Ringwald, Sid Luckman, Gale Sayers, Jim McMahon, the Hooters, *Scarecrow*-era Mellencamp, Lucy Dawidowicz, Joey Cora, Marvin Gaye, Jeff Agoos, Stevie Ray Vaughan, Roy Harper, Cat Stevens, Luc Longley, Public Enemy, Jens Lekman, Sufjan Stevens, ABBA, Studs Terkel, Cameron from *Ferris Bueller,* Arthur Miller, *Trading Places, Diner, Moonlighting*-era Bruce Willis, *Bachelor Party*–era Tom Hanks, Kibbutz Alonim, my favorite football writer of all time Simon Kuper, David Grossman, God Shammgod, David Simon, Wilfred Owen, David Ben-Gurion, Tibor Kalman, Charlie Rose, and Svetlana Alexievich.

In terms of life and meaning on the football pitch: Bob Latchford, George Wood, John Bailey, Paul Bracewell, Trevor Steven, Duncan Ferguson, Tony Hibbert, Li Tie, Leighton Baines, Tim Cahill, Thomas Gravesen, Joseph Yobo, Johnny Heitinga, Stevie Pienaar, Denis Stracqualursi, Royston Drenthe, Marouane Fellaini (now dead to me), Tom Davies, Ademola Lookman.

Jonathan Williamson, Producer JW, is the single greatest work partner I could have. Everything we do, we do because of him. It is incredibly rare to find someone who is both creative-minded and patient in equal measure. JW is both the muse and wartime consigliere of *Men in Blazers*.

Jamie Glassman. My best friend from the age of zero. A fellow Blue Belly. I value your love, support, and humor, even though I cannot believe you meekly sat by and allowed your kids to support Arsenal. To Mrs. Barton, Mrs. Simpson, and Mrs. Lindsey, for raising and schooling me. To Liverpool. There is no city in the world I would rather be from.

To my family: my in-laws, the Krolls, especially Celia. All Bennetts, especially my beautiful mum. Judge Ivor for making me a Blue; my sister, Amy; and my brother, Nigel, who somehow became a Red. I miss my grandparents every day, especially my grandfather Sam, who was a history buff and adored America as much as I do.

To my kids, Samson, Ber, Zion, and Oz. I love you with every atom in my body. To my wife, Vanessa. It is the singular achievement of my life to have met and married you, the greatest human being in the world—and, yes, I am including Leighton Baines in that sweeping statement.

Finally, thanks to Philip Larkin, for so much. Especially these lines: "We should be careful. / Of each other, we should be kind. / While there is still time." In the darkest times—footballing or otherwise—those words give me the strength to pretend to carry on. Courage.

DAVO WOULD LIKE TO THANK

All of my agents past and present, but particularly Sean Perry at WME and Jeremy Zimmer at UTA, who have been there for me for my entire career.

Mark Shapiro and John Skipper, who encouraged and enabled my moonlighting as a football writer for espn.com back in the early 2000s.

All of my bosses at Disney, ABC, and Sony, who have tolerated my obsession with the world game and my frequent disappearances into said world to cover it. Most notably to Mort Marcus, Lloyd Braun, and Steve Mosko, who in every aspect of my career have supported me beyond any reasonable level of expectation.

To all of my colleagues at Sony Pictures Television and Embassy Row, with special thanks to Jen Patton, Tammy Johnston, Jen Simons, Deirdre Connolly, Ruth Chen, Julia Cassidy, Amanda McPhillips, Ana Mijich, Britton Schey, Lisa Rechsteiner, and Bari Jean Dorman.

To my assistants during the course of writing this book, Kaylen Cumana, Louisa Keil (who has a mean stepover and drag back), and my rock, Francesca Henriques.

To Jimmy Kimmel, Regis Philbin, and Andy Cohen, who at different times have literally changed the course of my career.

To all my friends and especially my best friends in a life of watching and talking about football and sport: Ben, Scoops, George, Simon, Ruth, Joe, Bruce, Pete, Andy, and Michael ("Bloomface").

To Steve Parrish, Will Salthouse, and the Hard Core Ibiza crew, who have been the greatest gift brought to me by my adventures in football. And in Steve's case, brought back to me by *Men in Blazers*.

To Claude, who endured not just one but both of my career obsessions.

To Laura, my favorite GFOP ever, who has suffered too much.

To the staff and membership of my golf and tennis club, The Bridge, for constantly allowing me to switch the channel in the bar to the EPL.

To Barbara, who has been more important to me over the last twenty years than she will ever know. The midfield general of the Davies family.

To my big brother, Will, and big sister, Bec, who achieved so much so young that they gave me no room not to achieve something myself.

And Will, I owe you so much for all the help you gave me early in my career. If one entry in this book is written a tenth as well as you could have written it, I have overachieved.

To my nephews, Harrison and Luke, whom I love even more than we all love Chelsea. To Lizie, for thirty years of outrageous behavior and generosity. To Sarah, Jess, Joe, Eva, and Romy, because when it comes down to it, all we really have and care about is our family. Even though Jess supports Arsenal.

To my dad and in memory of my mum. You gave me my work ethic and my sense of humor. The only thing that I regret about moving to the United States twenty-nine years ago is how much time I missed with both of you.

And finally to my exceptionally talented and well-behaved daughters, Brea, JJ, and Ingrid, who make just enough effort to cheer for Chelsea and England that I actually believe you care, and to my son, George, who was born with my love of football and the left foot of Paolo Maldini. You four are my inspiration, why I am who I am, and the reason I do everything I do.

Illustration Credits

Illustrations on pages 4, 7, 13, 18, 19, 31, 43, 45, 46, 51, 53, 58–59, 67, 77, 85, 88, 111, 115, 118, 119, 122, 125, 126, 130 (bottom), 138, 142–143, 146, 154, 156, 168, 169 (top), 177–178, 193 (left), and 209 by Bonnie Gayle Morrill.

Photographs/Ephemera

a, viii: Subbuteo created and painted by Terry Lee

3: Popperfoto/Getty Images

8: (Gervinho) Laurence Griffiths/Getty Images; (Di Stefano) S&G/PA Images via Getty Images; (Yordan Letchkov) Bongarts/Getty Images; (Archie Gemmill) Bob Thomas/Getty Images; (Bobby Charlton) Peter Robinson/EMPICS via Getty Images; (Arjen Robben) Alexander Hassenstein/Bongarts/Getty Images; (Roberto Carlos) Angel Martinez/Real Madrid via Getty Images; (Frank Leboeuf) Matthew Ashton/EMPICS via Getty Images; (Jaap Staam) John Walton—EMPICS/PA Images via Getty Images; (Maicon) Stuart Franklin/Getty Images; (Brad Friedel) Alex Livesey/Getty Images; (Zidane) Laurence Griffiths/Getty Images

16: (left) SSPL/Getty Images; (right) Bob Thomas/Getty Images

17: Duncan Raban/Allsport/Getty Images

18: (top) Gregory Warran

25: MSI/Mirrorpix/Mirrorpix via Getty Images

27: Alpha/PA Images via Getty Images

30: Culture Club/Getty Images

34: (bottom) Rolls Press/Popperfoto/Getty Images

35: Peter Robinson/EMPICS via Getty Images

36: Tommy Hindley/Professional Sport/Popperfoto/Getty Images

37: (left) Mike Egerton—EMPICS/PA Images via Getty Images; (right) Express/Getty Images

38: (top) HGL/GC Images; (bottom) Ben Radford/Getty Images

41: Popperfoto/Getty Images

48: (bottom three photographs) Robert Davies (robertwdavies.co.uk)

65: (Nicolas Anelka) Scott Heavey/Getty Images; (Djibril Cissé) Ryan Pierse—FIFA/FIFA via Getty Images; (George Best) © Hulton-Deutsch Collection/CORBIS/Corbis via Getty Images; (Andrea Pirlo) Shaun Botterill—FIFA/FIFA via Getty Images; (Ricky Villa) Peter Robinson/EMPICS via Getty Images; (Xabi Alonso) David Ramos/Getty Images; (Tim Howard) OLI SCARFF/AFP/Getty Images; (Adam Clayton) Lynne Cameron/PA Images via Getty Images

69–70: Figurine Panini are reprinted with permission of Panini America.

80: (David Fairclough) Bob Thomas/Getty Images; (Louis Saha) Adam Davy—EMPICS/PA Images via Getty Images; (Paul "Ginger Prince" Scholes) ANDREW YATES/AFP/Getty Images; (Jack "Ginger Pirlo" Colback) Ian Horrocks/Getty Images; (Alan "Ball of Fire" Ball) Express/Hulton Archive/Getty Images; (Gordon Strachan) David Cannon/Allsport/Getty Images; (Alexi "Big Red" Lalas) Bob Thomas/Getty Images; (Wes Brown) John Peters/Manchester United via Getty Images; (Gary "Ginger Pelé" Doherty) Adam Davy/EMPICS via Getty Images; (John Arne "Ginge" Riise) Jon Buckle—EMPICS/PA Images via Getty Images; (Adam "Wolf" Bogdan) Paul Gilham/Getty Images; (Sean Dyche aka Ginger Mourinho) Charlie Crowhurst/Getty Images

105: (Gai Yigaal Assulin) Nigel French—EMPICS/PA Images via Getty Images; (Ronny Rosenthal) Dave Munden—EMPICS/PA Images via Getty Images; (Johan Neeskens) Peter Robinson/EMPICS via Getty Images; (Yossi Benayoun) Rebecca Naden/PA Images via Getty Images; (Eyal Berkovic) Matthew Ashton/EMPICS via Getty Images; (Edgar Davids) OLIVER HARDT/AFP/Getty Images; (Jeff Agoos) Scott Halleran /Allsport; (Avi Cohen) Bob Thomas/Getty Images; (Juan Pablo Sorin) PIERRE-PHILIPPE MARCOU/AFP/Getty Images; (Bela Guttman) S&G/PA Images via Getty Images; (Dudu Aouate) Alex Livesey/Getty Images; (Jose Peckerman) Stuart Franklin—FIFA/FIFA via Getty Images

125: (bottom) Courtesy of Mercersburg Academy

127: (top left) Peter Robinson/EMPICS via Getty Images; (bottom left) Jason Hawkes

130: (top corner, top left) Peter Robinson/EMPICS via Getty Images; (top corner, bottom left) Bob Thomas/Getty Images; (top corner, right) Photo by Central Press/Getty Images

131: (top corner, right) Janette Pellegrini; (bottom left) Andrea McCallin/ABC via Getty Images;

(top corner, bottom left) Allen Berezovsky/WireImage; (bottom right corner) Courtesy of NBC Sports

132: Courtesy of Trevor Barley

163: (right) MSI/Mirrorpix/Mirrorpix via Getty Images

164: (top) Rolls Press/Popperfoto/Getty Images

165: (bottom) Popperfoto/Getty Images

166: Chris Coleman/Manchester United via Getty Images

167: Mark Leech/Getty Images

169: (bottom right) The Print Collector/Getty Images

170: Jurgen Schadeberg/Getty Images

171: (top) © Hulton-Deutsch Collection/CORBIS/Corbis via Getty Images; (bottom) Douglas McFadd/Getty Images

172: Tom Kingston/WireImage

191: Courtesy of Tyler DeBoer

Images on pages 12, 20, 21, 29, 31, 39, 45 (top), 55, 73, 76, 79, 86–87, 94–96, 116, 117, 123, 140–141, 145, 153, 162, 181, 182, 191 (right) and 193 (right) are from Rog and Davo's collection.

Images on pages 6, 9, 11, 14, 42, 44, 50, 62, 84, 90, 98, 103, 110, 111, 134, 135, 136, 137, 139, 151; 152, 159, 163, 173, 174, 175, 176, 183, and 192 are from Rog's collection.

Images on pages 22, 47, 72, and 100 are from Davo's collection.

A Note About the Authors

Men in Blazers are Roger Bennett and Michael Davies, two men whose paths first crossed during short, mediocre, ultimately tragic football careers in the late 1940s. Their athletic apex was being fringe squad players on the England team that bravely lost 1–0 to the United States at the 1950 World Cup. Rog then spent four decades bouncing between the merchant navy and the Mossad. Davo became a nightclub owner and noted ornithologist in Marrakech. The pair reunited in 2009 after having a fender bender, and subsequent fistfight, on the streets of SoHo, New York. They agreed to salvage their relationship by attempting to pivot into careers as twin bald back-of-head models, but work was slow. So they started a podcast about football, love, First World War poetry, kitchen hardware, Scotch, and death. It has become quite popular.